CUPBOARD LOVE

Tom Norrington-Davies is a cook and ~~writer~~. He was part of the team at the pioneering Eagle pub in London and his first book, *Just Like Mother Used To Make*, was published in 2003. Tom writes the cookery column in the *Daily Telegraph* on Saturday.

Cupboard Love

How to get the most out of your kitchen.

Tom Norrington-Davies

Photographs by Jason Lowe

HODDER

Text © 2005 by Tom Norrington-Davies
Photographs © 2005 by Jason Lowe

First published in Great Britain in 2005 by Hodder & Stoughton
A division of Hodder Headline

The right of Tom Norrington-Davies to be identified as the Author
of the Work has been asserted by him in accordance with the
Copyright, Designs and Patents Act 1988.

A Hodder paperback

1

This book has in no way been endorsed by any of the brand owners featured in it.

A CIP catalogue record for this title is available from the British Library.

ISBN 0 340 83527 3

Page makeup by Craig Burgess

Printed and bound by Clays Ltd, St Ives plc

Hodder Headline's policy is to use papers that are natural, renewable
and recyclable products and made from wood grown in sustainable
forests. The logging and manufacturing processes are expected to
conform to the environmental regulations of the country of origin.

Hodder & Stoughton Ltd
A division of Hodder Headline
338 Euston Road
London NW1 3BH

For Léonie. May your cupboard never be bare.

CONTENTS

HOW TO GET THE MOST OUT OF YOUR KITCHEN.

When was the last time you walked into your kitchen and found inspiration? Is it fulfilling its potential? Do you enjoy being there? And does being there inspire you to cook? Questions, questions. I sound like one of those awful self-help-manual authors. I should be talking with a soothing (and vaguely Californian) accent. And this book should be called . . . *Love Your Cupboard, Love YOURSELF!* by Dr Paddy Fields M.B.S.

It's time to change the relationship between you and your kitchen. How would your kitchen feel if it was the person you lived with? When did you last make time for each other? Be honest with yourself because I mean real, quality time. Not just nipping in and out to put the kettle on. Not just over cereal in the morning when you are all sleepy and grumpy. And definitely not popping something ready made into the oven and gawping at the telly.

Damn. I kind of lost the Californian accent there. Do Americans use the word gawp? Never mind. I quite like this self-helpy thing . . .

Let's face it. Your relationship with your kitchen has got to the point where you only really make an effort when there are others around. And do you remember the last time the two of you had people over? It was supposed to be a fun night but it got a bit stressful. You got positively scratchy with one another. You resented having to do all that last-minute shopping when you were the one out earning all day. You felt you made all the effort and never got to relax with your friends. An angry little part of you felt that your kitchen was cramping your style.

It's not as if you haven't tried to spice things up a bit. You bought all the right books and (admit it) a fair few gadgets. You even bought your kitchen a fantastic makeover a couple of years back. There was gleaming stainless steel everywhere, but the sad truth is that your relationship has gone 'off the boil' . . .

Joking aside, this is a book about building a new relationship with your kitchen; about turning it into a place that makes you want to cook. Don't worry, it isn't about expensive makeovers. If you will forgive a rather old-fashioned piece of vernacular, it is about putting a larder into the modern kitchen. You won't need a big, flagstoned room full of chipped enamel bread bins and jars with gingham bonnets, though. Neither are you about to read a book full of 'fun things' to do with corned beef or Spam. The 'larder' in this book can be as small or large a corner of your life as time, space and inclination allow. It will manifest bits of itself in your fridge and freezer, and squeeze itself into the slimmest of cupboards. In fact, I intend to abuse the word larder all the way through the book. I'm going to drag it kicking and screaming from its rather quaint place in our collective memory and into the contemporary home.

Many cookbooks pander to our fantasies and aspirations. They tell us as much about the fashions and fads of society as they do about the food we eat. They are often described as manuals but in reality they inhabit a strange space between genuine instruction and flight of fancy. This is nothing new. Even the title of a venerable tome like Mrs Beeton's *Book of*

Household Management speaks volumes about the aspirations of the nineteenth-century woman at home. I wonder how many of Mrs Beeton's readers actually got to test-drive the chapter about keeping house in colonial India? I imagine the answer is about as many as are living a life remotely like that of the friend of a friend (of a friend) of mine, who ran off to farm olives in Provence and is currently living the dream . . .

As the rat race gets faster and our free time ever rarer, who can blame us for wanting to escape to a rural idyll? Of course, most of us know that we never will, which is why fantasy cookbooks make enjoyable reading and can be great fun to cook from. They allow us to bring a little escapism into our kitchens. That escape from everyday life doesn't have to take the form of tilling the soil. There is a sizeable cookery section in even the smallest branch of Books-U-Like, offering any number of fantasy lifestyles to choose from. Today's celebrity chef is something of a lifestyle guru.

The downside is that the culinary standards of celebrity chefs are not always easy to live up to. Most of us don't spend much 'quality' time in the kitchen, despite our admiration for those who do. Modern life simply conspires against it. In the UK we are obsessed with food yet we spend very little time preparing it compared with our neighbours on the Continent. We fill our kitchens with more gadgets and frills than anyone but we use them about twice before consigning them to the cupboard under the sink. We do buy *a lot* of cookbooks. Yet, almost across the board, we only pull them off the shelf for special occasions. That's when we scour the contents list hoping that something will leap out at us, spend a small fortune buying all the ingredients we didn't have in, sweat over the recipes for hours, impress our friends and swear we'll never do it again – at least, not until the next time.

This book is *not* a fantasy cookbook. There are enough of those on the shelves already. Instead I hope it will remove that slightly overwhelming sense of occasion from cooking – which, after all, should be an enjoyable, simple, everyday activity. Feeling intimidated by the idea of cooking leads many of us to fall back on something else we spend a lot of money on in this country: convenience food.

A NEW LOOK AT 'CONVENIENCE' FOOD.
The way food is marketed today, and the ubiquity of pit-stop shops full of ready-made meals, means that you can eat food that requires little or no preparation all the time. Here's a common sight: young urbanites in suits, asking their loved ones over a mobile phone what they fancy for dinner. Chinese, Indian, pizza; low fat, no fat; 'treat yourself', 'we're the best' . . . the list is endless. Whatever your particular craving, the chances are it can be indulged whenever you like. These meals used to crowd the freezer sections but now they are sold as 'fresh'. Advances in technology have blurred the boundary between fresh and preserved food to the point where it is hard to know what has been tampered with for the so-called benefit of lasting 'freshness'.

Are all these 'fresh' ready meals a good thing? On the face of it, the answer might be yes. They are promoted as some kind of culinary cure-all – saving time, cutting calories and basically taking care of all the work for you. Nothing wrong with that, you might argue. We all love having someone else take care of the cooking for us once in a while. And there's the rub. In a weird reversal of the way things should be, cooking is in danger of becoming something we do once in a while, and having someone else take care of it is the norm. A staggering 51 per cent of all ready-made meals produced in Europe are consumed in the UK.

No other country on the Continent comes close to eating that amount of convenience food.

The relationship we have with this food is not always easy. Very few people would claim that it makes them happy. Quite the reverse, in fact. The vast majority of fast food is a triumph of merchandising over content. The meal that ends up on your plate rarely looks as good as it does on the packet. The nutritional value of most pre-prepared food is, at best, questionable. And so are the ingredients. Look at the back of any ready meal and most of the time you will find yourself reading through a list of unfamiliar ingredients. Many of them don't sound very appetising and, unless you are completely *au fait* with the language of E-numbers and modified fats, starches, sugars and proteins (or whatever), they are downright bewildering.

Bewildering is not good news right now, in an age when most of us want to be reassured about what we eat. Lately, we seem to have become as addicted to food scares as we are to ready meals. Many of us worry about the amount of fat, salt, sugar and additives we consume. We are concerned about the effect of food production methods on the environment and our health. The food scare (or perhaps it is just scary food) is the new bogeyman, lurking in the takeaway joint or chilling in the supermarket aisle.

If you turn to the same pre-prepared food again and again but are unhappy with it, or if you have become a regular reader of ingredients lists because you worry about the issues I have just touched upon, there is a simple solution: take the bull by the horns and cook for yourself.

Every time we turn to ready-made food, every time we let someone else take care of what we eat, we make a leap of faith. We trust the producers to have our interests at heart. Yet with the best will in the world, any company that needs to turn in a profit is not going to have your happiness and well-being at the top of its list of priorities. No matter what it says on the packaging.

This is why it is crucial that you learn to cook your own food. Don't think that it can't be convenient, because it can. If you make a bit of a change to the way you shop, this book can provide you with the building blocks for cooking food that tastes good, is easy to make and can often be done on the spur of the moment. The recipes I have included are meant to tackle our preconceptions about convenience food head on. Lots of them can easily be cooked in roughly the time it takes to heat up a plastic tray of mediocrity in a conventional oven. Most of them are a doddle.

However, I think it is also important to point out what this book can't promise you. I can't offer you the 'bargain-bucket cookbook'. Not at first glance, anyway. When you start using recipes for meals you don't ordinarily make for yourself and you have to buy all the ingredients, it can appear to be an expensive project. Just remember, though, that any ready-made meal is a one-off, whereas a kitchen full of the right raw materials enables you to make several meals without much further outlay. I say this because convenience food, especially fast food, seems so cheap these days. Fast-food outlets in particular want you to think that they are offering you a bargain. In reality, the plan is to make you eat their food more often, so that you regularly spend your hard-earned money on it. If you are eating a lot of this food, don't forget that when you buy anything pre-prepared you are paying for the marketing, the packaging, the labour and a whole host of other things. Worryingly, the ingredients are likely to be the least important consideration in the cost of your meal. Buying your own food, on the other hand, puts you in charge of quality control. I believe that this is the most important difference between home-made and convenience food.

I can't promise you a book full of lean cuisine, low-carb, fat-free or calorie-controlled meals (although some of the recipes in this book will fit some of these criteria, if that's what interests you). The food I eat is probably moderately fatty, sometimes sugary and occasionally completely indulgent. But I can promise you olive oil and butter in place of hydrogenated vegetable fats. Honey and golden caster sugar in place of corn syrup, dextrose, glucose and other 'hidden' sugars. Once again, cook for yourself and you will be in control of the ingredients.

Neither can I promise you the definitive store-cupboard cookbook. Rather than choosing recipes that rely entirely on what's in, I've used plenty of store-cupboard ingredients supplemented with easy-to-find fresh produce.

I can't promise you that the food in this book will look as pretty or colourful as some of those enticing pictures on the packs of ready meals (but neither do the contents of the pack, in most cases). So, here is my trade-off: living with those packets less and less will give you something no food manufacturer is able to sell you. When you sit down to eat with something good on your plate, something that you made, everything about that meal changes. The preparation might have been minimal but the sense of achievement you feel is out of all proportion to the labour involved. Cook a meal for yourself and you get this snug (and mildly smug!) feeling inside. Cook a meal for a group of friends or family and you might also get a chorus of compliments.

HOW TO USE THIS BOOK.

By now it should be clear that this book is supposed to help you turn your kitchen into a place where you make spontaneous decisions about what to eat. To show you how straightforward this can be, I first want to describe the way I shop and cook. I'm going to start by basically talking you through my kitchen, since this is where I cook and eat. This will make you think either that a) my lifestyle is gloriously uncomplicated and therefore extremely covetable, or b) that I'm a very sad person who spends too much time thinking about food.

ME AND MY KITCHEN.

I live in a small flat in southeast London. I'm only saying this because I don't want you to think that I have acres of kitchen space, an enormous larder and a walk-in fridge at my disposal. My kitchen is fairly basically equipped. I have a four-burner gas hob and an electric oven with a grill function built in. I have two smallish store cupboards available for food, as well as a fridge-freezer. I have two large saucepans and three small ones. The lid of at least one has gone AWOL.

I also have a wok, which I pretty much live out of. I have a heavy-bottomed frying pan with an ovenproof handle, which means I can put it in the oven or under the grill, and a smaller, lighter version. I own two roasting trays and a ridged cast-iron griddle. There are cake and pie tins knocking about because I like baking, but I won't urge you to do much of that.

I have a couple of gadgets I use all the time. One is a food processor (a Magimix) and the other is a venerable Kenwood Chef mixer (but a hand-held electric beater is a cheaper alternative if you want something for mixing up cakes and puddings). I could probably live without one of these. That really is it. No blowtorches or pasta makers or ice-cream machines or blah blah blah – no room. I don't need a bigger space. What I could do with, perhaps, is more time to spend there, but I've yet to find it.

WHERE TO SHOP.

What unites us all in the twenty-first century, whether our kitchen is large or small, is lack of time. This creates the dilemma facing so many of us when we go shopping for food: whether to fall into the convenience-food trap or buy 'proper' food. It's easy to go from one extreme to the other. How many times have you decided that you're going to spend the next few weeks eating completely healthily and crammed your fridge full of fresh food, only to lose track of half of it and let it perish?

I have been down both routes. Over the years I have built up a modern 'larder'. Much of it is kept in my cupboards, some in my fridge and some in the freezer. I'm a serial deli raider. I love foods that keep well, and my store is now such that I can shop for perishables, i.e. meat, fish, fruit and vegetables, pretty much as I need them. Shopping this way is not time-consuming, and it is rewarding. It also allows you to be more adventurous about where you shop.

I used to be a supermarket's dream come true, since I would try to live off one monthly binge in a superstore. It would be too simplistic to say that I've since become anti-supermarket. We all love being able to get everything under one roof, complete with free parking. You can't help but be amazed by the sheer range of produce on offer in these places, either. A modern supermarket tries to be all things to everyone, from unscrupulous bargain-hunter to concerned ethical shopper. I'm slightly perturbed by the marketing of ethical produce in large stores.

A few bags of Fairtrade bananas or free-range eggs next to a mountain of cheaper alternatives looks like nothing more than a gimmick to me (a less cynical person might call it 'a good start'). However, if the ultimate goal of supermarkets is to offer convenience and a huge range of products, they have certainly achieved it.

What really bothers me is the impact this has had on our high-street culture, which is becoming homogenised. Many small-scale outlets simply haven't been able to compete with the supermarket chains and, as they go out of business, the chains appear in compact 'metro' or 'local' versions in their place. The effect is to reduce our choice of where to shop.

I think it is becoming increasingly important to strike a balance between high street and superstore. We are a society that has lost touch with the people who produce our food. For all its good points, the supermarket on the edge of town is not going to reverse that. You would be surprised at how quickly you can build a friendly, informative relationship with smaller shops. With this established, most are willing to source more unusual ingredients for you. You might also be surprised by the diversity of produce available on your high street – if you take a closer look at it.

It is these smaller shops that I would, ideally, urge you to get out and visit when buying ingredients for this book. Food shopping can be hugely enjoyable this way. So I recommend you try Italian delis, Asian supermarkets, and those mysterious 'continental stores' for the larder, plus markets, baker's, fishmonger's and butcher's for shopping to order. This will supply you with all the diversity that so-called convenience food and convenience shops offer you. I'm aware that not everyone can do this, so I have made sure that pretty much everything in this book can be bought from supermarkets too. People who live far from big cities could also investigate mail-order suppliers, the Internet, farm shops and delivery boxes.

HOW THE CHAPTERS WORK.

Each chapter opens with a brief introduction to the style of food it deals with. Then there is a short section called 'The Kit', which will read something like a shopping list. This should help you build up a collection of all the right bits and bobs – generally items you can buy and then store medium to long term, so that next time you return to the recipes in that chapter, much of what you need will be handy. Most of the time, 'kit' refers to foodstuffs, although on occasion I will also point out what hardware you might like to have around as well. None of it will be too outlandish or gadgety. I recommend that you shop for most of the kits in this book only as and when you need them, and build up your store slowly.

Scattered throughout the book there are 'DIY' recipes aimed at cooks who want to make items one might normally buy in. These range from curry pastes, chutneys and preserves to home freezing. There are also recipes for 'scratch cookery' enthusiasts, such as alternatives to canned products like coconut milk and tuna.

Pasta.

THE LONG AND THE SHORT OF IT: PASTA.

With so much written about pasta, I had to think quite long and hard about where to go with it in this book. Actually, it is probably easier to think about where not to go. If we are talking about pasta as a convenience food, then we are talking about what Italians call *pasta asciutta*, the dried stuff. This is what the overwhelming majority of Italians eat from day to day. Fresh egg noodles and sheets of lasagne with rich, slow-cooked sauces are another story, eaten mainly on special occasions.

We have readily adopted pasta in the UK. This is hardly surprising, considering that it is quick and easy to cook, and filling too. However, although we have claimed pasta as our own we haven't taken up an Italian attitude to it. In Italy pasta is usually eaten in fairly small quantities, either as the focus of a light meal or at the start of a larger one. This is very different from the way we tend to serve it, in great bowlfuls. We swamp our pasta dishes with sauce, whereas Italians use the sauce almost as a seasoning. Have a look at the first recipe in this chapter and you'll see what I mean. Eaten this way, the pasta is a vehicle for a mix of flavours, sometimes simple, sometimes complex. In fact, without wishing to sound as if I'm trying to tell you something profound, the pasta is *part* of the combination of flavours.

It is this kind of pasta dish that a lot of us miss out on – which is a shame, because not only are the recipes delicious but they are a cinch to cook, too.

At least one or two of the recipes in this chapter are very well known in the UK. Unfortunately they are mostly consumed out of jars and, like so much else that we buy 'ready made', the flavours and ingredients tend to be indifferent. Considering the overwhelming ease of a sauce like carbonara (see page 29), I find it bizarre that anyone would want to buy it ready made. We don't buy bacon and eggs pre-cooked for breakfast, yet a fry-up is actually harder to get right than pasta carbonara. No joke! If you are a jar junky, you have no control over the quality of what you're eating when it comes to your carbonara. It should be the freshest eggs, the crumbliest Parmesan and bacon from the happiest of pigs. This kind of pasta sauce is about the quality of the ingredients, not your dexterity in the kitchen.

THE KIT.

PASTA. Talking of quality, the pasta must be good. It should be made with 100 per cent durum wheat flour, water and salt. Nothing else. You can almost guarantee your pasta will be good if it is an Italian brand. My favourite is De Cecco, made distinctive by its yellow and blue packaging. Many supermarkets sell it. Artisan pasta, hand made by small companies, contains top-notch ingredients (right down to mineral water in some brands). It's worth checking out if you're after interesting shapes. What I can't be doing with is the chintzy way it is packaged half the time. I haven't space for that kind of nonsense in my cupboards.

Italians tend to choose the pasta shape according to the sauce. This is the best advice I can give you, too, and I'll specify the shape with each recipe. But you will have your favourites before long. I always have spaghetti, linguine and penne around, as I use them the most.

PARMESAN CHEESE. The word Parmesan is a bit of a misnomer. Most people would use it to refer to one of two similar cheeses: grana padano and parmigiano reggiano. The latter is considered superior, since it can be made only in Emilia Romagna with unpasteurised milk from grass-fed cows, and it is aged for a long time, giving it a complex flavour. It is a protected product, like champagne, and is therefore the more expensive of the two cheeses, but it's worth it for the slightly more rounded flavour. Grana padano is the same style of cheese as parmigiano, but with fewer restrictions on its production.

You might prefer to use a sheep's milk cheese in some pasta recipes. It makes an excellent replacement for Parmesan if you are intolerant of cow's milk. Pecorino romano is the one most similar to Parmesan in texture but it is harsher and saltier. Sometimes that's just what you want.

Because both these types of cheese tend towards dryness, always buy them ungrated. Purists will tell you not to grate the cheese until the pasta is actually cooking. This is sound advice. Buy small pieces and keep them well wrapped in baking parchment in the fridge. If you're lucky enough to have a cool larder, Parmesan will keep well in it and it's worth buying an eighth of a wheel from a big supplier.

It's a myth that all pasta dishes (or risottos, for that matter) require Parmesan. It is never served with fish, and many tomato recipes don't call for it either. I must admit that I'm in agreement with traditionalists about the fish but otherwise, add it when you want it. It is not always essential.

BUTTER, OIL AND SEASONING. Good unsalted butter and a fruity extra virgin olive oil will stand you in good stead for all pasta recipes. So will salt, black pepper and chillies (nearly all the recipes that follow favour the dried red type). Other than the odd fresh herb, most of the seasoning in this chapter is pretty much down to the above ingredients. I never add dried herbs to pasta sauces with short cooking times. They don't have long enough to cook and they dominate the other ingredients. The worst culprits are the herb mixes. You will not find a single recipe in this book that suggests you use dried mixed herbs. Throw. Them. Out!

COOKING EQUIPMENT. You will need a large saucepan, the deeper the better. One that holds at least 5 litres of water will be a safe bet for cooking two to five servings of pasta. A large colander is essential for draining the pasta. It might be worth considering the pasta saucepans you sometimes see on sale with the colander built in. A pair of tongs comes in handy for serving pasta, especially the long ribbon varieties. I am suspicious of the rather clumsy, faux-rustic, wooden tongs. Better to have a metal pair with a hinge. These come in handy for grilling and roasting meat, too. A roasting fork is also a handy tool for stirring pasta.

A WORD ABOUT PORTION SIZES. I mentioned earlier that we tend to eat massive portions of pasta compared to our Italian cousins. This is because it is often served as a starter over there. Personally I think there is a lot to learn from this. I rarely eat big bowls of pasta these days. I used to when I was younger and haring around all the time, and I think you'll find that a marathon runner can get through a fair bit of the stuff. These days, I prefer to balance a smaller portion with a good, robust salad. Some ideas for these are included at the end of this chapter.

Eaten with a light accompaniment, 100g pasta per person is a healthy portion. You could also open a more formal meal with a pasta dish as a starter and go on to serve grilled meat or fish as the main course in the Italian style. Head for the chapter on short-order cooking for more ideas (see page 143). As a starter, I'd say 75g pasta per person is fine.

COOKING DRIED PASTA. All you need to cook pasta successfully is lots of water at a rolling boil. Allow a litre of water per portion if possible, and no less than 500ml. Adding salt to the water will raise the temperature at which it boils and season the pasta as it cooks. Adding oil to the water, however, is a complete waste of time. It does absolutely nothing to stop pasta sticking together. That is why you need plenty of water, so the pasta can move around.

No two brands of pasta cook in the same amount of time, just as no two pans of water boil at exactly the same rate. So I have deliberately omitted precise cooking times for pasta from the recipes. I would go so far as to recommend ignoring the cooking times printed on the packet, which are always overcautious. And don't get hung up about the expression *al dente*. It describes how Italians like to eat pasta – with some 'bite' left in it, which enhances the flavour and texture. At home you can decide just how *al dente* you like it and how long that takes. Throwing pasta at a wall to see if it sticks is a pointless way of telling if it's ready. Who came up with that one?

Once the pasta is done, don't drain it too thoroughly. Many of the oily sauces in this chapter benefit from some residual water around the pasta causing a bit of emulsification. I'll point out where.

Lastly, don't cook pasta in advance. It will go sticky unless you douse it in oil, then it will fry when you reheat it. A pointless exercise. Where a sauce requires cooking, you should do it before anything else and devote all your attention to the pasta once the sauce is done. If the sauce is really quick to prepare, you could put the water on as you do it but make sure you always cook the pasta last – and not before everything, including any audience you may have, is ready at the table.

SPAGHETTI AND TINNED PLUM TOMATOES.

It doesn't sound very glamorous, does it? In fact it sounds like a bad joke. But in an Italian household it wouldn't. The joke would be on us and the fact that we would eschew the wonders of a tin of tomatoes for something truly awful in a jar that pretends to be fresh. We want there to be something almost tantric about the secret of good pasta sauces, 'lika mamma usta maka' – which is why we fall for images of rustic wooden tables groaning under the weight of a mountain of tomatoes. Come off it! Most of those bottled sauces are thick with modified starch and choked with vinegar and dried mixed herbs, but the reason they fly off the shelves is the misapprehension that few things in life are as dull as tinned tomatoes.

Well, what if I told you that the much-prized long variety of plum tomato is grown in Italy for the express purpose of cooking and canning? Fresh off the vine, it's not really much of an 'eater' but once canned, the flavour becomes a great deal more intense, so that it really holds its own in the pot. And there you have it. You shouldn't treat a tinned tomato like a fresh tomato. I'd go further: this sauce wouldn't be half as good if you made it with a fresh tomato. If you try this sauce wrapped around a portion of spaghetti, I swear you will know the almost childlike simplicity of true tomato sauce.

Try this on your own, or for a maximum of two of you, so that it seems as insanely easy as possible. It will take about 20 minutes.

For 200g spaghetti you need:
★ 400g tin of peeled plum tomatoes
★ 1 teaspoon olive oil and 2 teaspoons butter
  (or use just butter or just oil)
★ ¼ teaspoon salt
★ ½ teaspoon sugar
★ more salt and maybe some freshly ground
  black pepper to hand for later

The following are optional (don't be put off by them if you really are having a 'Mother Hubbard' moment):
★ 2 garlic cloves
★ 3–4 basil or sage leaves, roughly chopped

While you wait for the water to come to a rolling boil for the pasta, plonk a colander in the sink or over a bowl and tip the entire contents of the tin of tomatoes into it. Squash the tomatoes with your hands until all the juice has gone and you have a pulp.

Gently heat a fairly wide pan (a frying pan is fine) on the hob. Add the oil and half the butter. When they are just fizzing against the side of the pan, add the garlic, if you want. There's no need to chop it; just put it on a board and thump it. The skin will fall off easily now it is 'bruised' and it will flavour the sauce perfectly well this way. Give the garlic 2 minutes or so in the pan on its own but keep the heat gentle so it doesn't go brown. Now add the tomatoes and give everything a good stir. Add the salt and sugar, keeping the heat nice and low, and stir again. Now you could add the herbs, if you have any to hand. Don't use dried mixed herbs or oregano. They are too strong and will swamp the flavour.

You can leave the sauce to fizz, not bubble, away gently while you cook the pasta. Follow the instructions on page 19 if you are not a confident pasta cooker!

As soon as the pasta is done, drain it, return it to the pan (off the heat), add the remaining butter and stir through, just once. Add the tomato sauce and mix it in gently. You can pick out and discard the garlic or you can eat it, like I do. Taste another piece of pasta. If it seems bland, add more salt and some pepper.

That's it. Simple ingredients, stationed in the home for when you need or want them. This is convenience food and you made it. Of course, you might have more in than the lonely tin of tomatoes. The recipe above is deliberately Spartan. If you are the kind of person who keeps a small wedge of Parmesan in the fridge, then of course you would want to grate some over the top of the pasta.

JAZZED-UP TOMATO SAUCES.

With so many regional variations, there must be hundreds of tomato sauces for pasta in Italy. The following are my favourites. Some require more ingredients than others but they are all very easy to make.

GARLIC AND TOMATO SAUCE (AGLIO DORATO).

This takes a little longer than the other sauces in this chapter but it is really easy and it makes enough to put some aside. It is an unusual and addictive way of cooking a tin of tomatoes. Don't be put off by the amount of oil, as you only use some of the resulting sauce. It will keep for a couple of weeks in the fridge.

For 200g spaghetti or linguine you need:
★ 400g tin of peeled plum tomatoes
★ 250ml olive oil
★ 8–10 garlic cloves, peeled but left whole
★ salt and freshly ground black pepper

As with all tinned tomato sauces, tip the tomatoes into a colander and squish them with your hands until the juice has gone and you have a rough pulp.

Heat the oil gently for about 5 minutes in a small saucepan. Use a really, *really* low flame. When the oil is warm, add the garlic cloves and let them cook gently in the oil for about 20 minutes, until soft and golden. You *must* keep the heat low, otherwise you'll spoil the oil. After that time, test the cloves with a skewer or fork to make sure they are really tender. If not, let them have another 10 minutes or so. Add the tomatoes, gently so that you don't splash yourself, then bring the heat up a little and simmer for 15 minutes or so. Remove from the heat and leave to cool for about 10 minutes. Then transfer the sauce to a food processor and blend until you have a smooth emulsion. Season to taste with salt and pepper.

Cook the pasta and drain it only briefly. Two shakes of the colander as soon as you have tipped in the pasta should do the trick. Return it quickly to the pan you cooked it in, away from the

heat, and add about 4 tablespoons of the emulsion to the pasta.
Toss together thoroughly and taste to see if you like it. Add
more sauce by all means, and season with salt and pepper if
necessary. You can serve this with Parmesan, but it's best just
left on the table for people to help themselves.

CHILLI, BASIL AND ALMOND SAUCE
(PICCI PACCI).

Picci pacci is a sort of nonsense expression meaning, I imagine,
'this and that'. The sauce can be made with fresh tomatoes but
only at the height of summer when they are ripe and plentiful. If
you are using tinned tomatoes, you need to squash out the
juices really well.

For 200g spaghetti you need:
★ 50g blanched almonds
★ 400g tin of peeled plum tomatoes
★ 3 tablespoons extra virgin olive oil
★ 2 garlic cloves, finely chopped
★ 2 tablespoons chopped basil (or parsley, if you like)
★ 1 teaspoon red wine vinegar or balsamic vinegar
★ ½ teaspoon salt
★ a pinch of sugar (optional)
★ ½ teaspoon dried crushed chilli

This sauce doesn't need cooking as such, although you need
to roast the almonds until golden brown and crunchy (about
10 minutes in a moderate oven). When they are cool, chop
them coarsely.

Tip the tomatoes into a colander placed over the sink and
squash them with your hands until all the juice has gone and you

have a pulp. Combine them with the oil, garlic, herbs, vinegar and seasonings and, if you have time, allow them to steep for a couple of hours before you cook the pasta.

Cook the spaghetti, drain it and then combine with the sauce. Sprinkle the chopped almonds over the top.

TOMATO, BACON AND ONION SAUCE (AMATRICIANA).

This is a very rich sauce for something so simple. The main key to success here is not to use plonk for the wine. Since it is the kind of dish that goes down very well with a glass or two of an intense red, treat yourself to a bottle on the grounds that the recipe calls for it, and tip the first glassful into the pot.

For 200g penne you need:
★ 400g tin of peeled plum tomatoes
★ 1 tablespoon olive oil
★ 100g pancetta or smoked dry-cured bacon
★ 1 onion, chopped
★ 5–6 sage leaves
★ a good splash (i.e. about 100ml) of red wine
★ 1 tablespoon butter
★ about 50g Parmesan cheese, freshly grated
★ salt and freshly ground black pepper

Tip the tomatoes into a colander and squish them with your hands until the juice has gone and you have a rough pulp. Heat the oil in a frying pan and throw in the bacon. Fry over a medium heat until it is quite crisp, then add the onion and the whole sage leaves. Fry until they begin to brown a little as well. At this point pour in the wine and let it bubble up for a minute or so. It should reduce a little. Now add the tomatoes and season to taste with salt and pepper if you wish. Allow the sauce to simmer while you deal with the pasta.

Cook the pasta, then drain it and return it quickly to the pan you cooked it in, off the heat. Throw in the butter and toss to give the pasta a good coating. Now add the sauce and half the Parmesan. Serve the rest of the cheese at the table.

TOMATO AND BABY CLAM SAUCE (VONGOLE).

Food snobs take note: this is not a cheat's version of the famous dish where fresh clams are steamed and then tossed with pasta while still in their shells. This is a totally different, well, kettle of fish.

The best clams to use are Italian brands, sold in jars. But you will also find good tinned clams in oriental supermarkets. They are very small and sweet and go brilliantly with tomato sauce. If you want to buy fresh clams, steam them by all means, shell them if you like, and reserve the juices to add to the sauce.

For 200g linguine you need:
★ 400g tin of peeled plum tomatoes
★ 1 tablespoon olive oil
★ 1 tablespoon butter
★ 2 garlic cloves, chopped
★ 200g jar of baby clams
★ a small bunch of parsley, preferably flat-leaf
★ salt and freshly ground black pepper

Tip the tomatoes into a colander and squish them with your hands until the juice has gone and you have a rough pulp. Heat the oil and butter in a wide pan, add the garlic and fry gently until soft and translucent. Don't let it brown. Add the clams with all their stock from the jar and turn the heat up so that the juices bubble up and reduce by about half.

Separate the parsley leaves from the stalks and chop the stalks as finely as possible. Add them to the pan and simmer for about 5 minutes. The juices will have reduced quite a bit. Add the tomato pulp and simmer for 15 minutes or so, during which time you can attend to the pasta.

When the pasta is cooked, drain it quickly and return it to the pan, off the heat. Wrap the clam and tomato sauce around it, season to taste and toss with the parsley leaves before serving.

PASTA WITH PESTO.

The ultimate fast food for me is a bowl of pasta and pesto. But be warned: once you make your own pesto, the stuff in jars will cease to appeal. Another warning: Italians like rules when it comes to certain dishes. I learned this when the formidable chef who taught me to cook risotto used to clamp her hand over mine and make me stir it her way! Innovation is often accidental, but on the other hand rules are the reason Italians can produce something as simple yet refined as this. Sometimes you just have to surrender to tradition.

Pesto will keep for about a month in the fridge, well covered with oil, so this amount makes 4 servings.

In winter basil is either hard to come by or just plain awful (it likes the sun, so buy it in December and it will have travelled, believe me). For a winter version, you can replace the basil with flat-leaf parsley and the pine nuts with walnuts. Roast the walnuts in a moderate oven for about 10 minutes first and, while they are still warm, shake them in a colander for 5 minutes or so to help them lose as much of their (bitter) skin as possible.

For 200g spaghetti or linguine you need:
- ★ a large bunch of basil (at least 50g)
- ★ 2 tablespoons (about 50g) pine nuts
- ★ 2 garlic cloves, peeled
- ★ 100ml extra virgin olive oil (a mild one is best)
- ★ 3 heaped tablespoons freshly grated Parmesan cheese (or pecorino, if you prefer)
- ★ salt and freshly ground black pepper

Here are the rules. Pesto should be a textured green sauce, not an emulsion. So chop the basil, pine nuts and garlic roughly by hand and then crush them to a paste in a pestle and mortar OR blitz them in a food processor, using the pulse button. Only then do you add the oil and cheese, folding them in by hand, not in the machine. No more blitzing! Now you can season to taste with salt and pepper, adding more oil to loosen the sauce if it seems at all dry.

One more rule: to get the best from pesto, don't shake the pasta too dry after cooking. You need a little water to hit the pesto with the pasta to emulsify the sauce. So, drain the pasta, but not too thoroughly, then return it to the pan, off the heat. Add 2 heaped tablespoons of the pesto and toss well. Serve with extra cheese, if you like.

VARIATION.

A traditional way of serving pasta and pesto is to pair it with green beans and potato. Try this version using broad beans. It sounds a little odd, but it works. For 2 people, cut a couple of medium-sized waxy potatoes into small cubes, boil until just tender, then set aside. Next blanch a couple of handfuls of broad beans (frozen are fine) in boiling water for 1 minute, then drain and leave to cool. Pop the green bit out of the wrinkly, pale skin with thumb and forefinger. Cook the pasta (I recommend farfalle or orecchiette) and put the potato and beans into the pan with the pasta at the last minute to warm them through. Drain the pasta, but not too thoroughly, and mix everything with 2 tablespoons of pesto. Season to taste and serve with grated Parmesan or pecorino.

PASTA WITH EGGS AND BACON (CARBONARA).

In a classic carbonara, the sauce just happens by itself when egg yolks hit the warmth of just-cooked pasta. You will find ready-made carbonara sauces in shops and they are all a waste of your money. For roughly the same amount, you should buy really spanking-fresh free-range (and organic, for that matter) eggs and dry-cured bacon or pancetta. The speed and ease with which this meal comes together is something I've never managed to get blasé about. Make it tonight.

For 200g penne you need:
★ 100g pancetta or smoked dry-cured streaky bacon, cut into small strips
★ 1 heaped tablespoon butter
★ 3 egg yolks
★ 50g Parmesan cheese, freshly grated
★ salt and freshly ground black pepper

While the pasta cooks, simply fry the pancetta in half the butter until it is as crisp as you like. Do it on a fairly gentle heat so that you don't caramelise the butter too much. Keep the bacon and all its juices to one side when done. Beat the egg yolks in a small bowl with half the Parmesan. Drain the pasta and return it to the pan, off the heat. Add the remaining butter and the egg yolk mixture and quickly stir them into the pasta with the bacon. As soon as the pasta looks glossy, season to taste and serve, accompanied by the remaining Parmesan.

VARIATIONS.

There are alternatives to bacon for this sauce. Peas, broccoli and asparagus can be used in just the same way. Add peas or broccoli to the pasta just a minute before it is cooked and proceed from there. With asparagus, fry it like the bacon. With all three, add fresh basil to the finished dish.

THREE PASTA DISHES WITH ANCHOVIES.

Anchovies and pasta were made for each other. I like to buy whole anchovies packed in salt. Not only does this preserve their flavour better than oil, it means you can keep reusing a jar from the fridge. If you like anchovies in oil I still recommend buying the salted kind and marinating them yourself. Whole salted anchovies need filleting, but this is easy to do. Simply rinse them gently with water until all the salt has dissolved, then rub the skin off with your fingers. Lay each anchovy out flat and prise the fillet away from the tail and bone with your thumb.

ORECCHIETTE WITH BROCCOLI AND ANCHOVIES.

Orecchiette means little ears. It is the perfect pasta for broccoli sauces. Be warned: this dish is seriously addictive. Don't omit the nutmeg, which really intensifies the whole thing. For broccoli, you could also use spring greens or cabbage.

For 200g orecchiette (or pasta of your choice) you need:
★ 1 tablespoon unsalted butter
★ 1 tablespoon olive oil
★ 2 garlic cloves, chopped
★ ½ teaspoon dried crushed chilli
★ ¼ nutmeg, grated
★ 4 sprigs of thyme (tweak the little leaves off the stalks)
★ 1kg (or thereabouts) broccoli, cut into very small florets
★ 4 anchovy fillets
★ juice of ½ lemon
★ 50g Parmesan cheese, freshly grated
★ sea salt

Gently heat the butter and oil in a wide pan (preferably one with a lid) and, when it is fizzing, throw in the garlic, chilli, nutmeg and thyme. After about a minute, add the broccoli and anchovies. Sprinkle with 3 tablespoons of water and a scant pinch of sea salt, then cover and cook on a low heat for about 10 minutes, until the broccoli is soft.

Meanwhile, cook the pasta. Drain it thoroughly and return it to the pan, off the heat. Throw in the broccoli mixture and stir a couple of times until everything is mixed up. Squeeze in the lemon juice, throw in the Parmesan and stir again before serving.

LINGUINE WITH SARDINES, ANCHOVIES AND PARSLEY.

Linguine goes well with this sauce but spaghetti or bucatini works, too. You really need tinned sardines to get the rich texture. Without wanting to sound gory, the soft bones of tinned sardines break down, bringing an almost creamy nature to the dish.

For 200g linguine or spaghetti you need:

★ 1 garlic clove
★ 3 anchovy fillets
★ ½ teaspoon dried crushed chilli
★ juice of ½ lemon
★ 2 tablespoons well-flavoured extra virgin olive oil
★ 1 tin of sardines in olive oil, drained
★ salt and freshly ground black pepper
★ a very generous fistful of parsley, finely chopped
★ more lemon halves, if you like

This is easy; you're essentially making an infusion. Chop the garlic and anchovies as finely as you can, then add the chilli, lemon juice and olive oil and mix thoroughly. Place in a bowl and leave for about half an hour, if you have time (don't worry if you don't). Then drop in the sardines and mash gently with a fork.

Cook the pasta and drain, then return it to the pan, off the heat. Fold the sauce around the cooked pasta and season to taste with salt (and pepper, if you like). Serve with lots of parsley and let people add more lemon juice if they want.

SAPORI FORTI.

I couldn't complete this chapter without including this sauce. *Sapori forti* translates as 'strong flavours'. The combination of ingredients looks bizarre but it works, and the results are surprisingly subtle. You have to trust me! I like to serve this with linguine or spiralli (the pasta that looks like chopped-up telephone cord), but it works with most shapes. Because the ingredients are very salty, it is a good idea not to salt the pasta cooking water.

For 200g pasta you need:
★ 2 tablespoons olive oil
★ 1 onion, thinly sliced
★ 2 garlic cloves, chopped
★ 4–5 anchovy fillets
★ 50g (a handful) black olives, roughly chopped
★ 1 tablespoon capers, roughly chopped
★ 50g raisins, soaked in warm water until soft and plump, then drained
★ 1 tablespoon pine nuts
★ 1 tablespoon roughly chopped mint or oregano
★ extra virgin olive oil, to finish

Heat the olive oil in a fairly wide pan and add the onion and garlic. Fry quite hard for at least 5–10 minutes, stirring constantly. It doesn't matter if the onion catches a bit. When the onion has really softened, lower the heat, throw in the anchovies and cook until they melt down. Add the olives, capers, raisins, pine nuts and herbs and remove the pan from the heat. Loosen the sauce with as much extra virgin olive oil as you like (a couple of tablespoons should do it).

Cook the pasta, then drain and return to the pan, off the heat. Fold the sauce around the pasta immediately. This is best served without cheese.

THREE CHEESE SAUCES FOR PASTA.

The simple combination of pasta and cheese makes for almost instant comfort food. Here are three contrasting cheese 'sauces'.

SPAGHETTI WITH RICOTTA AND HERBS.

This is based on a recipe in Patience Gray's wonderful account of rustic life in the Mediterranean, *Honey from a Weed* (Prospect Books, 1986). Traditionally made with sheep's milk, ricotta is a mild and creamy Italian cheese that is often the by-product of making pecorino. The name refers to the twice-cooked (ri-cotta) curds. Unfortunately many of the commercially produced brands available are made from cow's milk and err on the side of blandness. If you find ricotta bland, try halving the amount stipulated in the recipe below and adding a tablespoon of grated Parmesan or pecorino. The recipe also works with goat's curd. Funnily enough, it is one of the few dried pasta dishes that works with fresh pasta, too.

For 200g spaghetti you need:
- ★ 2 heaped tablespoons ricotta cheese
- ★ 1 tablespoon extra virgin olive oil
- ★ 1 tablespoon lemon juice
- ★ 2 tablespoons chopped mint, basil or oregano (or a combination of any two)
- ★ ½ teaspoon dried crushed chilli or black pepper
- ★ salt, to taste

It doesn't get much easier than this. Boil the pasta in plenty of salted water. Just before it is ready, decant about 50ml

(3 tablespoons) of the cooking water into a small bowl and add
the ricotta. Stir a few times until the ricotta melts into the water.
Season with the oil, lemon juice, herbs, chilli or pepper and salt.
Drain the pasta, return it to the pan and toss with the sauce, then
serve quickly.

VARIATIONS.

There are all sorts of possible variations on this, but one of the
most delicious (and easy) is to throw a couple of handfuls (about
50g) of frozen peas or broad beans into the boiling water about
2 minutes before the pasta is ready. You could also use broccoli
or asparagus, or just add roughly chopped rocket or baby
spinach to the cooked pasta and ricotta.

PENNE WITH GORGONZOLA AND WALNUTS.

Another frighteningly easy pasta dish. While the ricotta sauce in
the previous recipe tastes light and summery, this one has wet
November evening written all over it. I have used Gorgonzola but
there is nothing to stop you trying something else. Dolcelatte
(a modern hybrid of Gorgonzola) springs to mind, as it is milder
and creamier, but a Roquefort would do the trick, too. If you're
shy of blue cheese, use a fairly soft cheese such as fontina or
Gruyère. You might want to up the ante, tastewise, in that case:
try adding a sprig of thyme or a scant grating of nutmeg.

Incidentally, at Christmas this is a great way of using up
pickings of leftover turkey. Just add it to the cream when you
start cooking the sauce.

One more thing: don't be alarmed if this sauce goes a little
bit pink. It is something that can happen when walnuts and
cream are cooked together. Some would say that the subtle
colour is part of the charm of this concoction.

For 200g penne you need:

- ★ 100g walnuts
- ★ 50g Gorgonzola cheese (or similar)
- ★ 100ml double cream
- ★ 3–4 sage leaves
- ★ 1 tablespoon butter
- ★ salt and freshly ground black pepper

Spread the walnuts out on a baking sheet and roast them in a moderate oven for about 10 minutes. If the walnut pieces are very chunky, rough them up a little in a pestle and mortar or wrap them in a tea towel and bash with a rolling pin. Don't beat them up too much.

Cut the Gorgonzola into small cubes, if you can. The way to do this is to get it as cold as possible in the fridge. If you don't have time, just break it up with your hands. It's a messy old cheese and once it hits room temperature it sticks to knives. You'll only end up trying to nudge it off the blade with your fingers.

Cook the pasta in plenty of boiling salted water. Meanwhile, heat the cream gently in a small pan and add the walnuts and sage leaves. Simmer for about 3 minutes, add the Gorgonzola and remove from the heat immediately.

Drain the cooked pasta and return it to the pan, off the heat, along with the butter. Toss the pasta and butter together, then add the sauce. Season it cautiously; Gorgonzola can be on the salty side.

PASTA WITH PARMESAN.

It might be daft, but when it comes to recipes I always think that three is company. Which is why you will find little culinary triptychs all through this book. I wanted a third cheese sauce, but I was struggling with which one to pick (the choice with any kind of pasta sauce is so vast that it's bewildering). This one actually came to me last night, as I ate it. I make it so often but would never have thought of it as a recipe.

The simplest of all pasta dishes, this is comfort food at its most basic. Because there was always pasta at the Eagle, the pub where I used to work, we served this to toddlers, as the unofficial kiddie meal. Children love it, but so do grown-ups.

If you are going to make something this simple, spend the extra pennies on the best cheese and decent butter. We are, as a nation, still in our infancy when it comes to understanding Parmesan. It is a complex cheese, whose reputation took a real bruising when it was sold dried and ready grated. Follow my advice in The Kit (see page 17), or go one further and look for a small piece of really well-aged parmigiano reggiano from an Italian deli. Oh, and don't cook the cheese, as doing so changes its character. Follow these minimal instructions to the letter!

For 200g spaghetti or linguine you need:
★ 50g unsalted butter, cut into small chunks
★ 50g parmigiano reggiano cheese, freshly grated
★ salt and freshly ground black pepper

Cook the pasta in plenty of boiling water and at this point (not before), grate the Parmesan. As soon as the pasta is done to your liking, drain it but literally just shake the colander a couple of times before returning the pasta to the pan, well away from the heat. Immediately, vigorously stir in the butter and leave it for a good 20 seconds or so. Now fold in the cheese, plus any seasoning. You should eat this, greedily, straight away. I always have it with a salad. In fact, a glass of good red wine is also compulsory here (unless you're a toddler, of course).

VARIATIONS.
You can enjoy the above as it is, but sometimes I'll add sage, in which case I chop 3 or 4 leaves of it and mix it in with the butter. Another option, which children like, is a teaspoon of tomato purée, added with the butter. It doesn't (and shouldn't) make the dish taste of tomatoes, but it brings something slightly pink and sweet/sour to the whole thing.

FIVE SALADS TO GO WITH PASTA.

A good leaf salad tossed with nothing more than extra virgin olive oil and salt is perfect with a bowl of pasta, but sometimes you want a little more. The salads below all contain vegetables. Eating them with pasta makes the meal seem more balanced. The following recipes are not strict instructions so much as suggestions. The quantities given will easily serve two people.

FENNEL AND PEAR SALAD.
A bulb of fennel, thinly sliced, and a crunchy pear, peeled, cored and thinly sliced. Mix with the leaves from a head of chicory and dress with the juice of ½ lemon, a pinch of salt and a teaspoon of olive oil.

COURGETTE AND SPINACH SALAD.
Thickly slice 2 smallish courgettes, blanch them in salted water for about 30 seconds, then drain and leave to cool. Dress with a teaspoon of balsamic or red wine vinegar, a pinch of salt and a

teaspoon of olive oil before tossing with a handful of rocket and/or baby spinach.

CARROT AND WATERCRESS SALAD.
Peel 2 carrots and, when the skin has gone, keep going with the peeler until you have thin, flexible strips. Dress them immediately with the juice of ½ lemon, a teaspoon of sesame oil and a pinch of salt. Slice a handful of radishes and toss them with the carrot strips and a bunch of watercress. If you can get your hands on some chervil, a few sprigs thrown in will add another, very welcome, dimension to the taste.

FRENCH BEAN AND AVOCADO SALAD.
Blanch or steam 100g French beans for about 2 minutes; they should still be quite crunchy. Drain and leave to cool, then toss with slices of avocado, 2 roughly torn heads of Little Gem lettuce, the juice of ½ lime, a teaspoon of olive oil and a pinch of salt.

TOMATO AND RED ONION SALAD.
Slice 3 really good, ripe tomatoes and a red onion. Dress with a tablespoon of olive oil, a teaspoon of red wine vinegar, a pinch of sugar and a generous pinch of salt. Allow to macerate together for at least half an hour, and toss with basil leaves. I wouldn't recommend this salad with tomato-based pasta dishes, for obvious reasons.

Risotto.

FAST BUT NOT FURIOUS:
POOR, MISUNDERSTOOD RISOTTO.

Make no mistake, risotto is easy, fast food. It is a meal in a bowl, as simple or as complex as you want it to be. If there's a box of short grain Italian rice in your store cupboard you are roughly half an hour away from a nourishing, comforting meal. I'm telling you this because if I had to name one type of food that seems to get people in a tizzy about making it for themselves, this is it.

The reasons are legion, but generally most cookery writers find it hard to give recipes for risotto without being a bit pedantic. I'm going to try very hard not to be, but you do need to follow a small number of golden rules – each of which I qualify below. This next bit is really only for the risotto novice. If you are a seasoned, confident risotto cook you should skip all instructions and just have a look at the recipes to see if you fancy any of them. And if you do, you should probably just use them as ideas and not even follow the methods I prescribe, because they may well annoy you.

1. You must use short grain Italian rice, such as Arborio, Vialone Nano or Carnaroli. Paella rice, sushi rice and pudding rice, although similar, do not behave in the same way. Since risotto rice is easy to find, this hardly presents a problem.

2. You need to give risotto your full attention. However, it doesn't take long to cook.

3. You need to be gentle with it. This is pretty much true of any kind of rice dish.

One more golden rule, which is not authentic Italian risotto lore but just an attempt to make cooking risotto very easy and enjoyable:

4. If you are a risotto virgin, make it for no one but yourself and/or a loved one. We have an alarming tendency to invite a horde of people into our homes before cooking something we have never attempted before. Which is fine if you are an adventurous, confident cook, but very stressful otherwise. All the recipes below serve two.

The principle of a risotto is simple: everything is stirred together during the cooking so that the rice becomes flavoursome, tender and creamy as it swells with the stock. It is when trying to describe the exact nature of a finished risotto that some writers unwittingly stress people out. Basically it is down to the nature of the rice (which is why you must use an Italian one). The outer part of the grain breaks down faster than the middle, which results in the creamy texture.

You don't actually have to add much or do too much to aid and abet this process. What you mustn't do is cook the rice too long or too hard – that's all. Besides, there is no way of describing the perfect risotto because personal tastes and regional practices mean that there are all sorts of idiosyncrasies. Venetians like their risotto loose and almost soupy. Milanese risotto is stiff enough to hold a soft peak like whipped cream. You will find out how you like yours. Worry less about texture and more about flavour, I say.

Here is how to bluff your way through a risotto, then. You start by gently frying a base – anything from onions to aromatics such as celery or fennel. Sometimes meat or fish is added, too. This is usually done with butter but it may be olive oil. Next you add the rice and coat it with the base. At this point many risottos have a little alcohol added to them to intensify the flavour. The heat is raised briefly to burn off (but not flambé) the alcohol. The hot stock (or water), which should be simmering next to the risotto pan so that it remains at a similar temperature to the rice, is added next. The rice absorbs it bit by bit until the middle of the grains is just soft enough to eat. Many Italians like the middle of their rice to be *al dente* (to have some 'bite'), like pasta. Throughout the cooking time, the heat beneath the risotto is kept low so that the rice simmers very gently. Italians will tell you that the cooking liquid should shimmer as if it has a breeze over it, which is an excellent guideline. In addition to this gentle simmering, the rice is also stirred. Think of a stir that matches the simmer: softly, softly. You see people churning away at risotto, which can turn it to porridge.

When the rice has absorbed enough liquid, the risotto is seasoned. Butter, salt and, more often than not, cheese are stirred in (although cheese is never added to a fish risotto). Then the ingredients are left together for just a few minutes before being served. You shouldn't make risotto in advance and reheat it, since it will just get thicker and stodgier as it sits around.

THE KIT.

THE RICE. You are most likely to find Arborio, a variety of short grain rice famous for risotto. You will probably also come across two other types of risotto rice: Vialone Nano, which some people say is the best one for seafood risottos, and Carnaroli, which is my favourite. Having harped on earlier about using Italian rice only, I have to say that Carnaroli is in fact a fairly modern hybrid (a cross with a Japanese strain), but it behaves very well. A word about quantities: I recommend about 100g risotto rice per person for a generous portion.

THE WINE. Many risottos start with wine. Don't use plonk; it will be too harsh. Some people say it is good to use a glass of whatever you plan to drink with the risotto. I keep vermouth in my larder for the express purpose of risotto-making. It's a good all-rounder.

THE STOCK. You can use stock but you don't always need to (I imagine risotto purists flinging the book across the room as I write this, which is why I told them to skip this section). Like my soup recipes (see pages 171–96), I believe that for the purposes of simplicity you can flavour a risotto superbly by sweating the base gently to coax juices and flavours from it before adding hot water. I'd be stupid if I claimed that adding stock to a risotto instead of water would not do anything more for it, and if you like making stock by all means use it. On the other hand, don't be put off these recipes if you have no stock handy. Whatever you do, don't use a really potent stock. Chicken or vegetable stock will do. Lamb and 'gamy' stocks would dominate everything else. Fish and some meat stocks can become gelatinous when reduced and can make risotto taste gluey.

I do sometimes use Marigold bouillon powder, which is a great cupboard standby for any recipe that needs stock. You can also buy fresh liquid stocks from many good stores. Avoid stock cubes at all times. If you are wondering why, read the ingredients list next time you see one. Adding a stock cube to anything makes it taste like a Pot Noodle. Enough said.

THE PAN. As wide and thick-bottomed a saucepan as you have (preferably with a lid, for sweating the base ingredients). As long as you remember that the cooked risotto will be about three times the size of the amount you put in the pot to begin with, then you will always have enough room. Incidentally, my favourite risotto pan is an old Le Creuset casserole. It has a heavy base and, being built for long, slow cooking, is perfect for sweating onions.

LEMON RISOTTO.

Try this, the simplest risotto I can think of, first. It isn't here just because it is easy. It might come as a pleasant surprise to you that the simple fragrance of a lemon can do so much for a dish. Use a really good lemon, organic and unwaxed, because you primarily need the zest. Most supermarkets sell them.

For 2 people you need:
★ about 1 litre water
★ 2 tablespoons light olive oil
★ 1 onion, finely chopped
★ ½ teaspoon salt
★ 200g risotto rice
★ juice and grated zest of 1 lemon
★ 1 tablespoon butter
★ 50g Parmesan cheese, freshly grated
★ salt and freshly ground black pepper

Have the water simmering on the hob next to the risotto pan. Gently heat the oil in a wide, heavy-based pan (ideally one with a lid), add the onion and salt and stir until well coated with the oil. Now cover the pan and let the onion sweat in the oil for a good 10 minutes, until soft and opaque. Don't let it brown. Add the rice and stir it around until it is well coated with the onion and oil. Add the lemon juice and zest and stir again. Add about a third of the water and briefly raise the heat so it comes quickly back to a simmer. Lower the heat again and cook, stirring gently but often, until all the liquid has been absorbed – this will take a good 10 minutes; if it takes any less, the heat is too high. Add about a third of the water again and keep going. By the time it has absorbed this second quantity, the rice is probably ready. It should look grainy and creamy all at once, not dry exactly, but not soupy either. Taste a grain to see what you think. If it is not done, add some of the remaining water and cook for a little longer, but the chances are you won't need it.

Remove from the heat, stir in the butter and half the cheese, and check the seasoning. Cover and leave for about 3 minutes, then serve with the remaining cheese as a garnish.

VARIATIONS.

The above risotto is, of course, very simple. You can add to it to make it more complex. In the spring, sweat 5 or 6 asparagus spears, cut as small as you can, with the onion. Let the woody end of the spears simmer with the water to make an impromptu stock. Or simply stir a generous bunch of chopped basil into the finished risotto. The taste is extremely summery.

CHILLI AND HERB RISOTTO.

The herb here is really a matter of personal choice. Basil or oregano would be sweet and fragrant, while flat-leaf parsley is surprisingly punchy. You could also use a leaf such as rocket or baby spinach. The chilli can be fresh or dried, and the saffron is entirely optional.

For 2 people you need:
★ about 1 litre water or stock
★ a very scant pinch of saffron
★ 2 tablespoons light olive oil
★ 1 onion, finely chopped
★ 1 fresh red chilli, deseeded and finely chopped
  (or ¼ teaspoon dried crushed chilli)
★ 2 garlic cloves, chopped
★ ½ teaspoon salt
★ 200g risotto rice
★ 1 teaspoon tomato purée
★ 100ml white wine or vermouth
★ a bunch or fistful of herbs, roughly chopped
★ 1 tablespoon butter
★ about 50g Parmesan cheese, freshly grated
★ salt and freshly ground black pepper

Have the water or stock, with the pinch of saffron added, simmering on the hob next to the risotto pan. Gently heat the oil in a wide, heavy-based pan (ideally one with a lid), add the onion, chilli, garlic and salt and stir until well coated with the oil. Now cover the pan and allow the ingredients to sweat for a good

10 minutes, until the onion is soft and opaque. Don't let it brown.

Add the rice and tomato purée and stir thoroughly. Add the wine or vermouth and bring the heat up so that it bubbles vigorously. When the liquid has evaporated, add about a third of the hot water or stock and bring it to a gentle simmer. Lower the heat and cook, stirring often but gently, until the liquid has been absorbed – this will take a good 10 minutes; if it takes any less, the heat is too high. Add about the same amount of liquid again and continue. By the time this is absorbed the rice should be about ready, but taste a couple of grains to see what you think. If it's not done, add some of the remaining liquid and cook for a little longer, but the chances are you won't need it.

Remove from the heat, fold in the herbs, butter and about half the Parmesan, and check the seasoning. Cover and let everything rest for about 3 minutes, then serve with the remaining cheese as a garnish.

DRIED MUSHROOM RISOTTO.

Dried porcini mushrooms seem expensive, but they go a long way. You can buy quite small sachets of them in Italian delis. When the porcini (or cep) mushroom is fresh, it has a sweet, subtle flavour. As it dries, the flavour becomes very intense. It tastes nothing like other mushrooms.

You need to soak the mushrooms before cooking and the resulting liquor acts as a stock, so don't discard it. If you like, combine the dried porcini with a couple of handfuls of fresh mushrooms. You could use a mixture of cultivated and wild. That option is included in the recipe below.

For 2 people you need:

★ 50g dried porcini mushrooms
★ 1 litre hot water
★ 2 tablespoons light olive oil
★ 1 onion, finely chopped
★ 6–7 sage leaves
★ 2 garlic cloves, chopped
★ ½ teaspoon salt
★ about 100g mixed fresh mushrooms, chopped (optional)
★ 200g risotto rice
★ 1 teaspoon tomato purée
★ 100ml white wine or vermouth
★ 1 tablespoon butter
★ 50g Parmesan cheese, freshly grated
★ salt and freshly ground black pepper

Soak the porcini mushrooms in the hot water for about 30 minutes, then drain, reserving the liquid. Strain the liquid, which can be gritty, through a sieve lined with kitchen towel. Put the liquid into a pan and bring it to a simmer. Blitz the mushrooms almost to a paste in a food processor and set aside.

Gently heat the oil in a wide, heavy-based pan (ideally one with a lid) and fry the onion, sage and garlic in it. Add the salt and the fresh mushrooms, if using them. Cover the pan and allow the ingredients to sweat for about 10 minutes. Do not let them get dry or catch. Add the rice, tomato purée and blitzed mushrooms and stir thoroughly. Add the wine or vermouth, turn up the heat and let it bubble away. When it has evaporated, add about a third of the liquor from the soaked mushrooms and bring it to a gentle simmer. Lower the heat and cook, stirring often but gently, until the liquid has been absorbed – this will take a good 10 minutes; if it takes any less, the heat is too high. Add about the same amount of liquid again and continue. By the time this is absorbed, the rice should be about ready, but taste a couple of grains to see what you think. If it's not done, add some of the remaining liquor and cook a little longer, but the chances are you won't need it.

Remove from the heat, stir in the butter and half the Parmesan, and check the seasoning. Allow the risotto to rest, covered, for 3 minutes or so, then serve with the remaining cheese as a garnish.

PEA AND PRAWN RISOTTO.

Starting this risotto by sweating leeks very gently complements the flavour of the prawns. The peas are a handy addition, as in my household they tend to share the freezer with prawns. Thus this is my standby risotto. You could use broad beans instead of peas, if you like, or finely diced courgettes.

For 2 people you need:
- ★ about 1 litre water or stock
- ★ 2 tablespoons olive oil
- ★ 3 leeks, finely sliced
- ★ 2 garlic cloves, roughly chopped
- ★ 100g frozen cooked peeled prawns, thawed
- ★ 100g frozen peas (optional)
- ★ 200g risotto rice
- ★ 1 teaspoon tomato purée
- ★ 100ml white wine
- ★ 1 tablespoon butter
- ★ salt and freshly ground black pepper

Have the water or stock simmering on the hob next to the risotto pan. Gently heat the olive oil in a wide, heavy-based pan (ideally one with a lid), then add the leeks and garlic, plus a tiny pinch of salt. Stir the leeks a couple of times, cover and leave to sweat for about 10 minutes. When the leeks are soft and juicy, add the prawns and peas, stir them a couple of times, then add the rice and tomato purée. Stir until the rice is coated with the other ingredients, then add the wine, raise the heat and let it bubble up fiercely and evaporate. Stir the rice just enough to prevent it sticking. Add about a third of the water or stock, bring to a simmer, then lower the heat. Cook, stirring often but gently, until the liquid has been absorbed – this will take a good 10 minutes; if it takes any less, the heat is too high. Add about the same amount of liquid again and continue. By the time this is absorbed, the rice should be just about ready, but taste a couple of grains to see what you think. If it's not done, add some of the remaining liquid and cook a little longer, but the chances are you won't need it.

Remove from the heat, stir in the butter and season to taste. Leave to rest, covered, for about 3 minutes before serving. You could garnish this with lots of chopped parsley, if you wish. In summer, basil is also good.

VARIATIONS.

One unusual but delicious variation on this dish (risotto purists, avert your gaze, please) is to use potted brown shrimps – the kind Morecambe Bay in Lancashire is famous for. They are usually sold in 50 or 100g tubs. Omit the oil and butter from the recipe above. Start the risotto by frying the shrimps in their own butter, then add the leeks and garlic before continuing. Be careful with the seasoning, since potted shrimps can be salty.

You could also replace the prawns with bacon, in which case I would factor in about 50g grated Parmesan at the end of the cooking time.

LEEK AND SHEEP'S CHEESE RISOTTO.

This is a rich and wintry meal. Pecorino is a fairly broad Italian name for any number of sheep's cheeses and your choice should depend on how strong you want the flavour to be. Pecorino romano is very hard, like a salty, brutal Parmesan. You can usually find it in supermarkets these days. Some Tuscan and Sardinian versions are subtler. I hesitate to be too prescriptive with cheeses for recipes, since I find people can be put off if they think they can't follow the ingredients to the letter. If you have access to a deli with a healthy range of cheeses, pop in and ask them for a good sheep's cheese. Tell them it's for a risotto and they might give you something unusual. You could also use a Spanish Manchego or a British sheep's cheese – I am a big fan of Berkswell and Ticklemore at the moment.

For 2 people you need:
★ about 1 litre water or stock
★ 1 tablespoon olive oil
★ 2 tablespoons butter
★ 4 leeks, chopped
★ 2 garlic cloves, chopped
★ 1 sprig of rosemary, leaves stripped from the
   stem and chopped
★ 200g risotto rice
★ ½ teaspoon tomato purée

* 100ml white wine
* about 100g hard sheep's cheese, grated
* salt and freshly ground black pepper

Have the water or stock simmering on the hob next to the risotto pan. Gently heat the oil and half the butter in a wide, heavy-based pan (ideally one with a lid), then add the leeks, garlic and rosemary. Stir them just a couple of times and add a really scant pinch of salt. Cover and allow the ingredients to sweat for about 10 minutes.

Add the rice and tomato purée and stir so that the rice is coated with the other ingredients. Add the wine, turn up the heat and let it bubble up and evaporate, stirring so that the rice doesn't stick. Add about a third of the water or stock, bring to a simmer, then lower the heat. Cook, stirring often but gently, until the liquid has been absorbed – this will take a good 10 minutes; if it takes any less, the heat is too high. Add about the same amount of liquid again and continue. By the time this is absorbed, the rice should be about ready, but taste a couple of grains to see what you think. If it's not done, add some of the remaining water and cook a little longer, but the chances are you won't need it.

Remove from the heat, stir in the remaining butter and about half the cheese, and season to taste. Cover and leave to rest for about 3 minutes, then serve with the rest of the cheese.

Toast.

THE LATE, LATE BREAKFAST SHOW: EGGS AND TOAST.

As long as you have half a dozen eggs in the larder, you are never more than a few minutes away from a good meal. And by that I don't necessarily mean breakfast. Take omelettes, for example. An omelette is one of the fastest, most effortless foods you can produce. Annoyingly, it is also one of those culinary sacred cows, like risotto, which some cooks find intimidating. If you do, you might take heart from the words of Elizabeth David, who quite rightly points out that the only infallible omelette recipe is one's own. I couldn't agree more, so if you have an omelette recipe that you know and trust, please ignore mine. I include guidelines only for those who feel they might need them.

It is hardly surprising that we love meals on toast. From the parathas and naans of northern India to the bewildering array of loaves on offer in our supermarkets, bread is a worldwide staple. There was bread before there was anything to serve it on, so old habits, I guess, die hard. In medieval Britain, food was eaten off baked discs of something like bread called trenchers. The disc was consumed at the end of the meal, impregnated with all the juices, or given to the poor as a 'sop'. The modern pizza is a distant relative of the trencher.

As long as there has been bread, there has been toast, since grilling a stale loaf was a way of making it edible. This might be why meals on toast have long been associated with the pauper's kitchen – think of the student and his or her baked beans.

Actually, that image is well and truly dated. Toast has become something of a fashion statement in our new Med-mad restaurant culture. Bruschetta and crostini have been to the last decade what garlic bread was to the Eighties.

I'm not surprised by the bruschetta, pita, or burger-in-a-bun craze. Like our poor plateless ancestors, we like food that we can hold in our hands. Perhaps it takes us back, not to the Middle Ages, but to the first time we picked up food as infants. There is a release from starchy table manners in holding a precarious and overloaded slice of bread in front of our open mouths. But it isn't just table manners we have escaped from; it is cooking. Somehow, you feel as if you have managed to skive out of kitchen duty if you are sitting in front of the telly enjoying a meal on toast. It needn't be beans, cheese and ketchup or scrambled eggs – not all the time, anyway. I have discovered that this sense of culinary defiance will stretch to any number of toasty preparations, some of which can end up looking and tasting pretty highbrow, even if I say so myself. A few of them follow in this chapter.

THE KIT.

EGGS. I have few set-in-stone rules in my cookery, but one is: never buy battery-farmed eggs or chickens. Battery farming is not only cruel – it produces eggs that are mediocre at best, dangerous to eat at worst. Every extra penny you spend on truly free-range chickens and their eggs is worth it.

BREAD. There is a loaf of sliced white bread (square loaf, and it must be thick cut) and a loaf of brown (actually, Granary) in my freezer at all times. I am thus ready for any eventuality. As far as

I'm concerned, there are brown bread toppings and white bread toppings and never the twain shall meet etc . . . but you might think differently.

Lots of the recipes that follow are perfect for a slice of dry or buttered toast. However, some are not, and for these you need bruschetta. Although it is a bit trendy, sometimes you cannot beat a slice of bruschetta. In fact, it has to be one of the sexiest things to have hit our shores since the olive oil slick of the early Nineties.

Here's how you make bruschetta. First of all, you need a less than fresh (yesterday's) loaf of rustic-style white bread. Sourdough is best, because of its dense texture as much as anything. It seems expensive at first glance, but it keeps for days, especially for toasting. Round loaves are the best option for long, slightly oval slices. So, if you have access to a clued-up deli, ask them if they sell Pugliese, or the more expensive pain Poilâne. Your next best bet is one of the Mediterranean-style loaves such as ciabatta or pain de campagne. You may as well slice the whole loaf up (I suppose it will come as no shock to you that I also stash bruschetta-friendly slices of bread in my freezer). Strictly speaking, bruschetta is grilled bread rather than toast. If you have one of those ridged grill pans and you have the patience to let it get hot enough, by all means use that. If not, then grill the bread conventionally. We're not in the River Café now. It's what you do once it is hot that matters most. You need to bruise a clove of garlic and rub it over one side of the grilled bread. Then drizzle a surprisingly generous amount of extra virgin olive oil over the same side. Use the best oil you have. Season the bruschetta with a scattering of sea salt.

The Spanish, and in particular the Catalans, have their own version, where the cut side of a tomato is squished on to and

rubbed into the bread along with the oil. And so it becomes
pa amb tomaquet – the best breakfast in the world, just as it is
or with ham and cheese.

Crostini are crispy little toasts, related to croûtons and often
associated with finger food. They needn't be restricted to polite
partying. You could make large slices of crostini and pile 'em
high with anything you like. There is something very satisfying
about the way they almost explode or collapse (or both) as you
bite them. I love to make big crostini for eating with soup. Use
stale bread again, and avoid ciabatta, which most people seem
to think is good for this purpose. Far too many holes for the
filling to fall through! For small crostini you are hard pushed to
beat yesterday's baguette, sliced thinly. Lay the slices flat on a
roasting tray, drizzle them with olive oil and scatter with salt, then
bake in a low oven (150°C/Gas Mark 2) for 20 minutes or so,
until they are crisp all the way through.

THE OMELETTE PAN. You need the smallest non-stick frying
pan you can get your mitts on. Omelettes shouldn't spread out
too much and cook through too quickly. It follows that a normal
(20cm) frying pan is fine for a four-egg (two-person) omelette but
a bit big for a two-egg one. I keep a 15cm frying pan handy,
which is perfect for two-egg (one-person) omelettes.

A BASIC OMELETTE.

The best time to try this (and I'm talking here to only the most
spooked, uninitiated 'omeletteer') would be any time that you're
alone. And hungry, naturally. A weekend breakfast when you're
in the mood.

The most common failing of an omelette is blandness. You need to season the eggs before you cook them, even if there is a filling. A pinch of salt (and pepper, if you like) should be enough.

This omelette and the ones that follow are great with toast, but don't forget chips. An easy recipe for your own oven chips can be found on page 208.

You need:
★ 1 tablespoon butter
★ 2 eggs
★ a pinch of salt (plus some black pepper, if you wish)

In a small, non-stick frying pan, warm the butter over a moderate heat until it begins to fizz. Break the eggs into a cup or small bowl, add the seasoning and, using a knife, just 'cut' the eggs so that the whites and yolks fuse together but are not beaten. Now pour off any excess, fizzing butter from the pan into the egg and fold it in. The pan should just be lined with a film of butter. Turn the heat up high, wait 20 or 30 seconds and add the egg. When it hits a hot pan like this, it should dance about on the surface rather than clinging, limpet-like, to the base. There's your non-stick working. It's about the heat of the pan as much as anything else.

Once the omelette has danced, reduce the heat to moderate. Let it cook for a minute or two, until the base is set but the top is still runny. To help the omelette set, you could gently nudge the edges back towards the middle (really, just a nudge) with a spoon or spatula. This allows runny egg to creep into the space you have created and cook. Don't overcook a simple omelette like this by putting it under a grill to finish. Like scrambled egg, an omelette is best when only just set.

Some people, myself included, like to fold an omelette in two. This is particularly good if you are jazzing up the ingredients (see below), as some of the egg should remain slightly runny. This gives an omelette a richer centre. You can't beat that. To fold the omelette, simply cook it as above until the base has set. Gently lift one edge of the omelette with a spatula or palette knife and bring it over to meet the opposite edge. Do this in a gentle but decisive movement. The sure-fire way to break an omelette is to dither when folding it.

JAZZED-UP OMELETTES.

The possibilities are endless when it comes to elaborating on a basic omelette. Here are a few very simple suggestions to get you in the mood for doing so. Omelette enthusiasts might want to get a copy of *Larousse Gastronomique* (Hamlyn, 2001), where there is a terrifying number of ideas.

HERBY OMELETTE.

Classic *omelette aux fines herbes* contains a mixture of chervil, tarragon and parsley, but a few leaves of basil are equally lovely. I've also got a thing going for chives in an omelette at the moment. For 1 omelette you need about a tablespoon of herbs. Scatter them over the basic omelette as it cooks.

CHEESE AND TOMATO OMELETTE.

Scatter a tablespoon of freshly grated Parmesan over the basic omelette when the top is nearly set. Deseed and chop a tomato and throw that in, too. Cook as above and finish by throwing basil over the omelette. My favourite summer breakfast.

BACON OMELETTE.

Fry 3 rashers of bacon with the butter. Remove once they are done to your liking and set them aside with the excess butter, instead of pouring it into the eggs. Make the basic omelette and, as soon as the base starts to set, drape the bacon and butter over the centre of the liquid part. When there is almost no runny bit left, fold the omelette in half.

VERY SIMPLE VEGETABLE OMELETTES.

Fry 50g sliced mushrooms or a finely diced courgette with the butter. Remove and set aside. Make the basic omelette following the instructions above. When the omelette has almost set on top, add the cooked vegetables and fold the omelette in half.

ELIZABETH DAVID'S TUNNY OMELETTE.

Elizabeth David was a world-class omeletteer. Since her time tunny fish has come to be known as tuna. Which is a pity since tunny is such a cute word. Here is another recipe where tinned tuna (or tunny fish!) produces something that might seem studenty but is, in fact, mildly elegant.

For 2 people you need:
- ★ 1 tablespoon butter
- ★ 1 tablespoon olive oil
- ★ 1 onion, chopped as finely as possible
- ★ juice of ½ lemon
- ★ 100g tinned tuna, drained of oil
- ★ ½ teaspoon salt
- ★ ½ teaspoon black pepper
- ★ 2 tablespoons chopped parsley
- ★ 4 eggs

Heat the butter and oil gently in a small, non-stick frying pan and add the onion. As soon as it has warmed through, add the lemon juice, tuna, salt, pepper and parsley. Warm everything through but don't sauté it as such. As soon as it is hot, remove from the pan and set aside.

Wipe the pan clean and return it to the heat. Barely beat the eggs with just a turn or two of a wooden spoon and add them to the hot pan. As soon as the egg begins to set, add the tuna fish mixture. Serve immediately.

VARIATION.
You could replace the tuna with good tinned sardines or smoked salmon. To enrich the meal even further, you could garnish the omelette with chopped olives or tomatoes.

OMELETTE GORDON BENNETT.
Silly name, but sometimes I think that when you start busking a famous dish at home, taking all the shortcuts a lazy cook is prone to, it is only respectful to acknowledge the dumbing-down process with a new title. This one, I admit, is slightly smart-assed. The real thing is from the Savoy Hotel in London, named in honour of the famous novelist, Arnold Bennett. To be truly authentic it requires both béchamel and hollandaise sauce. Which is why I'm happy to leave it to the chefs of the Savoy Grill.

Talking of grills, this omelette should be flashed under one, if possible, as it is meant to be eaten unfolded. So make sure the pan has a suitable handle (i.e. not a plastic one).

For 2 people you need:
- ★ 1 smoked haddock fillet
- ★ 2 tablespoons butter
- ★ 4 eggs
- ★ 1 tablespoon double cream
- ★ 50g Parmesan cheese, freshly grated
- ★ salt and freshly ground black pepper

You will need to poach and flake the smoked haddock. This is easy. Simply boil a kettle full of water, place the haddock in a shallow dish and pour the hot water over it. Cover and leave for a good 10 minutes. After that, drain it and leave until cool enough to handle. Remove the flesh from the skin, discarding any bones.

Preheat the grill. Heat the butter in a small, non-stick frying pan. Beat the eggs only slightly and season them with very little salt and some pepper (the haddock will be salty). Add them to the pan and cook the omelette until it is just beginning to set but is still runny on top. Flake the haddock over the top, then cover with the cream and Parmesan. Place the omelette under the grill until it is lightly browned.

SPANISH OMELETTE (TORTILLA).

The famous Spanish omelette is really a potato cake (the root of the word is related to the French *torte*). This is the simplest version, although you can add all sorts to it. Some people like peas, spinach or fried peppers in theirs.

A word about authenticity: this is going to bug tortilla 'experts' everywhere, but over the years I have stopped frying the potatoes for this omelette. If you don't have a deep-fat fryer, the process can be laborious. And at the end of it, you are left with a glut of used oil, which isn't much fun to deal with. These days I blanch the potatoes instead, and those of you scowling, take note: this is nothing to do with low-fat cookery. I have a way of making sure the whole thing is still oily and flavoursome *and* I've got it past my Spanish friends several times. Some of them even copy me, so there.

This recipe makes a 20cm omelette, which is enough for 4 to 6 people. If there are fewer of you, make this size anyway and enjoy the leftovers tomorrow.

You need:
★ 250ml olive oil
★ 2 large onions, thinly sliced
★ about 4 large potatoes (waxy varieties are best),
   peeled, halved and cut into slices about 5mm thick
★ 6 eggs
★ salt and freshly ground black pepper

Heat the oil in a wide pan and throw in the onions. Once they are bubbling away, turn the heat down low and simmer them for a good half an hour, until they are soft and sweet but not coloured, stirring every 10 minutes or so to prevent them catching.

When the onions are about half way through their cooking time, start the potatoes. Wash the slices vigorously to remove excess starch, then place them in a pan with enough water just to cover, chuck in a generous pinch of salt and bring to the boil. Simmer until the potatoes are tender but not breaking up (this doesn't take long, so lurk near them and keep testing them once simmering). Drain them thoroughly in a colander. You really don't want any excess moisture left, so ideally leave them sitting there for at least 5 minutes.

Strain the onions but keep all the oil and juices. Gently mix the potatoes and onions together in a large bowl. Add at least 4 tablespoons of the oil from the onions, plus a good pinch of salt, and mix again. Everything should look pale and glossy. Check the seasoning. In another bowl, beat the eggs, but only briefly, then mix them with the potatoes and onions.

Heat a good non-stick or well-seasoned frying pan, about 20cm in diameter, over a fairly high heat. When you see faint wisps of smoke from the pan, add 2 tablespoons of the onion oil (skim the top of the oil with the spoon rather than catching the onion juices underneath it). Coat the pan all over with the oil and gently tip in the omelette mixture. It should fizz at the sides and you will be able to jig it about a little, which stops it sticking. Turn the heat down low and let the omelette cook gently. After about 7–8 minutes it will be ready to flip. This isn't difficult. Grip the pan handle in one hand with a cloth. With your other hand, place a large flat plate over the top of the omelette. Now, holding the pan and the plate in each hand, invert everything so the omelette is on the plate. Return the pan to the heat and gently slide the omelette back into it with the cooked side on top. Cook for another 4–5 minutes. The omelette will feel solid when it is ready. You should neither eat nor attempt to move the omelette from the pan while it is piping hot, so leave it for at least 10 minutes before serving. This also helps prevent sticking, by the way.

If you're nervous about flipping the omelette, you could cheat. Cook it on the hob for just a few minutes, until it is set underneath but still liquid on top, then – assuming you have a pan with a metal handle – transfer it to a preheated oven (on full whack) and leave for 8–10 minutes, by which time it should be cooked through. For aesthetic reasons, you might want to turn it over as you serve it, so it looks like a traditional omelette. In Spain, they always seem to be displayed pan-side up.

VARIATIONS.

★ Perhaps the best addition to a Spanish omelette is sliced peppers. I use 1 green and 1 red, substituting them for one of the onions and frying them for the same length of time. They should really wilt, so don't rush this bit.

★ Herbs can be delicious, particularly dill and parsley. In the privacy of your own home, with all traces of authenticity banished, try a dill-flavoured Spanish omelette with slices of smoked salmon served on the side. This is a great picnic version of smoked salmon and scrambled eggs.

THE OMELETTE SANDWICH.

Anyone who has been on holiday to Spain may have come across this, perhaps the starchiest sandwich on the planet. It is fantastic. Slap yesterday's tortilla between slices of bread and butter by all means, but for the real Spanish version use a roll or a section of a loaf such as ciabatta (Italian, I know, but you can get it anywhere). Cut a good, ripe tomato in half and rub the inside of the roll with the cut side, squishing the tomato slightly as you go. Season the bread with a little salt and olive oil before sandwiching the omelette in it.

PORTUGUESE OMELETTE.

Writing up the recipe for Spanish omelette reminded me of this lesser-known curio, which actually comes from Sri Lanka but is also served in southern India. Quite how it gained its nickname is one of those charming foodie mysteries, but it could be because it contains chillies. The Portuguese were the first to colonise the island of Sri Lanka, and would have bought chillies native to the Americas with them. Before that, they were not known in Asia.

For 2 people you need:
- ★ 1 firm tomato, deseeded and finely chopped
- ★ 1 red onion or shallot, chopped as finely as possible
- ★ 1 garlic clove, finely chopped
- ★ 1 small fresh chilli, finely chopped (or ½ teaspoon dried crushed chilli)
- ★ 2 tablespoons milk or yoghurt
- ★ 4 eggs
- ★ ½ teaspoon salt
- ★ 1 tablespoon chopped coriander

In a large mixing bowl, combine the tomato, onion, garlic, chilli and milk or yoghurt. Fold in the eggs, making sure you don't really beat so much as just break them up. Now add the salt. Heat a little oil in a frying pan until good and hot and add the omelette mix. Follow the instructions for cooking a basic omelette on page 62. I don't fold this omelette but serve it, only just set, scattered with the coriander.

EGGS ON TOAST.

I think eggs on toast is one of the best combinations for fast food. And it isn't just fast food. It's comfort food, eat-in-front-of-the-telly food, have-friends-over-for-brunch food or even feeling-under-the-weather food. There are so many recipes you will be familiar with; I've tried to suggest a few that might be new to you.

CURRIED EGGS ON TOAST.
This is based on a dish from Madhur Jaffrey's first book, *Indian Cookery* (BBC Books, 1982). As authentic as the recipes are,

it's good to eschew oriental veracity now and again. So serve this paraphrased version of her recipe on toast. It is lovely on a bed of wilted spinach as well.

For 4 people you need:
- ★ 2 tablespoons vegetable oil
- ★ 1 large onion, chopped
- ★ a smallish cube of ginger (about 2cm), grated or finely chopped
- ★ 1 fresh chilli, chopped (deseeded, if you like)
- ★ 275ml single cream (you can also use yoghurt, but not a low-fat one as it curdles)
- ★ 1 tablespoon tomato purée
- ★ 1 tablespoon lemon juice
- ★ 1 teaspoon ground cumin
- ★ a pinch of garam masala
- ★ a pinch of salt
- ★ 6–8 hard-boiled eggs, shelled and halved
- ★ chopped parsley or coriander, to garnish

Heat the oil over a medium heat in a largish pan. Fry the onion in it for about 3 minutes, until slightly browned and softened. Add the ginger and chilli and fry for another minute or so. Now add the cream, tomato purée, lemon juice and spices. Mix thoroughly and allow to simmer for 1–2 minutes.

Add the halved eggs and cook for a further 5 minutes, until the sauce has thickened. Check the seasoning and serve garnished with flat-leaf parsley or coriander. Leftovers of this dish can be chopped up and eaten in a sandwich, like egg mayonnaise. I love to stuff pita bread with this mixture.

VOLCANO EGGS.

Is there a cookbook that does all the best cinematic meals?
I have been eating this on and off ever since I saw Rose
Castorini (Olympia Dukakis) make it for her daughter Loretta
(Cher!) in *Moonstruck*. Great movie.

Children love volcano eggs, partly because of the name and
the presentation. I've included instructions on how to grill fresh
peppers for this recipe but I love to use tins of small, roasted
piquillo peppers, which you can find in Spanish and Italian delis
and some supermarkets. They have a slight astringency to them
and a very subtle, peppery kick. You don't need to include the
peppers, of course, although they add to the Vesuvian feel of the
dish with their vivid red colour. Grilled tomatoes are just as good,
as are slivers of streaky bacon.

For 2 people you need:
- ★ 1 large red pepper
  (or 2 from a jar of grilled peppers in oil)
- ★ 1 tablespoon olive oil
- ★ 1 tablespoon butter
- ★ 2 long slices of rustic-style bread
- ★ 2 eggs
- ★ salt and freshly ground black pepper

If using a fresh pepper, place it under a hot grill (or char it over
a gas flame) until it is soft and collapsed and the skin has
blackened. Pop it into a bowl and cover so it 'steams' for 10
minutes or so. This will loosen the burnt skin and allow you to
peel it off by rubbing it with your fingers. Don't do this under a
tap or you will lose the flavour of the pepper. It's better to have
the odd bit of skin around, which is why you sometimes see little

bits of carbon in tins of roasted peppers. Once you've skinned the pepper, cut it into thin strips.

To cook the volcano eggs, heat the oil and butter in a large frying pan. Using a small scone cutter, punch a hole in the middle of each slice of bread (if you don't have a scone cutter, use the rim of an egg cup or espresso cup). Now start to fry the bread in the pan over a medium heat. After a couple of minutes, turn the bread over. Break the eggs into the holes and cook until they are done as you like. Just remember to keep the heat moderate so that you don't burn the bread. Serve with the peppers.

EGGS ROYALE.

Or, poached egg, smoked salmon and hollandaise sauce. The name is surely a pun around its more famous counterpart, eggs Benedict – smoked salmon being (historically) more expensive than ham. It's worth pointing out that cheap smoked salmon (or ham, for that matter) is best avoided.

If you are a fan of smoked salmon and scrambled eggs, you will love this dish. I would imagine tradition dictates serving eggs royale on a muffin but please let me coerce you into a slice of rye or sourdough toast instead. I have also eaten this served without any kind of toast, on a bed of wilted spinach.

For 2 people you need:
- ★ 1 tablespoon vinegar
- ★ 1 tablespoon salt
- ★ 2 top-notch eggs for poaching
- ★ 2 slices of toast
- ★ 4 slices of smoked salmon

For the hollandaise sauce:
★ 3 egg yolks
★ juice of 1 lemon
★ 1 teaspoon white wine vinegar
★ 125g butter
★ salt and freshly ground black pepper

This recipe is deceptive. It looks simple but actually it could be stressful if you ended up doing everything at once. The trick is to make the hollandaise sauce first and keep it warm (pop it into a Thermos flask or a plastic bowl with a lid and leave it next to the hob). Have the toast ready, with the smoked salmon draped generously across it, before you poach the eggs.

Now, I cheat with the hollandaise, so my method is totally back to front. Beat the egg yolks, lemon juice and vinegar together until the mixture is smooth and pale. Bring the butter to a good fizz in a small pan and simmer gently for a minute or so. Now slowly (but not too cautiously) add the hot melted butter to the egg and lemon mixture, whisking it in as you go. The heat of the butter will cause it to emulsify. Ideally, have someone hold the bowl as you do this. Finally, season to your liking (remember that smoked salmon is salty) and keep warm.

To poach the eggs, put about 2 litres of water in a wide pan with the vinegar and salt. Allow it to come to a good rolling boil, then turn the heat right down so that it is just at a simmer. Grab a whisk or spoon and stir the water so that it is spinning into a central vortexy kind of thing, as if it was going down the plughole. Into this vortex, break one egg. About 30 seconds later, add the second. The vortex keeps them tight and round, but it isn't absolutely necessary. A perfect poached egg usually takes about 3 minutes. If it is too soft for your liking, allow

another minute for the yolk to start setting. Then remove
with a slotted spoon and drain briefly on kitchen paper.

Put the poached eggs on top of the toast and smoked
salmon, pour over the hollandaise sauce and serve straight
away.

SIX SAVOURIES FOR TOAST.

Old-fashioned 'savouries' on toast are part of our culinary
heritage. They seem to be back in fashion at some restaurants
and pubs these days. The most famous is probably Welsh rabbit
(or rarebit, as it is often called).

WELSH RABBIT.

I make no apologies for lifting this recipe from my last book, *Just
Like Mother Used to Make* (Cassell Illustrated, 2003). It's one of
the best meals on toast there is. You should use the crumbliest
cheese you can get: Cheshire, Lancashire or, if you're lucky, a
Welsh cheese like Caerphilly.

For 2 large slices of bread you need:
★ 125g cheese (see above), grated
★ 1 teaspoon butter
★ 3 tablespoons stout (or ale)
★ 1 teaspoon wholegrain mustard
★ a splash of Worcestershire sauce
★ a bag of plain flour on standby

Put the cheese, butter, stout, mustard and Worcestershire sauce
in a small saucepan over a low flame and leave until melted.

Sometimes the sauce looks as if it has curdled. This only happens rarely. If so, add either a touch more mustard or a teaspoon of flour to help it become a paste. Allow the paste to cool completely before you even think about grilling it.

Heat the grill and toast the bread on both sides. When it is done to your liking, spread one side generously with the paste. Return the toast to the grill and cook until the topping is golden brown.

VARIATIONS.

★ In *Just Like Mother Used to Make*, I wrote about some regional variations of rabbit (or rarebit). In Scotland a rabbit is spread on buttered toast. In England it contains red wine. I have since had some correspondence that alerted me to a couple of other variations. Buck rabbit is Welsh rabbit served with a poached egg on top. Try this, it's good. And I received another Welsh idea from my friend John Williams, who stirs cooked onions into his rabbit paste.

★ By far the tastiest variation I have come across was in a tea room in York. Make the rabbit paste and set aside. Poach a fillet of smoked haddock or a kipper: simply immerse it in a pan of simmering water, or pour boiling water from a kettle over it in a shallow dish, then cover and leave for about 10 minutes. Drain and leave until cool enough to handle, then flake the flesh roughly, removing the skin and bones. Add the fish to the rabbit paste, loosening it with a little milk if it seems stiff. Spread over the toast and grill briefly before serving.

SCOTCH WOODCOCK.

Or rather, scrambled eggs with anchovies. Like Welsh rabbit, this is an olde worlde recipe, though not the refined version you sometimes see in cookbooks today. It is a homely supper dish, but it also makes a good starter if you are entertaining.

For 2 large slices of bread you need:
★ 2 tablespoons butter
★ 5 anchovy fillets
★ 3 tablespoons double cream
★ 4 eggs
★ 1 tablespoon chopped parsley
★ salt and freshly ground black pepper

Melt the butter in a small saucepan, the kind you would scramble eggs in. When the butter fizzes at the edges, add the anchovies and cream. Now remove from the heat and leave to infuse for about 10 minutes. This gives the anchovies a chance to dissolve in the butter without frying, which can make them bitter.

Return the pan to the heat and break in the eggs. Stir them gently and cook like scrambled eggs. If you're eating this with someone else, warn them that it will be 3 minutes away tops. Basically you need to serve this just as the eggs start to set, not become truly scrambled. As you serve them, fold in the chopped parsley and some salt and pepper. Serve over hot buttered toast.

DEVILLED SHRIMPS.
This is based on a Claudia Roden recipe from Morocco. I hope she will forgive me for messing around with it. When I was young, our local pub used to serve devilled shrimps. They warmed me up as I sat in the chilly beer garden, hating pubs (how times have changed). I could never imagine what the recipe was. If you can get hold of small brown shrimps for this,

they work really well here. If not, use peeled, cooked Atlantic prawns. I buy them frozen, let them thaw completely, then squeeze them gently to get rid of the rather salty water they can accumulate.

For 2 large slices of toast you need:
★ 1 garlic clove, chopped
★ 1 tablespoon olive oil
★ 1 tablespoon butter
★ ½ teaspoon salt
★ ½ teaspoon paprika
★ ½ teaspoon ground cumin
★ ¼ teaspoon ground ginger
★ 300g peeled shrimps or prawns
★ 1 tablespoon chopped coriander
★ lemon wedges, to serve

Fry the garlic in the oil and butter until it is golden. Add the other seasonings and the shrimps or prawns and let them sizzle over a medium heat for 2–3 minutes. Add the coriander for the last minute or so. Serve this with lemon to squeeze over the shrimps when they are on the toast.

BEANS AND SAUSAGES.
I use slices of the hot little Napoli sausages you can get from delis and supermarkets these days. You could use another kind, or bacon. The choice of beans is up to you but I like cannellini beans from a tin (this is supposed to be a quick supper). If you wish to soak dried beans for this meal, you will find instructions for cooking them on page 191; 200g dried beans will roughly equal the contents of a 400g tin.

For 2 large slices of toast you need:
- ★ 1 tablespoon butter
- ★ 200g Napoli sausage or similar, sliced
- ★ 1 tablespoon Worcestershire sauce
- ★ 1 teaspoon sherry vinegar or cider vinegar
- ★ 1 tablespoon chopped parsley
- ★ 400g tin of cannellini beans, drained
- ★ salt and freshly ground black pepper

You can do a lot worse than make this dish in a wok, if you have one. Otherwise a frying pan or sauté pan is fine. Heat the butter in the pan until it fizzes and add the slices of sausage. A minute later, add the Worcestershire sauce, vinegar and parsley. Let everything bubble for half a minute or so, then mix in the beans, heat through and check the seasoning. You might want more Worcestershire sauce.

Let everything rest in the pan while you make the toast. Serve the sausage and bean mixture on the toast.

ROAST TINNED TOMATOES.

Now, to me this was a revelation. It comes courtesy of my friend, Gaetano Uzi, from Sicily, and the flavour is quite intense. It is supposed to be pretty oily but you can tone that side of it down, if you like. I love it with cheeses like mozzarella or halloumi and it's also good with bacon and eggs or in a cheese sarnie. The tomatoes keep quite well in the fridge for 3 or 4 days if you don't eat them all. Smashed up, they make a decent, impromptu pasta sauce.

For a small roasting tin you need:
- ★ 4 tablespoons olive oil

* 2 x 400g tins of peeled plum tomatoes
* ½ teaspoon balsamic vinegar
* ½ teaspoon salt
* a couple of sprigs of rosemary

Preheat the oven to 180°C/Gas Mark 4 and grease a small roasting tin with 1 tablespoon of the oil. Carefully tip the contents of the tins of tomatoes into a colander and lift out the tomatoes, trying not to let them break. Discard the juice. Lay the tomatoes in the roasting tin and season them with the rest of the oil, plus the balsamic vinegar, salt and rosemary. Bake for about 25 minutes, then see how they are getting on. They should be slightly wrinkled and may have caramelised ever so slightly around the edges. Serve on toast. You can eat the tomatoes hot or cold.

TUNA AND FETA 'MELT'.

This comes from my local Turkish café. I've never seen it anywhere else and the pairing of tuna and feta isn't an obvious one, but it is lovely. Calling it a 'melt' is a bit rich, since the feta doesn't, really. It behaves like a young goat's cheese, and simply becomes softer. The flavour will intensify slightly, too.

For 2 large slices of bread you need:
* 200–250g tin of tuna, drained
* 2 tomatoes, deseeded and diced
* 1 red onion, diced
* ½ cucumber, deseeded and diced
* 50g feta cheese, roughly crumbled
* 1 tablespoon olive oil
* ½ teaspoon black pepper
* lemon wedges and chopped mint, to serve (optional)

Put all the ingredients in a bowl and stir together gently so that you don't break up the feta too much.

Toast the bread on one side and then transfer it to a baking tray. Load the uncooked side generously with the tuna mixture and grill for about 3 minutes, until the topping has warmed and the feta has softened (remember that it won't actually melt). Serve with lemon wedges and chopped mint, if you like.

THE CLUB SANDWICH (AND ITS COUSINS).

You could argue that the club is, strictly speaking, a sandwich and not a meal on toast. So sue me. It's a meal in toast! It's also the best hangover cure in the world. Did they know that when they first put it together at the Saratoga Club in New York? I often wonder about the great hotel and club dishes and drinks of the early twentieth century, from Singapore slings to Waldorf salads. Were there fiercely competitive chefs trying to come up with timeless signature dishes? I doubt it. I suspect the club sandwich, for example, was entirely improvised but then stuck, because the ingredients were made for each other. Some dishes do that to such an extent that people are afraid to tamper with them, as if it were some kind of foodie blasphemy. The premise is, I suppose, if it ain't broke don't fix it – with the added afterthought, woe betide you if you try! Back in the early Nineties I remember Nigel Slater confiding to his readers that he liked to make his club sandwich with brown bread. You could almost imagine him mouthing, *'Brown bread!'* in a declamatory fashion, but I know exactly what he meant.

Brown bread, white bread, it's up to you. If I was advising a restaurateur who planned to serve clubs, I'd tell him or her not to mess with the classics and to stick to neat triangles of toast, complete with cocktail sticks to hold them together (a good club is vertiginous enough to need help in that department). In the comfort of your own home, it's a different story. Actually, because I think you need to roast a whole chicken to make a decent club sandwich, I like to assemble a crowd to eat this. And so my own act of club heresy is to let people build their own at the table. I simply provide the materials. It's fun that way and, as with so many dishes like this, children have a ball making them. What follows is the classic club – or at least my attempt at it. Then I will give you a few variations on the theme.

For the classic club you need:
★ A roast chicken: choose one depending on the size of your crowd. For just one or two people, I recommend you still roast a whole bird, as the leftovers will come in handy. The flavour is so good if you get a mixture of dark and white meat. I've never found a better recipe for roast chicken than Nigella Lawson's in *How to Eat* (Chatto & Windus, 1998), partly because she makes it sound so pragmatic and easy.

Buy a decent bird (by which she means a free-range hen that got to run round a yard and eat real food; don't touch anything else). Smear the breast of the chicken with oil or butter. Use as much as if it were expensive hand cream. Her words! Sprinkle it with salt. Shove half a lemon up the chicken's bottom and roast it at 200°C/Gas Mark 6 for 20 minutes per 500g, plus half an hour (thus, a bird weighing 1kg takes 1 hour 10 minutes). Allow the chicken to cool completely and then pick off the meat. Reserve all the juices (see below).

★ Crisp bacon: use dry-cured streaky, smoked or unsmoked. Allow at least 2 rashers per person. I cut mine into lardons (small strips cut across the rasher) before frying.

★ Little Gem lettuce (or the middle of a Cos): I use whole Little Gem leaves and dress them with the juices of the roast chicken.

★ Tomatoes, sliced as finely as possible: if they lack flavour, macerate them for half an hour before you eat them by tossing them with a drizzle of olive oil and some salt. This will cause even the most frigid tomato to get a bit sexy.

★ And finally, mayonnaise: I use this in lieu of butter and I would make my own for a club sandwich (see page 211 for the recipe). They hardly need my help advertising, but it has to be Hellmann's if you are using a shop-bought version. Don't even think about anything as silly as garlic mayonnaise or salad cream. Sacrilege.

I take all the above to the table on an enormous chopping board and let people dig in. Incidentally, my favourite bread for a club is toasted Mighty White (but don't tell anyone). I also like the caraway taste of New York-style rye bread with any sarnie that involves mayonnaise.

LOBSTER CLUB.
This is very decadent, of course, because it simply is all the above with lobster instead of chicken. Don't omit the bacon; it still belongs here. You can use fresh, tinned or frozen lobster meat, or crab.

BLT.

Or (as if you needed telling) bacon, lettuce and tomato. Which is a club without the chicken, I suppose. I prefer a leaner rasher for this, so I use back bacon. While the bread for a true club sandwich must be white, the BLT works brilliantly with doorsteps of Granary or wholemeal bread. I do like to make my own mayonnaise for it (see page 211). I always think that, like the club, the best way to serve a BLT is to take the constituent parts to the table and let everyone build their own. That way you don't have to try and present a sandwich that, well made, wants to collapse before you get it out of the kitchen.

HALLOUMI, ROCKET AND TOMATO 'CLUB'.

Some abbreviations work, some don't. This is a veggie BLT, because the halloumi cheese adds that salty, slightly fatty edge to an otherwise verdant sarnie. I'd go back to toast for this one or, even better, toasted pita bread, which you can stuff. A 250g block of halloumi will feed 3–4 people. You also need a bag of rocket and 3 thinly sliced tomatoes. I don't put mayonnaise in this sandwich but you could, of course. I like to imitate the smokiness of bacon by making a dressing with smoked paprika – vigorously whisk together the juice of a lemon, ½ teaspoon of smoky paprika and about 3 tablespoons of olive oil and toss with the rocket. Be aware that halloumi can be salty, so don't season the dressing.

Larder salads.

A HOLIDAY PACKAGE: LARDER SALADS.

Come Christmastime in Naples, they have a special dish. It may seem rather incongruous to us here in the chilly north, but it's a salad. To prepare *insalata di rinforzo*, cooked vegetables are combined with preserved items from the store cupboard. They enhance the vegetables and, in an age when you couldn't buy things outside their natural growing season, they also added taste and texture to the winter's paucity of fresh ingredients. The literal translation of *rinforzo* is 'reinforced' but it can mean 'topping up', too.

I was delighted to come across *insalata di rinforzo* while researching this book because it's what you might call a good, textbook example of a 'larder salad'. That's my catch-all name for those wonderful dishes you always seem to discover on Mediterranean holidays. There are hundreds of them, many centred round common ingredients such as olives, capers, anchovies and pickles. They'd make for a rather exhaustive and ultimately pointless book but I hope you will forgive my devoting one chapter to them. The reason is simple: these are salads as meals, not side dishes, palate cleansers or starters, as we tend to view them in this country. Not that we don't have fine versions of our own. If you think of a ploughman's lunch, it's based on a similar concept to a Greek salad. I haven't included it here, though. The food in this chapter is for those evenings when we sit outside and pretend we are like the Niçois or Athenians, lining the streets under awnings and harpooning olives with our forks.

THE KIT.

Your store cupboard can be your very own delicatessen if you keep a rolling stock of the following items. They will come in handy for many of the recipes in this section (and many others).

ANCHOVIES. The preserved anchovy, in one form or another, has been seasoning food since as far back as Ancient Rome. Even if you think you don't like it, you'd be surprised how much more there is to the little fish than a pizza topping (look at the ingredients of a bottle of Worcestershire sauce, for example). You will find lots of recipes using anchovies in this book and by far the best way to buy them is packed in salt. Jars of anchovies in salt are available from most Italian or Spanish delis. The Spanish ones tend to be the best. Escala, a town in northern Catalonia, is particularly famous for them. Anchovies packed in salt need to be filleted when you come to use them, but this is easy (for instructions, see page 30). If you prefer to buy anchovies in a tin, go for those kept in olive oil.

CAPERS. A caper is the bud of a bush that grows all along the coast of the Mediterranean. It works a bit like the anchovy and the olive, as a salty, bitter condiment. In Spanish shops you might also find the fruit of the same bush, caper berries, which are usually sold pickled with their stalks intact.

For cooking with capers, choose those packed in salt, like anchovies (see above), rather than the ones in vinegar. Once washed, the salted ones will give you a truer taste.

OLIVES. If you are lucky enough to live near a good deli, it is best to buy olives only when you need them rather than keeping them on spec. They do deteriorate, even in the fridge. I sometimes keep a stash of the dried black variety (they might be sold as date olives). Avoid tinned olives, and pitted olives in general. These are produced for convenience rather than flavour.

COCKTAIL GHERKINS (CORNICHONS). Not to be confused with the larger gherkin eaten as a pickle. These are smaller and saltier. They are usually pickled in vinegar, with or without dill and peppercorns.

TINNED PULSES. For the sake of this book, I'm assuming that you will probably use tinned beans rather than dried ones. At home, that's what I usually do. I must admit that I prefer to cook my own beans and lentils from scratch (see page 191), but I know myself well enough to keep a pyramid of what I call 'forgetful beans' in the corner of the larder. Lots of chefs are snobby about them, and certainly until recently it was hard to find decent ones. It was kidney beans (in a slippery brine of salt and sugar) or bust. However, there are now some excellent brands of tinned pulses available, especially some of the supermarkets' own organic ones. Do look at the ingredients when deciding which brand to buy. Many of the organic types are free of salt and canned in their own cooking liquor. And some beans 'can' better than others. Kidney beans, for example, are far less appetising from a tin than borlotti or cannellini.

TINNED TUNA. The French and Spanish are the world's best fish canners. I know it sounds pedantic, but you can have a bit of fun sourcing your tinned fish if you care to. Tuna should be cooked and canned in olive oil. It is worth hunting down the Spanish brand, Ortiz (identifiable by the rather jolly red and yellow tin), although some French versions are excellent. If you are a big tuna fan, look out for albacore (white tuna) and bonito (a near relative). Some Spanish manufacturers also sell tuna in a vinaigrette-type dressing (*escabeche*) – although I find this an acquired taste. And talking of taste, I never use tuna in brine. It reminds me of cat food. In fact, I've seen better-looking cat food.

PRESERVED VEGETABLES. I keep a running store of these especially for larder salads. Jars of artichoke hearts in oil and white asparagus in brine are not only essential for Catalan Salad (see page 99) but also make handy nibbles for impromptu guests. Look out for some of the more unusual delicacies like tiny pickled broad beans or wood-roasted peppers.

VINEGAR. I keep three vinegars on standby in my cupboard. This might seem excessive but I think each one brings something different to the table. For cooking and curing (and some dressings), I use red or white wine vinegar. Cider vinegar would also work, if you like it. Balsamic vinegar is dark and treacly. It should be made in the Modena region of Italy from Trebbiano grapes and well aged. However, its recent surge in popularity has led to large-scale commercial production, so beware of some brands, which are non-aged vinegars darkened with caramel. Your best guide is to check whether its age is on the label: ten to twenty years is a good sign. Be prepared to pay quite a hefty sum of money. You only need a small amount of it so if you are put off by the price consider how long it will last you.

Sherry vinegar is not produced commercially on such a large

scale. Like balsamic, it should be well aged. You are most likely to come across the Valdespino variety in this country, which is aged for ten years. It is a good, reliable vinegar.

THREE POTATO SALADS.

For me, these meals are the best of the larder salads. They are elegant in a nonchalant, thrown-together way. They are also at the heart of this collection of recipes – a triumph of good ingredients over effort. Perhaps that is why these are salads I'd be happy to give to dinner guests without feeling that I'd somehow 'skimped'. As soon as the weather warms up, I want to invite everyone I know over, sit them in my garden, ply them with rosé (yes, rosé) and make a salade niçoise . . . sort of.

SALADE NIÇOISE.
Only the most idiotic cook would lay claim to the actual recipe for a salade niçoise. I've yet to meet two aficionados of this wonderful dish who agree 100 per cent on how it should be done. Which is fine. It is hardly set in stone. Throughout France you find meat, fish and vegetables cooked à la niçoise, which means 'like they do in Nice'. It refers to the inclusion of anchovies, tomatoes and the famous little black olives of the region. A true salade niçoise, as far as I can make out, is based entirely on local produce and consists of tomatoes, cucumber, onion, garlic, young broad beans (raw), black olives and cured anchovies. With the possible exception of an egg, there should be no cooked ingredients at all. So, no tuna and no spuds. This, of course, disqualifies every single version I've ever eaten (three of which were in Nice, by the way).

So let's not get hung up on authenticity. If you have another recipe for this salad and you like it, don't start using mine. If you don't like anchovies but like tuna (or vice versa), leave them out. If you are a fan of neither, then try one of the near relations to this salad that I have discovered on my travels around the Med. Recipes for those follow this one.

Having said that we don't need to worry about authenticity, we do need to be vigilant about ingredients. These dishes are about celebrating provenance – of the fresh stuff and what's in the larder. So buy your ingredients judiciously and treat what you have with some dignity! Carelessness when shopping for this dish and lack of attention during the unfeasibly easy bit of cooking will spoil everything. Below are the most obvious pitfalls – the seven deadly sins of salade niçoise:

1. The wrong olives. By which I mean, principally, tinned, pitted black olives. I don't know why they taste of mouthwash, but they do. If you can, seek out the dry, slightly wrinkly olives that Nice is famous for. Buying olives over the counter of a deli where you get to taste one first is the safest way to obtain the best. Some supermarkets now stock an excellent range.

2. The wrong lettuce. By which I principally mean iceberg. Sorry, but there you go. A close second is anything frilly, like lollo or oak leaf. Potato salads need robust leaves. Cos and Little Gem are best but chicory will also work. Beware of leaves such as rocket that bruise easily – the salad will taste good but wilt fast.

3. The wrong fish. By which I mean tuna. I think seared fresh tuna in a salade niçoise is wrong. Just showing off. Spend money on posh tinned tuna, like they do just about everywhere except in the UK (or confit your own – see page 97). The Spanish produce the best stuff (see page 91). Beware cheap anchovy fillets, too. They shouldn't be 'hairy' or particularly 'fishy'. Again, the Spanish ones are the best.

4. Hard-boiled egg. The yolk should be creamy rather than hard, to help with the dressing. Time your eggs pedantically.

5. Unripe tomatoes. Hard to avoid completely, easy to overcome. If you end up with hard, watery tomatoes, macerate them for half an hour or more with the dressing in the recipe before adding them to the salad. This will bring them along a bit.

6. Cold potato. Not room temperature cold but straight out of the fridge. My teeth ache just thinking about it. I don't reckon leftover spuds are up to the mark for this salad anyway. The starch in a potato changes some time after it has been cooked, which is what makes yesterday's tatties taste the way they do. Save them for bubble and squeak.

7. Overdressing. Salade niçoise and all its cousins are naturally alive with flavours. Nothing swamps them like a ton of vinaigrette. Leave all pre-prepared dressings well alone and use a little oil and vinegar or lemon juice instead.

For 4 people you need:

* ★ 400g new potatoes (small ones such as
  Jersey Royals are best), scrubbed
* ★ 100g green beans (use your favourites; runners
  or broad beans are mine)
* ★ 4 eggs
* ★ 4 tomatoes
* ★ 75ml extra virgin olive oil
* ★ 1 tablespoon lemon juice, or red or white wine vinegar
* ★ ¼ teaspoon black pepper
* ★ 100g (about ½ tin) cooked butter beans or cannellini
  beans, drained and rinsed
* ★ 1 Cos lettuce or 2 Little Gem, leaves torn
* ★ about 200g tinned tuna in oil, drained
* ★ 100g black olives
* ★ 2 tablespoons capers
* ★ a small handful of basil leaves
* ★ 8 anchovy fillets
* ★ salt

First of all, cook the potatoes until tender. Leave to cool, then,
unless they are tiny, break them up by hand or slice them.

Next, cook the beans. Runners should be sliced and given
a good 5 minutes at a rolling boil; broad beans need no more
than 1–2 minutes. If the broad beans are not too babyish, they
look and taste fantastic when shucked. This means squishing
them out of their skins (use thumb and forefinger and don't
press too hard), which is fiddly but worth it. Fine French beans
are best cooked briefly and left fairly crunchy – 3 minutes tops.

Eggs next. For creamy yolks, bring a pan of water to the
boil, carefully put in the eggs, then cover and boil for exactly

6 minutes. Cool immediately by plunging them into cold water. Peel them as soon as possible, as the shell comes off most easily just after they have been cooked. Cut them into quarters.

Deseed the tomatoes by cutting them open from top (stalk end) to bottom, placing them on a chopping board and scooping out the seeds with a spoon. Not only are the seeds indigestible, but the watery seed cavity can bleed into salads, drowning the leaves. I promise you won't lose flavour by doing this. Then cut each tomato half into 4.

The rest of the preparation of this salad is about throwing it together. Whisk up the oil and lemon juice or vinegar with the pepper and some salt and dress the potatoes with some of it. Doing this while they are slightly warm is good, as they will absorb it better. If you have broken rather than sliced them as suggested, this is particularly prudent. Then toss everything except the eggs and anchovies together in a large bowl with the remaining dressing. Top it off with very un-arranged quarters of the eggs and slivers of anchovy. *Et voilà*.

DIY: CONFIT YOUR OWN TUNA.

Good tinned tuna in oil has been more or less confited (cooked slowly in the oil). If you have access to a good fishmonger's, you can ask for tuna belly (as opposed to the loin that steaks come from) and do this yourself. It is expensive but not time consuming, and the tuna keeps for a week or so in the fridge, as long as it stays in the oil.

You need:
★ 1 tuna belly
★ enough light olive oil to cover it in the pan
★ a handful of peppercorns and 1–2 bay leaves (optional)

Heat the oil and any seasonings to simmering point in a large pan and then immerse the tuna belly in the oil. Bring it back to a gentle simmer but do not allow it to boil. Simmer for about half an hour, then remove from the heat and leave to cool completely. The tuna must be entirely covered by the oil. When the fish is cold, you can remove any skin and bones. This is much easier to do after cooking (like flaking poached fish). Return the fish to the oil if you do not wish to use it immediately and keep refrigerated until needed.

A TURKISH SALAD.

This is a slightly unusual salad, with a great variety of textures, including a crunchy topping of crushed almonds. The use of dill gives it a very distinctive taste.

For 4 people you need:
★ 400g new potatoes, scrubbed
★ 4 eggs
★ 6 tomatoes
★ 3 red or yellow peppers
★ 100g whole blanched almonds (or use flaked almonds, if you prefer)
★ 1 large or 2 small cucumbers
★ 2 Little Gem lettuces, leaves separated
★ 200g kalamata olives, pitted
★ 100g (about ½ tin) cooked butter beans, drained and rinsed
★ 3 tablespoons extra virgin olive oil
★ 1 tablespoon red or white wine vinegar
★ 1 tablespoon chopped dill
★ salt and freshly ground black pepper

Cook the potatoes and eggs and prepare the tomatoes following the instructions for Salade Niçoise (see page 97).

You can serve the peppers raw or grilled in this salad. I like them grilled, with the skins removed. To do this, char them over a gas flame or place under a hot grill until they have blistered and look 'collapsed', then leave them to cool in a covered bowl. This helps loosen the blackened skin. Peel the skin off with your fingers and remove the seeds. Cut the flesh into strips.

Roast the almonds in a moderate oven for 10 minutes, then leave to cool completely. Crush them roughly in a food processor or with a pestle and mortar.

Deseed the cucumber by cutting it in half lengthways and running a spoon along the seed cavity, then slice it. Combine with the lettuce leaves and tomatoes in a large bowl. Add the olives, butter beans, peppers and potatoes and dress with the oil, vinegar and dill. Season to taste with salt and pepper. Sprinkle the salad with the crushed almonds and garnish with the quartered eggs before serving.

CATALAN SALAD.

Here is a potato salad for carnivores, although if you don't eat meat it's still good without it. I often swap the charcuterie for anchovies. You needn't go mad searching for true Catalan *salchichón* or chorizo either. Use any cured sausage or salami you like.

This salad makes much of preserved vegetables. You could use the fresh versions in their place but the creamy blandness of white asparagus from a tin or jar and the slightly pickled taste of artichoke hearts in oil work very well here.

For 4 people you need:

★ 400g new potatoes, scrubbed
★ 4 eggs
★ 3 tomatoes
★ 50g pancetta or dry-cured bacon, cut into thin strips
★ 100ml extra virgin olive oil
★ 1 tablespoon sherry vinegar, or red or white wine vinegar
★ ½ teaspoon salt
★ ½ teaspoon black pepper
★ 50g chorizo or salami (or similar), thinly sliced
★ 1 red or green pepper, thinly sliced
★ 2 heads of chicory, leaves separated
★ 50g (about ¼ tin) white beans of your choice,
   drained and rinsed
★ a bunch of radishes, sliced if large
★ 100g artichoke hearts in oil, drained
★ 8 tinned white asparagus spears
★ 100g olives of your choice
★ 1 tablespoon capers

Cook the potatoes and eggs and prepare the tomatoes following
the instructions for Salade Niçoise (see page 96).

Fry the pancetta until crisp, then set aside. Mix the oil,
vinegar, salt and pepper together to form a loose dressing.

Basically the salad is built like the two above. You will get the
best results if you dress the potatoes while still warm, then allow
them to cool before tossing with the other ingredients. As with
the salads above, I reserve the eggs for garnishing, along with
the pancetta in this case.

TWO 'ENGLISH' POTATO SALADS.

There is more to a British potato salad than mayonnaise and chives. Here are a couple of suggestions, based on the same principles as the Mediterranean recipes above. Cook the potatoes as for Salade Niçoise (see page 96), then proceed as follows:

SMOKED TROUT AND SPINACH SALAD.

Add flaked smoked trout, baby spinach, sliced cucumber, cooked green beans and walnuts. If you can get hold of fresh or pickled samphire, add this as well. Dress with a simple vinaigrette made with 3 tablespoons olive oil, a teaspoon of mustard and a tablespoon of cider vinegar.

HAM AND CHICORY SALAD.

Add cooked ham, chicory, finely sliced fennel and green beans and include grated lemon zest in the vinaigrette above.

TWO BREAD SALADS.

We shop for bread very differently from our counterparts in the Mediterranean, where bread is not expected to 'keep' for more than a day. Once it has gone stale, it is not necessarily thrown out but is used in a specific way. Here the bulk of each salad is provided by that stale bread, which sounds very unglamorous indeed. Don't be so sure. In the same way that bruschetta (see page 61) absorbs the flavour of garlic and the best olive oil, so the bread in these salads takes on the surrounding flavours and becomes something far more special than a clever way of dealing with the sorry remains of a loaf.

PANZANELLA.

This is probably the snazziest thing you could ever make with stale bread. It is a wonderful lunch for a summer's day. The best bread to use is sourdough. Buy it a day ahead of using it, if you can. If not, the easiest way to contrive staleness is to tear it up (no neat cubes for this, please) and put it in a very low oven for an hour or so before you need it.

For 4 people you need:
★ 3 peppers (if one could be yellow, this looks great)
★ 8 ripe tomatoes
★ 100ml extra virgin olive oil
★ ½ teaspoon salt
★ 2 tablespoons red wine vinegar
★ 1 large or 2 small cucumbers
★ 1 tablespoon capers
★ 100g black olives
★ a generous fistful of basil leaves
★ 8–9 anchovy fillets (optional)
★ 1 small sourdough loaf, torn into very rough, bite-sized pieces
★ 5 tablespoons water

Char the peppers over a gas flame or place them under a hot grill until they have blistered and look 'collapsed'. Leave them to cool in a covered bowl. This helps loosen the blackened skin. Peel the skin off with your fingers and remove the seeds, then cut the flesh into slices. Don't wash the peeled peppers, as it is better to have little black bits than lose flavour.

Deseed the tomatoes by cutting them in half from top (stalk end) to bottom and scooping the seeds out with a spoon. Set the seeds aside. Roughly dice the tomato flesh and place it in a bowl. Put the seeds in a sieve, hold it over the bowl of tomatoes and run a spoon around the sieve to squish any juice out of the seeds. Discard the seeds.

Make the dressing by combining the oil, salt and vinegar. Deseed the cucumber by cutting it in half lengthways and running a spoon along the seed cavity. Cut the cucumber into crescent moon shapes on a slight diagonal. Toss the peppers, tomatoes, cucumber, capers, olives, basil and anchovies, if using, with half the dressing and set aside.

Now place the bread in a large mixing bowl. Pour over the remaining dressing and sprinkle with the water. Toss the bread around the bowl a few times and allow it to sit like this until it has softened.

Toss the 2 parts of this salad together just 10 minutes or so before serving.

FATTOUSH.

This salad comes from Syria but the final seasoning is Turkish in origin. Sumac is made from the dried leaves and berries of a shrub. These are ground down to a fine, purple powder and the taste is sharp, like lemon. If you can't get hold of it, don't let that put you off making this unusual dish – just leave it out.

You can use split, toasted pita bread as the base for this. However, if you have access to a Turkish or Middle Eastern deli, you will be able to choose from a wide range of flatbreads, some of which are sold vacuum-packed in thin sheets.

For 4 people you need:

★ 4 tomatoes, the firmer the better
★ ½ cucumber (or 1 small one)
★ 4 discs of flatbread, toasted in a low oven until crisp and dry
★ juice of 1 lemon
★ 100ml extra virgin olive oil
★ 1 teaspoon dried mint
★ 1 red or green pepper, finely diced
★ 2 red onions, chopped
★ 2 garlic cloves, chopped
★ ½ small cauliflower, cut into tiny florets
★ 4–5 small radishes, finely chopped
★ 400g tin of chickpeas, drained and rinsed
★ a bunch of flat-leaf parsley, chopped
★ ½ teaspoon sumac
★ salt and freshly ground black pepper

Deseed the tomatoes by cutting them in half from top (stalk end) to bottom and scooping out the seeds with a spoon. Set the seeds aside. Finely dice the tomato flesh and place it in a large salad bowl.

Deseed the cucumber by cutting it in half lengthways and running a spoon along the seed cavity, then chop it finely.

The premise of this is easy. Break the bread into bite-sized shards with your hands. Toss it with the lemon juice and olive oil to soften it ever so slightly, then combine it with all the rest of the ingredients except the sumac. Sprinkle the sumac over the salad.

VARIATIONS.

Basically, this is one of those wonderful family dishes that you can modify to suit your own taste. If you don't fancy the raw cauliflower, for example, you could omit it. Some recipes contain no chickpeas either, and some combine the vegetables with finely shredded Cos lettuce. You could use dill instead of the mixture of dried mint and parsley. Go create!

TWO TINNED BEAN SALADS.

Pulses seem to be an integral part of many of the larder salads. It is in Italy that you find some of the best. Both these bean salads make great sauces for pasta. Don't use much – just 50g per person of a shape like conchiglie (shells) or orecchiette (little ears) will do. And don't worry about heating the beans any more than described below; the pasta will warm them through just enough. An alternative is to serve the salads over big pieces of toast or bruschetta (see page 61).

A WINTER BEAN SALAD.

Radicchio is sold as a salad leaf in the UK but it is often wilted in hot oil in Italian dishes. This takes the edge off its bitterness.

For 4 people you need:
★ 1 head of radicchio
★ 400g tin of cannellini or borlotti beans
★ 2 tablespoons red wine vinegar (or balsamic vinegar, if you prefer)
★ 2 tablespoons extra virgin olive oil, plus extra to serve
★ 100g good olives, roughly chopped
★ 1 tablespoon capers, roughly chopped
★ 2 tablespoons chopped flat-leaf parsley
★ 1 tablespoon chopped thyme or rosemary
★ 50g Parmesan or pecorino cheese, shaved or grated
★ salt

You will need to core and roughly shred the radicchio. Think of it as a spindly relation of cabbage; slice it in half from top to bottom and remove the solid white, triangular core. Now you can shred the leaves as roughly or finely as you please. Use your hands if you like; I'm always happiest when I can dump a knife. It makes preparing dinner feel totally effortless.

Drain the beans but reserve the liquor. In a saucepan, gently warm half the liquor with the vinegar and oil. Let it simmer for a couple of minutes, then add all the rest of the ingredients except the cheese, stir them through the liquor and remove from the heat. Don't let it cook! There is your salad. Dress it with as much extra virgin oil as you like (I like a lot) and the cheese. If you plan to serve it warm, I recommend you grate the cheese and stir it through, so it will meld with rather than melt over the beans. Trust me, the former is prettier than the latter.

TUNA, BEAN, LEMON AND OREGANO SALAD.

This is one recipe where I like to use dried oregano (against which I am normally very prejudiced). There are infinite possibilities with tuna and beans, as anyone who has ever been a student will know. This has a Sicilian twist to it, although I can't vouch for its authenticity; it just happens to be my favourite.

For 4 people you need:
- ★ 2 firm tomatoes
- ★ 200–250g tin of good tuna in olive oil, drained
- ★ 400g tin of white beans of your choice, drained and rinsed
- ★ 1 red onion, or a bunch of spring onions, finely chopped
- ★ 1 tablespoon capers, roughly chopped

- ★ 3–4 anchovy fillets
- ★ ¼ teaspoon dried crushed chilli
- ★ 2 garlic cloves, chopped
- ★ zest of ½ lemon and the juice of all of it
- ★ 1 teaspoon dried oregano
- ★ 2 tablespoons roughly chopped fresh oregano
  or flat-leaf parsley
- ★ 100ml extra virgin olive oil

Deseed the tomatoes by cutting them open from top (stalk end) to bottom, placing them on a chopping board and scooping out the seeds with a spoon. Chop them finely.

Combine the tuna with the beans, onion, tomatoes and capers. Then set to work on the dressing. Chop or pound the anchovies until they are almost a paste and combine them with the chilli and garlic. You could do all of this in a food processor if you have one with a small compartment. Don't use a blender, which is too powerful. Add the lemon zest and juice, herbs and oil and whisk until you have a rough emulsion. Add the dressing to the salad and allow everything to sit together for at least half an hour, if possible, before serving.

TWO CHEESE SALADS.

The cheese salad is really a very broad church. Think of ploughman's lunch or the famous trio of mozzarella, basil and tomato. For the sake of this chapter, I'm going to stick with the summer holiday theme, which makes the inclusion of Greek salad compulsory, really.

GREEK SALAD.

Of all the holiday dishes we remember, this one is probably the best known. Quite right too, because when made well it is fantastic. It is serious hot-weather food – real heatwave material. The vegetables are cooling and the 'larder' bits salty.

Like the salade niçoise, though, here is a dish against which all sorts of abuse has been committed. The worst, worst, *worst* is, once again, iceberg lettuce. You must use Cos, or omit leaves altogether. The second is Danish feta cheese. I'm sorry if any Danes are reading this. Once upon a time it was the only feta you could get in the UK, unless you lived near a Greek or Turkish deli. Made with cow's milk (feta should be a sheep's milk cheese) and devoid of any taste except a slightly overwhelming saltiness, it is a vacuum-packed piece of nonsense. If you can't get hold of proper Greek feta, use a crumbly goat's cheese. And if you prefer things a little blander, try making this with mozzarella. If you think about it, it's no less authentic than pretend feta.

This is probably stating the obvious, but the main ingredients of Greek salad will make a fine dish without cheese altogether. The intensity of the chopped tomatoes, mint, olives and onion in the vinegary oil is a great foil for seafood, especially prawns or squid (which love mint, as fans of Vietnamese food will know). But cheeseless Greek salad also goes very well with lamb. Grill a butterflied leg of lamb, leaving it pink in the middle and serve it thinly sliced next to the salad. You could swap a pile of chops for the leg. If meat or fish is not your bag, try chickpeas or broad beans.

For 4 people you need:
* ★ 8 tomatoes
* ★ 1 large or 2 small cucumbers
* ★ 2 tablespoons capers

- ★ 1 teaspoon dried oregano
- ★ 2 tablespoons red wine vinegar
- ★ 100ml extra virgin olive oil
- ★ 1 red onion, sliced as thinly as possible
- ★ 200g kalamata olives, pitted
- ★ 1 Cos lettuce, trimmed and roughly cut up
- ★ 200g feta cheese, broken into bite-sized chunks
- ★ a bunch of mint, leaves whole or roughly chopped
- ★ freshly ground black pepper (leave salt well alone)

Deseed the tomatoes by cutting them open from top (stalk end) to bottom, placing them on a chopping board and scooping out the seeds with a spoon. Then cut each half into 4.

Deseed the cucumber by cutting it in half lengthways and running a spoon along the seed cavity, then slice it. Chop the capers to a near paste and combine with the dried oregano, vinegar and oil. Toss half this dressing with the tomatoes, onion and cucumber. If possible, allow this lot to marinate for half an hour.

When you are ready to serve, toss the olives and Cos into the salad. Roughly toss the feta with the remaining dressing and some black pepper and scatter it over the other ingredients. Serve strewn with the mint.

. . . AND SOMETHING FROM THE PUNJAB.

If Madhur Jaffrey ever reads this book, she will think she has a stalker. I have to pass this recipe on because the minute I saw it I was reminded of Greek salad. It was on one of those wonderful, part-food, part-travelogue shows she used to make. They were always slightly mad. If I'm not wrong, she made this in a paddy field complete with some obliging water buffalo in the background. Five minutes later she was sat, laughing, on the back of a lorry, tearing up the grand trunk road from Delhi to Amritsar, on the border with Pakistan (an experience she likened to bungee jumping). Why don't they make shows like that any more?

The obliging water buffalo would have been responsible for the cheese in this salad – paneer. It is often wrongly described as cottage cheese but, although the two are quite similar, paneer is strained. If it has a near relative it would be proper, buffalo-milk mozzarella, which is easier to obtain. You can also use feta or goat's cheese, though the taste will be stronger.

This salad, like many in South Asia, is oil free, but if you want to drizzle it with a bit of extra virgin it does no harm.

For 4 people you need:
★ 8 ripe tomatoes
★ 2 red onions, sliced as finely as possible
★ 1cm cube of fresh ginger, finely chopped
★ 2 garlic cloves, chopped
★ 2 small green chillies, chopped (optional)
★ juice of 1 lemon or 2 limes
★ 1 teaspoon salt (omit this if using feta)
★ ½ teaspoon freshly ground black pepper
★ ½ teaspoon ground cumin
★ 100g paneer or similar cheese, roughly crumbled or cut into small cubes
★ a bunch of mint, leaves whole or roughly chopped

Deseed the tomatoes by cutting them open from top (stalk end) to bottom, placing them on a chopping board and scooping out the seeds with a spoon. Then chop them roughly. Combine them with the onions in a bowl. Mix together the ginger, garlic, chillies, if using, lemon or lime juice, salt, pepper and cumin and scatter on top of the tomatoes and onions. Top this with the cheese and mint leaves and serve immediately. I like it with warm pita bread. Naan bread is easily available these days but I find it slightly sweet when made commercially.

DIY: MAKE YOUR OWN PANEER.

It is very easy to make paneer, and you will find your own much tastier than the commercial variety. This recipe makes enough for the Punjab salad above. You will need a piece of muslin, available from kitchen shops or haberdasher's.

You need:
* ★ 1 litre whole milk
* ★ juice of 1 lemon
* ★ ½ teaspoon salt

Heat the milk in a small pan until it reaches scalding point (it will fizz against the sides). Lower the heat so that it doesn't boil over and stir in the lemon juice and salt. Continue to simmer and the milk should curdle. You will now have curds and whey (in case you never saw them before).

Line a sieve with a piece of muslin, allowing plenty of excess to hang over the edge. Place the sieve over a pan or bowl, pour the curds into the sieve and leave to drain. Now pull up the excess cloth to form a little 'bag' with the curds (a surprisingly small amount) inside it. Twist the top or tie a knot in it and squeeze out any excess moisture, as if you were wringing out clothes. Alternatively put a weight on the cheese and leave it there for a good half an hour or so. The cheese is ready to use after this time. If you are making it in advance, shape it into small balls and keep it in its whey (which is how mozzarella is kept, incidentally).

For another recipe using paneer, see page 247.

Stir-fries.

FAST AND FURIOUS: STIR-FRIES.

Strictly speaking, this is not a chapter about Chinese food, but it is the place to look if you crave the snappy textures and flavours of oriental cooking. If you tend to eat ready-made oriental meals and takeaways, most of which are mediocre, you're denying yourself the true pleasures of what should be some of the healthiest, fastest food on the planet. Lurid, oversweetened sauces, thick with cornflour and 'flavour enhancers', don't do you any favours. When we think of oriental food we think of virtuous eating. We want it to make our bodies feel like temples. Bad oriental food lies in wait like a culinary Lorelei. It appeals by association. The easiest way to sidestep the indifferent stuff is to cook your own stir-fries. Do yourself the hugest of favours and, if you don't own one already, buy a wok.

The word stir-fry may have become inextricably linked with the cooking of China but in fact the practice is widespread all over Asia. The wok has been used for centuries as far west as India and Pakistan. The cooking of Southeast Asia is largely based on stir-frying. Even a Thai curry is essentially a stir-fry. The reason for such widespread use of the wok? Its shape. The unique curvature allows the entire surface area to heat evenly so that the sides are as useful to cook on as the base. This is pretty handy in one of the most densely populated regions of the world. Less fuel is used if cooking can be done rapidly.

If only we took this attitude in the West. We have a tendency to pile a heap of mysticism on anything that comes to us from the East. The way some people talk about woks, they might as well be Tibetan singing bowls. I know so many people who own woks and never use them because they think there is something complicated about them. They have an undeserved reputation for being high maintenance. They are, in fact, one of the simplest, handiest things ever invented.

You don't need an enormous amount of gear to be able to eat a different stir-fry every night of the week. Below is my basic oriental store cupboard. I really recommend you raid a Chinese supermarket to buy the following ingredients. Although most are available in Western shops, Chinese shops are usually cheaper.

THE KIT.

SOY SAUCE. Most oriental cookery uses sauces made from fermented soy beans or fish for seasoning. Whether it is an ingredient in a dish or served as a condiment, soy sauce is essentially used like salt. Think about this when you buy it, since whatever you get is going to be with you for a while. Make it a good 'un. There is a lot of bad soy sauce out there. When made properly it is naturally brewed. When not, it is artificially coloured and flavoured with all sorts of nonsense. You don't want to find caramel or flavour enhancers in a soy sauce. The best brand widely available in this country is Kikkoman.

I also keep a small bottle of the Indonesian soy sauce, *kecap manis*. This is thicker, darker and sweet. I like to add a sweet note to most of my stir-fries (which you can omit if you prefer), so I usually add a small amount of *kecap manis* to my seasoning. If I can't get hold of it, I use runny honey instead.

MISO. This is a paste made from fermented soy beans and it usually has a grain added to it as well (often rice or barley). It makes a great base for soups and I use it in one of my favourite stir-fries, Bean Curd with Bean and Pepper Sauce (see page 127).

THAI FISH SAUCE. As well as soy sauce, I keep a bottle of the Thai equivalent, fish sauce, or *nam pla* (see page 263).

COOKING OIL. I use a light, non-virgin olive oil for all my stir-fries. Some people will tell you that olive oil is too strongly flavoured for oriental food but the light versions available everywhere these days do fine. If you are dubious about cooking stir-fries with olive oil, buy groundnut oil instead. Sesame oil is mainly used as a seasoning, as it has a strong flavour. I keep a small bottle of the pure stuff for that purpose. Avoid the versions blended with vegetable oil: load of rubbish.

VINEGAR. Some dishes are sharpened with rice wine or rice wine vinegar and the Chinese often use a wine called Shaoxing that tastes rather like sherry. I must admit that, because I use them elsewhere, I tend to use sherry and sherry vinegar in my oriental cooking. I know, I know. I'll never reach enlightenment.

TOMATO KETCHUP. Don't be surprised by the inclusion of tomato ketchup in one of these recipes. The very name ketchup comes from *kecap*, Malay for sauce, and the real thing (sweet, sour and red hot with chillies) is still common in Southeast Asia. Incidentally I have seen the Heinz version used many times over there, too!

PEANUT BUTTER. The spicy peanut sauce so beloved of satay fans is easy to make if you keep a good peanut butter handy. For the texture to be right, you need a crunchy one. I like the brands that are unsweetened and not 'loosened' with vegetable oil. Sunpat and Whole Earth both make this type. Natural peanut butter should be kept in the fridge after opening. You do find ready-made satay-style peanut sauces but beware, westernised ones are often oversweetened, while some oriental brands are fiercely hot.

LIMES. Limes are more common for souring oriental food than lemons. I do like to use fresh limes, as their aroma is one of my favourite cooking smells in the world. But it is probably worth keeping a bottle of lime juice in the fridge. I do, and it is pretty good. Incidentally, there is a lovely Indonesian drink where lime is added to hot water. It has a very cleansing, astringent feel to it and is especially good if you feel like skipping caffeine for any reason.

THE WOK. This is one of the cheapest utensils you can buy if you know where to look. The best place is a Chinese supermarket, where a wok, ideally made from carbonised steel with a solid wooden handle, should cost less than a tenner. If you buy one from a trendy kitchen shop, the chances are you will see a big hike in the price. That shouldn't necessarily put you off. There are some very good non-stick woks available in department stores and the like. They could be worth the extra pennies if you don't fancy seasoning your wok (see below). Whatever you spend on a wok, don't fret too much. Mine is currently in its tenth year of service, so any wok, if well looked after, is a long-term investment.

First things first: your hob. If it is gas, then buy the traditional round-bottomed wok. If it isn't, buy a flat-bottomed one. This is the only type that will work on electric rings, or ceramic or halogen hobs. Don't be seduced by wok stands, as they keep the base of the pan too far from the heat.

Secondly, the seasoning. If you buy a traditional wok it will need to be washed and seasoned before use. Here is where the urban myths about woks being harder to look after than a Tamagochi (whatever happened to them?) kick in.

Give the wok a good scrub in warm, soapy water before you use it. It will probably have a lubricant on it to stop it rusting. To season it, you need some vegetable oil and a roll of kitchen towel. Add 2 tablespoons of oil to the wok and leave it over a low heat for about 20 minutes, regularly tilting the wok to coat the base and sides thoroughly with the oil. The oil will go black and start to smoke. After 20 minutes, quickly, while still hot (mind your hands), wipe off the excess oil with a wad of kitchen towel. The towel will go black. Without letting the wok cool down, add more oil and repeat the process until the kitchen towel no longer goes black. This does take a while, so set aside some time. And obviously don't wander off and leave the wok with hot oil in it. As you use the wok for cooking, it will slowly blacken; this is what you want. With time, use, and the correct care, the wok becomes more and more 'non-stick'.

Once the wok is seasoned, you shouldn't wash it with a scourer, nor, strictly speaking, detergent. If you watch oriental cooks, they simply use heat and water to sterilise the wok after each session. I have to admit that I regularly do throw my wok in with the other washing up but I don't scour it, as this spoils the seasoning. Neither do I let it drip dry. I either wipe it or return it to the heat. A wok must be put away thoroughly dry. I also keep one of those awful vegetable oil spray cans (originally marketed at dieters) by the sink to give the wok an occasional blast of oil.

Woks can rust inexplicably and it doesn't always mean that you haven't looked after them correctly. If you get a bit of rust on the wok just clean it gently, then dry it thoroughly before giving it a rub with some oil.

The wok heats up quickly, but this is not the only reason for the speed of a stir-fry. The principle is simple. Everything is cut small and vaguely evenly to enable quick cooking. Some people are intimidated by this quick cooking, so here are five steps to follow to enjoy stress-free stir-frying:

1. Have absolutely everything ready before you start. When I'm stir-frying, I like to play TV chef with all my ingredients laid out before me.

2. Make sure the wok is really hot before you start to cook, heating it even before you add the oil. When you add the oil, it should move freely around the wok, and not seem as viscous as at room temperature. Little wisps of smoke should appear. You are now ready to start cooking.

3. When cooking, make sure you add the ingredients to the wok in the right order. Even when cut small, some vegetables need a fraction longer than others to cook. I'll let you know the order in each recipe.

4. When stir-frying, don't so much stir as push the ingredients around the wok, making sure they all get a crack at the hot surface. You occasionally see cooks tossing vegetables deftly through the air over the wok with a flick of the wrist. Looks good; feels good; waste of effort. Never remove the wok or its ingredients from the heat or you will slow down the cooking time, which defeats the object of stir-frying.

5. One more thing: take a leaf out of the oriental book and don't load up the wok with tons of food. The principle to remember is 'big wok, small food'. That's how a stir-fry stays quick and easy. The following recipes are all for two portions. If you want to cook for a larger number, then it is more practical (and more fun) to do several different dishes than to try to feed everyone from a single stir-fry, so a good rule of thumb is: mix and match rather than multiply.

A BASIC VEGETARIAN STIR-FRY.

Here is the most basic of stir-fries, with ingredients that you can find pretty much all year round. The sauce is very, very basic. It's about balancing sweet with salty, but if you are not convinced by the honey, leave it out.

For 2 people you need:
★ 3 tablespoons soy sauce
★ ½ teaspoon runny honey
★ 2 tablespoons hot water
★ 1 tablespoon light olive oil
★ 1 red onion, sliced
★ 2 garlic cloves, finely chopped
★ 1cm piece of fresh ginger, finely chopped
★ 1 head of broccoli, divided into small florets
★ 2 carrots, sliced as thinly as possible
★ a shake of sesame oil

Make the sauce first. Combine the soy sauce, honey and water in something really small and handy (I use a coffee cup). Heat the olive oil in the wok on a high flame. As soon as it is hot, add the onion. Stir and fry for about a minute. Add the garlic and ginger and fry for another 30 seconds. Add the broccoli and carrots and stir-fry for another minute, then throw in the sauce. Only cook the sauce for about half a minute. The stir-fry is done. That's when I add the shake of sesame oil. Be very sparing with it because it can be strong. You can always add more. I tend to put sesame oil and soy sauce on the table when I serve this.

VARIATIONS.

Pretty basic, isn't it? I'm being deliberately Spartan. It doesn't have to be so 'bare necessities', but I often eat this stir-fry on a puritanical Monday night when I feel I may have had too much fun at the weekend. Don't stick to broccoli – I included it because it never seems to disappear from the shops. Other vegetables will cook in the same amount of time. Remember that the genius of stir-frying relies upon cutting everything small and cooking it fast on a high heat.

The combination of vegetables can depend on the time of year or your mood. Here is a summery combination: replace the carrots with a mixture of red and yellow peppers and use mangetout or sliced courgettes instead of the broccoli. In the depths of winter, use crunchy slices of red cabbage and wedges of fennel.

THE NO-KNIFE STIR-FRY.

If you are the kind of person who has never been put off
cooking for yourself by the thought of having to chop an onion
(or anything else, for that matter) after a long, bad day, then I
applaud you. The no-knife stir-fry is designed for the rest of us.

Bean sprouts are a great, low-maintenance way of adding
protein to a stir-fry. The commercially grown types are usually
from mung beans or soy beans. Ready to harvest within 5 days
of germination, they are cheap and packed with goodness. To
enjoy bean sprouts at their best, eat them on the day you buy
them and add them to a stir-fry no more than half a minute
before you serve it. In many Asian dishes they are barely cooked
at all, and in some they are practically a garnish.

For 2 people you need:
★ 1cm piece of fresh ginger
★ 2 garlic cloves
★ 1 lime
★ ½ teaspoon runny honey
★ a scant pinch of dried crushed chilli
★ 2 tablespoons soy sauce
★ about 50g oyster mushrooms
★ 1 tablespoon light olive oil
★ 200g mangetout
★ 200g bean sprouts

Using the finest blade on your grater (the one you might use for
Parmesan cheese), grate the ginger, garlic and lime zest into a
small bowl. Add the honey, the juice from the lime, the chilli

flakes and soy sauce and stir until the honey has dissolved. Tear the oyster mushrooms down their length into strips.

Heat the oil in a wok on a high flame. When it is just smoking, add the mushrooms. They should catch slightly, so don't be tempted to lower the heat. Fry them for 2 minutes or so. They take slightly longer than you think and can be chalky in the middle if left undercooked.

Add the mangetout and stir-fry for a further minute. Add the bean sprouts and stir-fry for just half a minute, then add the sauce. As soon as you stir in the sauce, remove the pan from the heat.

AN 'I'M FEELING EXPENSIVE' STIR-FRY.

I have chosen deliberately extravagant ingredients for this. Cashew nuts are a classic addition to stir-fries. Buy them unroasted and unsalted for the best results. In supermarkets, plain nuts usually loiter in the baking ingredients aisle. Cashews go particularly well with very fresh asparagus. You could use peas or beans instead, however, when asparagus is out of season, and there is nothing to stop you going for a more wintry vegetable, such as broccoli or cauliflower.

For 2 people you need:
★ 1 bunch of asparagus (about 400g), as skinny as possible
★ 1 bunch of spring onions
★ 1 tablespoon light olive oil
★ 2 garlic cloves, chopped
★ 1cm piece of fresh ginger, finely chopped
★ 100g cashew nuts

* ★ 2 tablespoons soy sauce
* ★ ½ teaspoon honey
* ★ 1 tablespoon sherry or Shaoxing wine

It's easy to prepare asparagus. The base of the stem is slightly woody and tough to eat, so should be discarded. To find out where the woodiness ends, simply hold a spear with the thumb and forefinger of each hand and bend it. The point at which the spear breaks is where the stem is no longer fibrous. If the asparagus is thick, peel the last inch or so with a potato peeler. Cut the asparagus into bite-sized slices on a slight diagonal and set aside. Cut the spring onions into similar-sized slices and set aside.

Heat the oil in a wok a shade more gently than usual and, when it is just hot, add the garlic and ginger. A minute later, throw in the cashew nuts and fry for a good minute or so or until they start to brown. Turn the heat up high and add the spring onions. A minute later, add the asparagus. Literally half a minute later add all the seasonings. The asparagus should be nice and crunchy.

VARIATION.

You might want to swap the cashew nuts for prawns, adding them with the garlic and ginger. A bag of good-quality frozen cooked peeled prawns is a great luxury to have in. It goes a long way, since you need only about 100g per person for this recipe. Here is what to do when adding prawns to stir-fries:

Put the frozen prawns in a large bowl, add a good litre of boiling water straight from the kettle and leave the prawns to sit in this for a minute. Then drain them in a colander, cool them with water from the tap and squeeze them dry. This is not just about thawing them out. It also removes the slightly frozen taste that even the best brands can have. If it doesn't bother you, then thaw them in the conventional way. Don't add them to the wok frozen, since there will be ice on them that will turn watery as soon as you start to fry them. To avoid this with thawed prawns, just squeeze any excess moisture from them with your hands.

TWO STIR-FRIES WITH BEAN CURD.

I call it bean curd because I'm nervous of using its other name, tofu. I can see meat-loving readers raising their eyebrows at this, the hippiest of hippy foods. Quite why it has such a bad reputation in the West is a bit of a mystery. It is bland but, used correctly, this is its strength rather than a failing. The nearest thing we produce in the West is cottage cheese or even mozzarella – silky and mild foils to stronger flavours. Like mozzarella, fresh tofu is kept in water.

For stir-fries, bean curd behaves best if fried beforehand. You can find it ready-fried in Chinese supermarkets. Simply slice the fried pieces and add them to your stir-fry near the end of cooking. If you are frying it yourself, you need to dry it thoroughly and press it for half an hour (a couple of plates sat on top of the curd, which should be wrapped in a tea towel, will do the trick) before cutting it into cubes. Another way to treat tofu for stir-fries is to freeze it raw. The texture changes after about 24 hours and becomes spongy, like the fried version. When it is thawed, you can simply cut slices from it and add it near the end of the cooking time.

The blandness of bean curd means it is ideal for some punchy stir-fries. Try the ones below (which would also be great with meat or fish).

If you don't fancy bean curd, the best alternative to use is an egg. It may surprise you that eggs make a welcome addition to stir-fries. Don't be shy of trying them. Break one or two eggs into a bowl and beat as if you were about to make an omelette. In a way, you are. Heat 2 tablespoons of light olive oil in a well-seasoned wok and, when it is good and hot, throw in the beaten egg. Leave for about half a minute, until the bottom of the egg starts to look 'omeletty'. Now gently start to turn and break the omelette with a wooden spoon. Continue with this kind of dry scrambling until the egg is fully cooked. Remove from the pan and set aside, then continue with the stir-fry. Add the broken egg just before serving.

You may not know the joy of a fried egg sitting on top of a simple stir-fry, spiked with a few flakes of dried chilli (particularly over a broccoli or cabbage stir-fry). If so, you haven't lived! I came across this habit in Indonesia.

BEAN CURD WITH BEAN AND PEPPER SAUCE.
Black bean sauce is a takeaway standard. It should taste salty-sweet and smoky and is often paired with chilli. I used to buy black bean sauce, but it invariably comes loaded with processed garlic and too much cornstarch for my liking. Miso, the Japanese bean paste, is a close cousin to black bean sauce and now I use it instead. You can find it in most supermarkets these days.

You can add plenty of chopped coriander to this dish, if you like.

For 2 people you need:

★ 2 tablespoons soy sauce
★ 1 heaped tablespoon miso paste
★ 3 tablespoons hot water
★ 1 tablespoon sherry vinegar
★ ½ teaspoon honey
★ 3 tablespoons light olive oil
★ 200g fresh bean curd, patted dry, pressed and
    cut into smallish cubes
★ 2 garlic cloves, roughly chopped
★ a pinch of dried crushed chilli
★ 3–4 spring onions, sliced
★ 1 green pepper, sliced

Mix the soy, miso, water, vinegar and honey together to
form a smooth sauce. Add a little more water if it seems
too thick.

Heat the oil in a wok until it is fiercely hot and fry the bean
curd in it, turning occasionally, until it is golden all over. It might
seem as if it is sticking at first; the trick is not to try and turn it
over too fast. Remove the bean curd from the wok and set
aside. Fry the garlic, chilli and spring onions for 1 minute, then
throw in the green pepper. After another minute or so, return the
bean curd to the wok with the sauce. As soon as it bubbles up,
the stir-fry is ready to serve.

BEAN CURD WITH PEANUT SAUCE AND CUCUMBER.
Peanut sauce (originally Indonesian) is often referred to as satay,
which is a misnomer. Satay means 'kebab'; it's just that the most
common sauce for skewered meat in the region is the spicy
peanut one we all know and love. You can use it for all sorts of

dishes and it makes a good dip, too. Mine is, naturally, a cheat's version, since I use crunchy peanut butter.

Don't be put off by the thought of frying cucumber. If you can get the smaller, Asian type, that is the best. If you are really unconvinced by the notion, however, use a courgette instead.

For 2 people you need:
★ 1 heaped tablespoon crunchy peanut butter
★ 100ml hot water
★ juice of ½ lime (or 1 tablespoon bottled lime juice)
★ 2 tablespoons soy sauce
★ 1 teaspoon honey or *kecap manis* (sweet soy sauce)
★ 1 teaspoon sesame oil
★ 1 small (or ½ large) cucumber
★ 2 tablespoons light olive oil
★ 200g bean curd, patted dry, pressed and cut into
  smallish cubes
★ 2 garlic cloves, chopped
★ 1 red chilli, chopped (or a pinch of dried crushed chilli)
★ ½ small (or roughly 200g) white cabbage, cored and chopped

Put the peanut butter into a small bowl or, better still, a mug. Add the hot water and leave for a minute or so. Then mix with a fork until the peanut butter has dissolved into the water. Add the lime juice, soy sauce and honey or *kecap manis*, then the sesame oil. Combine them thoroughly.

Cut the cucumber in half lengthways and scoop out the seeds. The best way to do this is to run a teaspoon gently down the seed cavity. Now slice the cucumber so that it falls into crescent shapes. If you feel like a smarty-pants you could do this on a slight diagonal, which looks '*très chinois, oui*?'

Heat the oil in a wok until fiercely hot and fry the bean curd in it until golden all over. Remove with a slotted spoon and set aside. Add the garlic and chilli and fry for 1 minute, then add the white cabbage. A minute after that, return the bean curd to the wok and add the cucumber. Stir-fry for a minute, then transfer everything to a plate or a wide bowl. This is slightly different from your average stir-fry in that the sauce is poured over the other ingredients.

Return the wok to the heat and pour in the peanut concoction. It will immediately start to bubble fiercely at the sides and darken slightly. Let the bubbling spread inwards towards the middle of the wok but as soon as it does this, pour it randomly over the stir-fry. If you don't get to it quickly enough, and it thickens, just loosen it with 1 or 2 tablespoons of water before you pour it.

VARIATION.

One more word on bean curd: if you have access to an oriental supermarket (or a healthfood shop), be sure to ask for tempeh, which is a punchier cousin to tofu. It can be substituted for bean curd in either of the stir-fries above. Originating from Indonesia, it is a fermented, pressed cake of hulled soy beans. The fermentation makes it even more nutritious than tofu. It has a mild-flavoured, mould-like skin (similar to Brie) and the whole lot can be cut into slices and fried.

GOOD COMPANIONS FOR STIR-FRIES.

If you want to make a stir-fry part of a more formal meal, try pairing it with a grilled, marinated cut of meat or fish. Below are my three favourites. For more information on simple grills, see pages 147–53. A really good-quality pork chop or duck breast with a simple marinade will enhance a stir-fry and this is a particularly good way to dish up a meal if you want to avoid rice.

I always grill the following dishes on a roasting tray lined with baking parchment. They all produce a fair bit of juice as they cook and the parchment is optional but it will slow down any 'catching' of the juices by the tray, so that you can pour them back over the meat or fish without deglazing.

SICHUAN PEPPER DUCK BREAST.

The taste of duck is so good, especially if you leave it a little pink, that I'm inclined to fiddle with it as little as possible – which means I leave the ubiquitous five-spice powder well alone. Instead, try this recipe using Sichuan peppercorns, which are pungent and spicy. You will find them in the spice section of most supermarkets. If you have trouble getting hold of them, look out for red or green peppercorns rather than the usual black kind.

For 2 people you need:
★ 2 duck breasts
★ 1 tablespoon sea salt
★ 1 teaspoon Sichuan peppercorns, roughly ground
★ 2 tablespoons light olive oil

With a sharp knife, score the skin of the duck breasts at least 3 times across. Mix together the salt and pepper and rub them on to the skin. Set aside to marinate for a couple of hours, if possible.

While the meat is marinating, preheat the oven to its highest setting. You could, if you prefer, grill the duck but the skin is fatty and it can spit, causing a spot of pyrotechnics. Using the oven is less stressful.

Use the wok to start cooking the breasts, skin-side down. Once the skin and the underside of the duck breasts are nicely browned, transfer them to a roasting tray (preferably lined with baking parchment) and cook for about 12 minutes, if you like it pink. Remove from the oven and leave to rest for at least 5 minutes before serving. I like to slice my duck and serve it on top of the stir-fry. It looks pretty elegant that way, but then I'm a sucker for that kind of thing. You can take the chef out of the restaurant . . .

LEMON CHICKEN.

The worst, worst, *worst* commercialised Chinese dish is lemon chicken. The sauce looks as if it belongs in a frozen lemon meringue pie. If you want chicken and lemon, you need zinginess, not gloop. Try this grilled version.

For 2 people you need:
★ 2 free-range chicken breasts, boned but not skinned
★ juice and grated zest of 1 lemon
★ ¼ teaspoon dried crushed chilli
★ 2 garlic cloves, roughly chopped
★ a generous pinch of sea salt
★ 2 tablespoons light olive oil
★ about 1 tablespoon chopped coriander

Combine the chicken breasts with the lemon juice and zest, chilli, garlic and salt. Leave to marinate for a couple of hours if possible, but less time will do.

Preheat the oven or the grill to its highest setting. Heat the oil in a wok or a large frying pan. Remove the chicken breasts from the marinade, but don't discard it. Start the chicken in the pan skin-side down over a high heat. When it has browned nicely, turn it over and transfer it to a roasting tray lined with baking parchment, adding what's left of the marinade. Place in the oven or under the grill and cook for about 10 minutes. You must cook chicken thoroughly. The short time I have prescribed should stop it going dry but ensure that it is not bloody. To check, make sure that the middle of the breast is nice and hot by inserting a knife or skewer, leaving it in for about 3 seconds and then touching it very gently to your top lip. You'll know if it's hot! Let the meat rest for about 5 minutes, then serve it with the coriander.

MACKEREL AND GINGER.
Mackerel, with its gamy flavour, is my favourite grilling fish, but you could use a number of other round fish instead. Red mullet and bream are good.

For 2 people you need:
★ 2 mackerel, weighing 200–250g each
★ a pinch of sea salt
★ 3 garlic cloves, roughly chopped
★ 1cm piece of fresh ginger, roughly chopped
★ 1 fresh red chilli, sliced (or ¼ teaspoon dried crushed chilli)
★ juice of ½ lime (or 1 tablespoon bottled lime juice)
★ 1 tablespoon soy sauce
★ 1 tablespoon sesame oil

Get the fishmonger to gut the mackerel for you, if necessary; otherwise it's easy to do yourself. Look at the belly of the fish and you'll see a small hole near the tail end. Starting from there, slice up as far as the gills and remove any guts with your hand. Wash and thoroughly dry the fish. There is no need to scale mackerel (yet another reason to love it).

Preheat the grill to its highest setting. Sprinkle the cavity of each fish with the sea salt and lay the fish on its side in a roasting tray. Sprinkle with the garlic, ginger and chilli. Squeeze the lime juice over the fish and drizzle it with the soy sauce, then the sesame oil.

Pop the fish under the grill. A medium-sized mackerel will cook in about 8–9 minutes (for larger fish, add another couple of minutes per 100g). There is no need to turn it. Serve the fish with any juices collected in the tray.

RICE.

Either I'm greedy or I was cursed with hollow legs. For me, the only way to eat a stir-fry is next to a ton of fluffy, slightly sticky rice. Throughout Southeast Asia, rice is the staple and I got hooked while living there. From Guangzhou to Jakarta, rice is never ordered; it just arrives, plain and unprompted, at the table. Its ubiquity is demonstrated by the fact that, from humble street café to fairly posh restaurant, you are rarely charged for it. Fried rice or noodle dishes are another thing entirely. They tend to be eaten as complete meals in themselves.

To cut a very long (and fascinating) story short, there are two main types of rice: long grain and short grain. Again in horribly simplistic terms, for short read 'sticky' (think of sushi, risotto and rice pudding) and for long read 'fluffy' (pilaus and biryanis). It is long grain rice that you would usually expect to find next to a stir-fry. In terms of flavour and being generally well behaved, I don't think it is possible to better basmati rice. Grown only in northern India or Pakistan, it has a slightly perfumed taste. It is pricier than other long grain rice – but don't forget that any rice you buy will go a long way. If you are not very experienced at cooking rice, you will be amazed how little you need for a portion (which also means that you and the rice you buy are stuck with each other for umpteen meals). Avoid American long grain rice, which is utterly tasteless. Some types of Thai and Chinese 'fragrant' rice are delicious and similar to basmati but they are stickier. This is not necessarily a bad thing – but it can come as a surprise to the uninitiated.

HOW TO COOK PERFECT RICE.

If you like rice and eat it a lot, it is probably worth investing in a small electric rice cooker. If I had to nominate my favourite gadget of all time, this would be the one. All a rice cooker does, really, is ape the oriental method of cooking rice by absorption, which is pretty foolproof. Here's how it's done.

You need a saucepan with a tightly fitting lid. Measure out the rice. A healthy portion for one person is 75g but it is far easier to work visually. If you have an espresso-sized coffee cup (or the American ⅓ cup measuring spoon), fill it to the brim for a good portion. Then tip it into a pan, measure out exactly 1½ times the amount of cold water to rice and add that, too. Place the pan over a high flame and bring it to the edge of boiling. Then lower the heat as much as you can. The rice should barely simmer from now on (think of a breeze ruffling the surface of a pond). Fit the lid on snugly and let the rice cook this way for about 12 minutes. Remove it from the heat and fluff it by gently nudging it around the pan with a fork. Then cover it again and let it rest for a few more minutes before serving. If you are making a stir-fry, then to eliminate stress altogether why not cook the rice first, so that you attack the stir-fry while it rests? It won't have time to go cold.

TWO STIR-FRIES WITH NOODLES.

I keep just two types of noodle as a catch-all. I like the Chinese-style egg noodles, but my favourite are the flatter rice noodles (which look similar to Italian tagliatelle), sometimes referred to as *ho fun* or rice stick in Chinese shops.

Basically you will find hundreds of different types of noodle on sale, especially if you visit a Chinese or Vietnamese supermarket. The best thing to do is try as many as you like and not get angst-ridden if recipes in other books are didactic about which noodle to put where. In oriental cooking, as in so many other cuisines, recipes can vary from one end of a street to the other.

As for portion size, the following recipes include a weight for the noodles but your eyes are the best judge of how much you want to eat. Added to that, any brand that sells noodles coiled into handy bird's nest shapes is a good bet to buy, as each nest makes a pretty foolproof portion.

You might prefer to eat all your stir-fries with noodles as opposed to rice but I personally think that noodle dishes have a distinct character of their own. Here are two good examples to demonstrate what I mean.

A THAI-STYLE NOODLE FRY-UP.

Phad thai, as it is known in the vernacular, has become very popular in the UK in recent years, and with good reason. It is, I suppose, the Asian equivalent of something like paella: holiday food, with a bold, outlandish combination of flavours. It should

SPAGHETTI AND TINNED PLUM TOMATOES, P20.

COURGETTE AND SPINACH SALAD, P38.

VOLCANO EGGS, P73.

DIY TUNA CONFIT, P97.

CATALAN SALAD, P99.

CRABBY NOODLES, BEFORE AND AFTER, P139.

LAMB CHOPS WITH GREEN SAUCE, P148.

be a perky, thrown-together affair, salty, sharp and sweet all at once. Made commercially, it is invariably sickly-sweet, with 3 curly-wurly prawns placed artfully on top.

This recipe is my version of pad thai. One of the best things about the genuine article is the crunchy topping of crushed peanuts. If you prefer, you could use cashew nuts. Should you resort to dry-roasted or salted nuts, watch the seasoning of the noodles, as Thai fish sauce is very salty.

For 2 people you need:
★ 2 nests (about 60g) rice stick noodles
★ 1 tablespoon light olive oil
★ 2 eggs, beaten
★ 4–5 spring onions, finely sliced
★ 3 garlic cloves, chopped
★ 2 fresh red chillies, finely chopped (or dried crushed chilli to taste)
★ 200g bean sprouts

For the sauce:
★ 3 tablespoons Thai fish sauce
★ juice of 1 lime (or 2 tablespoons bottled lime juice)
★ 1 tablespoon tomato ketchup
★ 1 teaspoon crunchy peanut butter
★ 1 teaspoon sugar

For the table:
★ a generous handful of roughly chopped coriander
★ lime wedges, or more lime juice
★ dried crushed chilli
★ 50g shelled peanuts or monkey nuts, roughly crushed

In a small mixing bowl or a mug, combine all the ingredients for the sauce until you have a very liquid paste. Set aside.

Put the noodles in a large bowl, pour over a kettle full of just-boiled water and leave to soak for about 5 minutes. Once they are fully malleable, drain them in a colander and cool them thoroughly under the cold tap. Set aside, leaving them in the colander.

Please note that noodles are just like pasta. If you want to have them ready more than a few minutes in advance you will need to toss them with a spoonful of oil to stop them sticking to each other.

Heat the oil in a wok and when it is almost smoking, throw in the beaten eggs. Leave to bubble until the egg has formed a skin underneath (as if it is becoming an omelette). Start to break it up gently with a wooden spoon, so that it is like dry scrambled egg. At this point, add the spring onions, garlic and chillies and stir-fry for 1 minute. Throw in the bean sprouts, stir-fry until they wilt, then add the noodles and the sauce. Stir and fry until the noodles have absorbed the sauce, which will take a minute, tops (this will not be a 'wet' dish; if anything it is slightly sticky). Check the seasoning. It should be slightly sweet and sour with a mild hit of chilli.

Serve the noodles in bowls. In Thailand you would never think of presenting noodles to someone without letting them tweak the taste for themselves, so it's fun to do the same here. A generous clump of coriander, extra lime, extra chilli and, of course, the crushed peanuts should all be left on the table for people to help themselves.

CRABBY NOODLES.

To get the best results from this, you really need fresh crab. A reputable fishmonger, and an increasing number of supermarkets, will sell dressed crabs, which sounds fancier than it is. Dressing really means that the crabs have been cooked and picked over for you. You can buy frozen crab but it tends to be white meat only and the brown meat has oodles of flavour. Better to create your own store of frozen dressed crab. Beware tinned crab. Some brands are okay but many contain unnecessary additives such as monosodium glutamate. As with commercially frozen crab, the tinned stuff is usually white meat only.

The base I like to use for this is a chilli and garlic sauce, which is dark, hot and very murky. It is made almost like a jam, and you will find it in most Chinese supermarkets. It keeps forever. On the next page there is a version of it you can make at home. Although primarily I keep it for stir-fries like this, it makes a good emergency ingredient for those days when you realise you used up your last garlic clove and chilli and didn't notice (happens to me all the time!). You needn't use the sauce at all, of course. You can start this dish by frying garlic and chilli from scratch.

For 2 people you need:
★ 2 nests (about 60g) rice stick noodles
★ 1 teaspoon chilli and garlic sauce
★ 4 spring onions, finely chopped
★ 1 courgette, finely chopped (or any green vegetable you like; broccoli and Chinese leaves are good)
★ 2 tablespoons Thai fish sauce
★ juice of 1 lime (or 2 tablespoons bottled lime juice)
★ 120g crab meat
★ 1 tablespoon chopped coriander

Put the noodles in a large bowl, pour over a kettle full of just-boiled water and leave to soak for 5 minutes. Once they are fully malleable, drain them in a colander and cool them thoroughly under the cold tap. Set aside.

Heat the chilli and garlic sauce gently in a wok and, when it is fizzing healthily, add the vegetables. You only need to fry them for about 2 minutes, so turn up the heat as you add them. Add the fish sauce and lime juice and stir-fry for a minute. When everything is hot, fold in the noodles and crab and toss well together until thoroughly heated through. Check the seasoning, stir in the coriander and serve.

DIY: MAKE YOUR OWN CHILLI AND GARLIC SAUCE.

Vatcharin Bhumichitr was one of the first Thai food writers to be published in the UK, and his books are still exciting to read today, the recipes coupled with beautifully illustrative descriptions of his country. This chilli condiment is based on one of his recipes. I've called it a sauce; in fact it looks like a very dark jam. I know of nothing else like it, and it has a distinctive, addictive taste. It keeps well in the fridge, which is a good thing as you use very little of it unless you are a total chilli head. Plus it makes a great emergency ingredient, as it can replace fresh chillies and garlic in stir-fries. A rescue remedy for Mother Hubbard moments. I sometimes toss it with plain noodles for a really instant snack.

You need a food processor to make this. Despite the small amount of sugar it isn't sweet. It is as dark and moody-looking as it is hot. Don't expect a pretty colour!

For a good jarful you need:

★ 4 tablespoons vegetable oil
★ 8 garlic cloves, chopped
★ 2 shallots or 1 small onion, chopped
★ 4 tablespoons dried crushed chilli
★ 2 tablespoons Thai fish sauce
★ 1 teaspoon salt
★ 1 teaspoon sugar

Heat the oil in a wok or a high-sided frying pan over a fairly moderate heat, then add the garlic and fry until it starts to turn golden brown. Remove the garlic with a sieve or a fine-slotted spoon and set it aside. Add the shallots to the pan and fry until golden brown and fairly crisp, then remove in the same way. Throw the garlic, shallots, chilli and fish sauce into a food processor and blitz until you have a paste. Add the salt and sugar, then return the paste to the oil in the pan. Stir it over a low heat until it starts to get really viscous. This doesn't take long and you end up with an oily, dark jam. Leave to cool and then store in the fridge.

Grills.

GRILLS AND SPILLS: SHORT-ORDER MEAT AND FISH DINNERS.

This chapter is about short-order cooking. I suppose that sounds a bit cheffy, but that's not to say it is flash or complicated. Instead it tells you how to get the best from quick-cooking cuts of meat or fish, then gives a number of thrown-together sauces that should go well with any or all of them. Thus you will be able to cook any of the cuts on pages 148–53 and pair them with any of the sauces that follow. All the sauces can be made in advance, well before you even think of turning on the oven.

THE KIT.

SALT . . . I have avoided being prescriptive about salt and pepper so far, but for grilling I think having the right kind of salt really makes a difference. It might seem mad to go on about the properties of salt, but actually it can be the most important ingredient in the kitchen. Most people find that food tastes pretty grim without it. And the character of the modern-day larder would be very different without the oldest preservative in the world. Preserving is only half the story – salt has been everything from a condiment to a currency. Considering the fundamental nature of it, I'm going to say little more. Only, spend a bit of money on the stuff. Refined, adulterated table salt is rubbish. So is low-sodium whaddyacallit. If you want to use less salt, buy a tastier one! Sea salt tends to have more flavour than rock salt and is usually unadulterated. Maldon sea salt is both a brand and a type of salt, made in the traditional way from sea water. When writing about food, it is almost compulsory now to mention Maldon salt crystals as if they were the champagne of salts. Some people think it tastes different from any other kind. To be perfectly honest, I think it tastes of, you know, *salt* but it does come in a very user-friendly form. The flakes are wonderful crumbled on to grilled meat or fish, or used to finish salads.

...AND PEPPER. I like to buy whole black peppercorns and grind them myself. As with any spice, keeping it whole preserves the flavour. If there is one condiment we have gone mad for in this country, it is pepper. It can overpower food, and I don't use it that much when I'm cooking. It really is best plonked on the table for people to add themselves. But it does enhance grilled meat and fish beautifully. Some Italians, by the way, never use it in the kitchen (which is why you get offered it by the waiter in more traditional restaurants).

THE PAN. I do all my 'grilling' in a cast-iron frying pan. This is because I use a method I call 'hot pan, hot oven'. To be honest, any well-seasoned or non-stick pan is good for cooking in this way but if you want to follow my method (see below) you will need a metal-handled pan that will fit in your oven, allowing the door to shut. A 20cm diameter pan is normally the biggest you will fit into a domestic oven.

A word about griddles or ridged frying pans: I don't recommend them over any other cast-iron pan. The ridges are really there for cosmetic reasons, to give the meat barbecue-style stripes. You can end up paying as much for a bad griddle pan as you would for a good, basic frying pan. Avoid any ridged pan without raised sides, as it will not retain the natural juices that you get from meat as it cooks. If you must have stripes, get a pan that can hold juices.

HOW TO GRILL MEAT AND FISH (THE HOT-PAN, HOT-OVEN METHOD).

A few words about the technique I use to 'grill' nearly all meat and fish (please note the inverted commas, because I suppose I am abusing the word a bit). I find that the best way to get really good, juicy steaks, chops, fillets of fish and the like is the hot-pan, hot-oven method – i.e. searing them in a very hot frying pan, then plunging them into an equally hot oven to finish them off. This isn't frying, because it requires little or no fat in the pan. And it isn't roasting, strictly speaking, because that implies a fairly leisurely cooking time. Perhaps it is pan-roasting, for want of a better name.

Why don't I use a grill? Because I think that the grill, which essentially heats food only from above, is a fairly blunt tool to cook with. It will brown a slice of cheese on toast beautifully, granted. But I'm not convinced that it does justice to a thick slab of meat or fish. Quite the opposite, in fact. What you need is a confined space with direct heat from below and above. Think of the pizza or tandoor oven. Putting a hot pan into a hot oven apes the intensity of this confined space with excellent results. Do try it to see what I mean. Preheating the oven for the short burst of cooking required for a chop might seem slightly extravagant, but if you have a fan-assisted oven, or are lucky enough to have a small, grill-sized oven as well as a conventional one, this doesn't take long.

The hot-pan, hot-oven method solves the problem of the fat

on some cuts (chops, for example), which seems to ignite easily under a grill. It also does a better job of thick cuts, which can take a while to cook through under a conventional grill or in a frying pan, drying out in the process.

Once your meat or fish is cooked to your liking, I would encourage you to leave it to rest for a few minutes before serving it. This allows the muscle tissue (the bulk of lean meat and fish) to relax after having been heated. Meat and fish tense up as they cook and resting is crucial for tenderness.

Many people are unsure when to season meat and fish during grilling. My general advice is, hold your horses. The recipes in this chapter assume you are using fresh meat and fish, not marinated. To get the best flavour out of the cuts listed below, leave seasoning until towards the end of cooking. I sprinkle lean meat and fish and cuts such as liver with salt and pepper only when I have finished cooking them, as they start to rest. Not only does this help flavour the meat, it encourages the juices to flow. With fatty cuts such as poultry breasts and legs or meat chops, it is worth rubbing the fat (or skin) with salt (and pepper, if you like) before cooking.

When buying cuts for short-order cooking, try to avoid cheap, intensively reared meat. Intensive farming is cruel to animals and produces mediocre-tasting food. The extra cost of free-range, pasture-fed meat that has been farmed on a small scale is worth every penny. The food scares of recent years serve to remind us of what cutting costs on the production of meat has done to the industry.

LAMB CHOPS.

I like to use loin chops for their lean meatiness. Preheat the oven to its highest setting. Heat a griddle or a heavy-based frying pan on the hob until it is almost smoking hot. Sprinkle a little salt on the fatty edge of each chop and sear it for half a minute or so by holding it against the griddle with tongs. Then lay the chops flat on the pan and sear them for 2 minutes on each side, still over a very high heat. Season with a pinch of salt and pepper, transfer the pan to the oven and cook for 5–6 minutes. Remove and leave to rest for 3 minutes or so, if you have the patience. This will give you a juicier, more tender chop.

PORK AND VEAL CHOPS.

Follow the instructions for lamb chops but cook the chops in the oven for about 12 minutes before resting.

CHICKEN BREASTS.

Chicken breasts can dry out easily, thanks to a certain fearfulness about eating them underdone. A quick turn in a hot oven will solve this. Preheat your oven to its highest setting. Heat a griddle or heavy-based frying pan until smoking hot. Rub the skin side of a boned chicken breast with oil and sear it for a good 2–3 minutes. Turn it over when the skin is browned and season the skin with salt and pepper. Put the chicken straight into the oven in the hot pan and cook for 8–10 minutes. Now take it out of the oven and allow it to rest in the pan for 3–5 minutes before serving. This will allow the meat to cook evenly and remain juicy all the way through.

DUCK BREASTS.

Duck is more like lamb than poultry, in that you can eat it pink. Preheat the oven to its highest setting. Heat a griddle or heavy-based frying pan and when it is good and hot put in the duck, skin-side down. Sear it over a medium heat for a good 5 minutes, or until it is really golden brown. Turn it over and season the skin side. Transfer it to the oven and cook for 5 minutes, then rest for 5 minutes before serving. This will give you pink meat. If you don't like it like this, allow another 3–4 minutes in the oven, but be careful that it doesn't become tough.

POULTRY ON THE BONE.

I have never been a big fan of boned-out poultry breasts. I think that they lack the flavour that cooking meat on the bone gives you. Instead I like to buy my chickens on the small side (1–1.5kg) and give each diner half a bird, with only the backbone removed. If you are nervous about doing this, ask your butcher to 'spatchcock' the bird for you. Season the skin liberally with salt, pepper and a splash of olive oil (or a knob of butter), then roast for about 25 minutes in an oven preheated to its maximum setting (there's no need to sear the chicken first). Baste half way through the cooking time. To check that the bird is cooked through, pierce the thickest point with a knife or skewer and apply a little pressure to make the juices run out. If the juices are clear and not at all bloody, the bird is ready. Rest for at least 5 minutes before serving.

Most farmed duck are too big for serving in halves (although you can get your hands on smaller mallard or teal during the game season). But you can buy the breast on the bone, or buy a whole duck and separate the legs from the breast. A decent butcher will be happy to do this for you.

STEAKS.

It is hard to dish out strict instructions for cooking steak. The degree of doneness is such a personal thing. I like mine rare and I can't bear them any other way, but to some people the thought of bloody meat is horrendous. However much or little you decide to cook steak, here are my tips for making it stress free:

First, add the steak to a very hot, dry frying pan. Rub oil on the meat first, by all means, to season it slightly, but don't fry steak. Once you have seared the meat on one side, turn it and only then add a seasoning of salt and/or pepper. Don't bother seasoning the side of the meat that is going to hit the base of the pan first.

For rare steak, 1 minute's cooking on either side of a thick (2cm) piece of meat will do, followed by a rest of at least 2 minutes. Medium rare will require double the cooking time, plus a 4-minute rest. For medium steak, it is best to lower the heat beneath the pan when you turn the meat and give it 5 minutes per side plus an 8-minute rest. For well-done steak, preheat the oven to its highest setting, sear the steak on one side in the pan, then turn it over and finish it by giving it 8–10 minutes in the oven, plus a rest of about 10 minutes.

Remember that fillet, T-bone and sirloin tend to cook faster than cuts like rump and rib eye. It is particularly easy to overcook sirloin.

Following cooking times is not always the best way to get what you want from steak. A very reliable chef's test is to use the palm of your hand as a guide to doneness. Prod the steak with your forefinger. A rare steak will feel like the base of the palm of your hand beneath your thumb. A medium rare steak will feel like the same place if you touch your forefinger with the thumb. Medium will feel like the same place when middle finger and thumb are touching. Well done steak will feel like old boots. Just kidding. It will feel like the same place when thumb and little finger are touching.

LIVER.

This must be one of the most underrated cuts of meat there is. And it has a reputation for being a bit pricy. Calf's liver is on the expensive side, but ox and lamb's liver are much cheaper, and full of flavour. The best way to cook liver is in thin (5mm) slices, quickly. Use a very hot griddle or heavy-based frying pan and a little oil or butter. Give the liver just 1 minute on either side, then rest it for at least 3 minutes before serving. Some people (me included) like to deglaze the pan to make a scant amount of sauce. Here's how: add a shake of balsamic or sherry vinegar to the pan immediately after you remove the meat and swirl it around.

SAUSAGES.

Buy premium sausages whenever possible. They are worth the extra cost, as they tend to be free of additives (which are there to add bulk and prolong shelf life, rather than help flavour or aid cooking). Because of their fairly high fat content, premium sausages benefit from the hot-pan, hot-oven method as much as chops, because under a conventional grill the fat can ignite a bit, spoiling the taste. To stop sausages splitting, prick them with a fork in at least two places; this allows steam to escape as they cook. Good sausages shouldn't need extra seasoning.

FISH.

It is important to buy line-caught rather than trawled fish, as this has less impact on the stock and its environment. Intensively farmed fish has a negative effect on seas and rivers. As with meat, good fish tends to cost more, but with a clear conscience comes tastier fish.

As pretty as griddle stripes are, fish can stick to these pans like limpets, so unless your griddle is well seasoned, use a conventional frying pan for all fish.

Steaks of large fish such as tuna, marlin, salmon and swordfish.
I tend to cook these much as I would steak, in 2cm-thick pieces cut from the loin. Heat a tablespoon of oil in a heavy-based pan until smoking hot and give the fish no more than 2 minutes per side. Like meat, fish will taste infinitely better if rested.

Whole, small round fish. Cook whole small fish such as mackerel, sardines, trout, sea bream and bass using the hot-pan, hot-oven technique. Heat a tablespoon of oil in the pan first until smoking hot and sear the fish on both sides. It is hard to give a precise cooking time because it will largely depend on the size of the fish. A rough guide is, after searing, for every 250g of fish allow 3 minutes in an oven on maximum setting, plus a rest of 2 minutes before eating.

Fillets of large fish such as cod, salmon, halibut and hake. These are easy to overcook, as they dry out quickly. Use the hot-pan, hot-oven technique and make sure the pan is smoking hot. Sear the fish first, skin-side down, in a tablespoon of oil. Don't season the skin, as salt will make it blister, encouraging it to stick to the pan and be left behind when you turn the fish. After about 3 minutes, turn the fillet over. Now you can scatter the skin with salt and pepper and transfer the pan to the oven. As with round fish, allow 3 minutes per 250g. Rest for at least 5 minutes before serving.

Squid, scallops and prawns. These do not need to go in the oven and should be seared for as short a time as possible, using 1 tablespoon of oil. Pieces of squid and whole scallops out of the shell will need no more than a minute on either side. Prawns in the shell will need about 2 minutes per side.

GREEN SAUCE (AND A NEAR RELATION).

These aren't sauces in the classic sense – they fall into a sort of hinterland between salad, sauce and side dish. Even salsa verde is essentially a very finely chopped salad. They are all very easy-going, without any of the last-minute flurry of preparation that you get with classic sauces such as hollandaise.

GREEN SAUCE (SALSA VERDE).

I am addicted to this stuff. I never get sick of making it and, besides, it never needs to be the same twice. It is not a million miles from a vinaigrette-type salad dressing. The basic principle is that it should be herby, oily and slightly sharp. In its most basic form, green sauce is chopped parsley, garlic, oil and vinegar. Everything else is optional. The complex taste of a really good green sauce is achieved by adding one or two more aromatic herbs to the parsley. Mint is fairly traditional, as is basil, but tarragon works brilliantly and so does dill – particularly if you pair the sauce with white fish. It's also an excellent accompaniment to lamb chops or sausages.

As well as the extra herbs, sharp and salty condiments from the larder are thrown in, too, as you will see below. The list is flexible. Vegetarians can leave out the anchovies, for example. Try this fairly classic version, using whatever herbs you like with the parsley.

Ever since I read Julian Barnes's *The Pedant in the Kitchen* (Guardian Books, 2003), I've been vaguely anxious about being, well, vague when it comes to measures of this and that. A handful, a pinch, etc . . . The trouble is, some recipes are meant to be open-ended. A handful of herbs means just that. If your handful is bigger or smaller than mine, it won't matter much here, trust me.

Loath as I am to admit it, the big supermarkets sell herbs by the (handy) handful-sized bunch. I'll qualify that by saying that they charge a disgraceful amount of money for such small quantities. A good grocer's (or market trader's) bunch of herbs is more like 2 handfuls. So why does it invariably cost less?

Two golden rules for green sauce:
1. No food processing! Chop everything by hand. The texture should be quite rough and loose. Whizzing salsa verde gives you lawn mowings in an oil slick.

2. Don't make it too far in advance. It keeps in the fridge, it tastes fine but the verdant herbs do eventually go a bit khaki, thanks to the acid in the condiments.

For 2–4 people you need:
★ 1 shallot or small red onion, chopped as finely as possible
★ 1 garlic clove, finely chopped or crushed
★ 2 anchovy fillets, chopped almost to a paste
★ 1 teaspoon capers, chopped
★ 4–5 cocktail gherkins (cornichons), chopped
★ 1 tablespoon English or Dijon mustard
★ a handful of roughly chopped parsley (flat-leaf is best)
★ a handful of roughly chopped mint, or tarragon or basil or dill
★ a handful of chives, chopped (optional)
★ 150ml olive oil
★ 1 tablespoon red or white wine (or sherry) vinegar
★ salt and freshly ground black pepper

There is a certain order to doing this. Start with the base, so mix the chopped shallot or onion, garlic, anchovies, capers, gherkins and mustard together in a bowl. Add the herbs next and stir them in. Then add the oil. By all means use less than I prescribe; the sauce can be dry enough to scatter over a piece of fish or runny enough to drizzle, if you see what I mean. Add the vinegar after the oil, which protects the herbs from being discoloured by the acid. Season the sauce only when you have the consistency you want. Feel free to add more vinegar if you like it sharper.

PINK SAUCE (SALSA RAPA).

This slightly sweet beetroot sauce is delicious. Try it next to liver or steak, or a piece of white fish. You simply need to add 1 small cooked beetroot, chopped as finely or as roughly as you like, to the ingredients for the green sauce above. If the beetroot has been pickled in vinegar, omit the vinegar from the recipe.

ITALIANATE BREAD SAUCE.

This looks weird written down, but please try it. As well as being a very pert accompaniment to white fish, it makes a fine dip for crudités. The original recipe is sweetened with a pinch of sugar, but I tend to use balsamic vinegar instead. Unlike the basic green sauce (see page 154), you can blitz this one in a food processor, although it is great left slightly rough and textured.

For 2–4 people you need:
★ 1 garlic clove, finely chopped or crushed
★ 2 anchovy fillets, chopped almost to a paste

* ★ 1 teaspoon capers, chopped
* ★ 4 or 5 cocktail gherkins (cornichons), chopped
* ★ 2 hard-boiled egg yolks
* ★ 1 tablespoon English or Dijon mustard
* ★ 2 slices of stale, rustic-type bread (ciabatta or sourdough is ideal)
* ★ 150ml olive oil
* ★ 2 tablespoons water
* ★ 2 tablespoons balsamic vinegar (you could use red or white wine vinegar instead)
* ★ a handful of roughly chopped parsley (flat-leaf is best)
* ★ a handful of roughly chopped mint (or basil, tarragon or dill)
* ★ salt and freshly ground black pepper

Put the garlic, anchovies, capers and gherkins in a bowl. Remove the egg yolks from the whites and crumble them into the bowl. Stir in the mustard and set aside.

Break the bread up into small pieces, put it in a bowl with half the oil, plus the water and vinegar, and leave until it has gone soft and squidgy. Mash it to a paste with a fork or blitz it in a food processor. Add the egg mixture, then the remaining oil and the chopped herbs, and stir together. Season the sauce only when you have finished it.

THREE PEPPER SAUCES.

The recipes that follow all use some form of preserved capsicum, but I should add that you could also use fresh red peppers or chillies where appropriate. Here is an extremely basic but tasty sauce to begin with.

GALLEGA SAUCE.

I feel cheeky calling this a recipe but it is so good. You will find the famous Galician tapa, *pulpo a la gallega* (octopus, braised until tender and dressed with this simple sauce) in many Spanish restaurants. I love octopus, but many people are spooked by tentacles. If you're not, be sure to try this with something like grilled squid (or indeed octopus and cuttlefish); otherwise, drizzle it over any grilled fish. Unsurprisingly, given its Spanish roots, the best meat to go with the sauce is pork.

For 2–4 people you need:
- ★ 1 heaped tablespoon smoked paprika
- ★ juice of 1 lemon (or 2 tablespoons sherry vinegar)
- ★ 100ml olive oil
- ★ ½ teaspoon salt

Whisk all the ingredients together like a salad dressing until they have emulsified. Your work is done. You can complicate things a little, if you like. An onion, sliced as thinly as possible, then left to marinate in the sauce for half an hour or so, is wonderful. To that you could also add a tablespoon of chopped capers. Toss warm potatoes in all the above and you should be smitten forever.

CHEAT'S ROMESCO.

Here is another famous Spanish sauce, this time from Catalonia. The real thing is made with dried, bell-shaped peppers (*nora*) and chillies, which require soaking. You can use fresh red peppers, grilled, skinned and deseeded, or make this quick version using tinned peppers (piquillos are best) and pepper paste, both of which you can find in many Turkish or Spanish delis and some supermarkets. Besides making a good accompaniment to grilled meat and fish, romesco sauce works well as a dip.

For 2–4 people you need:
- ★ 3 garlic cloves
- ★ 100g blanched almonds or hazelnuts
  (or a combination of both)
- ★ 1 tin of piquillo peppers
- ★ 1 generous tablespoon sweet pepper paste
- ★ ½ teaspoon paprika (smoked if possible)
- ★ ½ teaspoon salt
- ★ ½ teaspoon sugar (optional)
- ★ 1 dried red chilli, crushed (optional)
- ★ 100ml olive oil
- ★ 2 tablespoons sherry vinegar

In a moderate oven, roast the unpeeled garlic cloves for 15 minutes and the nuts for 10 minutes. Leave to cool, then peel the garlic cloves.

Blitz the nuts in a food processor until they are roughly ground. Remove them and set aside. Now do the same with the peppers, pepper paste, garlic, paprika, salt, sugar and chilli, if using, until you have a rough paste. Combine the pepper mixture and nuts in a mixing bowl and fold in the oil and vinegar. Check the seasoning. You might like to add more salt.

CARROT AND DRIED CHILLI.

This is startlingly good with prawns, squid or scallops, just shown a hot frying pan and served plain. It is inspired by a mezze-type salad from the Middle East, where it would be made with harissa, a fresh chilli paste. This version allows you simply to raid the spice rack. It is a bit rich to suggest that carrots are also a store-cupboard ingredient unless, like me, you always seem to have them around. Procuring some should not present a challenge. This makes another good dip, by the way. And you could try making it with sweet potato or pumpkin some time.

For 2–4 people you need:
★ 500g carrots, peeled
★ 1 teaspoon cumin or caraway seeds
★ ½ teaspoon coriander seeds
★ 1 teaspoon dried crushed chilli
★ 3 garlic cloves, chopped
★ 4 tablespoons extra virgin olive oil
★ juice of ½ lemon
★ ½ teaspoon salt
★ a handful of chopped coriander leaves (optional)

You could roast or boil the carrots. Roasting them adds an interesting, slightly caramelised note to the finished dish. The main thing to do is to get them really tender. Once the carrots are fully cooked, leave them to drain and cool, then purée in a food processor or mash them, depending on how smooth you want them.

Meanwhile, in a dry frying pan, roast the cumin or caraway and coriander seeds over a gentle flame until the heat unlocks their fragrance. You will smell this happening, in case that sounds a bit airy-fairy. Set them aside to cool. In a spice grinder or pestle and mortar, crush the seeds, then combine them with the chilli, garlic, oil, lemon juice and salt and stir thoroughly. Now stir half this mixture through the carrots. Check the taste before adding any more; it might be spicy enough already. You might

need more salt. If you are adding coriander leaves, just throw
them over the top of the whole thing as a garnish.

THREE ANCHOVY SAUCES.

It might seem surprising that anchovies go so well with meat.
Lamb is particularly good with anchovies and the two have a
long tradition of being paired with one another. You might be
surprised to learn that none of these sauces tastes fishy.

ANCHOÏADE.

The possibilities for this sauce are almost limitless. Try a dollop
of it next to a steak, chops or fish. Use it, loosened with a little
extra oil, as the dressing for a 'Caesar salad'. Toss it round some
pasta or simply smear it on toast. Although you'll see when you
make it that it behaves like a mayonnaise, it contains no egg.
This means that it will keep for up to 3 weeks in the fridge.

For 4 people you need:
★ 50g tin of anchovy fillets in olive oil
★ 1 tablespoon capers
★ 2 garlic cloves
★ a pinch of dried crushed chilli
★ 1 tablespoon Dijon mustard
★ 1 tablespoon red or white wine vinegar
★ 350ml olive oil

A food processor is ideal for this. Blitz the anchovies and their oil
with the capers, garlic, chilli, mustard and vinegar until they form
a paste, then slowly add the olive oil. You should end up with a

stiff, mayonnaise-type sauce. If it should refuse to come together (and there is the outside chance of this happening if you add the oil too fast), you can use it like vinaigrette. If you have your heart set on a mayonnaise consistency, remove the 'vinaigrette' from the food processor, pop in 2 egg yolks and start to add the vinaigrette as if it were oil. This is, by the way, a handy rescue remedy for any mayonnaise that refuses to do its thing.

WARM ANCHOVY, TOMATO AND ROSEMARY SALSA.

I like to make this with fresh (in fact, slightly underripe and firm) tomatoes, since they hold their shape well. Feel free to use tinned tomatoes but squish them thoroughly in a colander to remove any juices.

This salsa is another great topping for toast. Try it with fried eggs some time.

For 4 people you need:
- ★ 4 good-sized firm tomatoes
- ★ 50g tin of anchovy fillets, drained
- ★ 4 garlic cloves
- ★ 2 sprigs of rosemary, leaves stripped from the twig
- ★ 150ml extra virgin olive oil
- ★ 1 tablespoon red wine or sherry vinegar (or balsamic vinegar)
- ★ salt

Cut the tomatoes into quarters down their length and remove and discard the seed cavity. Now dice the flesh as finely as you can.

Chop the anchovies, garlic and rosemary leaves until they are one step away from a paste. Heat the oil very gently for about 2 minutes over a low flame. You want warm rather than 'frying hot' oil. Remove it from the heat and immediately add the anchovies, rosemary and garlic. Stir them into the oil. The anchovies will literally melt and fall apart a bit. Then add the tomatoes and vinegar. Allow the sauce to cool slightly, then taste and season it. You might need salt. A sprinkling of dried chilli is also good.

MUSHROOM AND ANCHOVY SAUCE.

This unusual combination tastes great, and is based on an old French recipe. The original version is slightly heavy, since it is made with a béchamel-type sauce. I have omitted this. You can enrich the sauce by adding a couple of tablespoons of double cream or crème fraîche if you are so inclined, but I like it just as it is. It is surprisingly light for such a punchy grouping of ingredients.

If you prefer, replace the anchovies with an extra shake of Worcestershire sauce, but whatever you do, don't avoid both.

For 2 people you need:
- ★ 2 tablespoons butter
- ★ 2 garlic cloves, chopped
- ★ 4–5 anchovy fillets, chopped
- ★ 200g field mushrooms or wild mushrooms, finely sliced
- ★ 1 tablespoon Worcestershire sauce
- ★ 1 tablespoon chopped dill
- ★ salt and freshly ground black pepper

Gently heat the butter in a small saucepan. When it is fizzing, throw in the garlic and anchovies. Lower the heat, cover and sweat for a couple of minutes. Add the mushrooms and Worcestershire sauce and cook, covered, for about 5 minutes. Finally, remove the lid, raise the heat and allow the sauce to reduce a little for a couple of minutes. Add the dill and season to your liking just as you are about to serve up. Fans of stews and casseroles, note: this is a great base for slow-cooked meat or poultry.

TWO PEAS AND A LENTIL.

I almost always serve these leguminous accompaniments with fish but in fact they go with just about anything. I think you know me well enough by now to have sensed that the peas are from the freezer. (By all means use fresh, if you prefer.)

BRAISED PEAS WITH RED WINE AND SAGE.

The long cooking time of this sauce makes it rich and dark. You could substitute a pulse such as Puy lentils for the peas to make it more wintry.

For 4 people you need:
- ★ 1 tablespoon olive oil
- ★ 1 tablespoon butter
- ★ 2 onions, finely sliced
- ★ 1 garlic clove, chopped or crushed
- ★ 6–7 sage leaves, roughly chopped
- ★ ½ teaspoon salt
- ★ 125ml red wine
- ★ 1 teaspoon tomato purée
- ★ 300g frozen peas, thawed
- ★ freshly ground black pepper

Heat the oil and butter gently in a pan, add the onions, garlic and sage, then the salt, and stir a couple of times. Cover, lower the heat and leave to sweat for about 10 minutes. Add the wine and tomato purée, turn the heat back up and let the wine come to a simmer. Add the peas and wait for the sauce to simmer again. Now lower the heat and cook until the peas are murky and very tender, which will take a good 20 minutes. Adjust the seasoning and serve with lots of good bread for the juices.

VARIATIONS.
You could add bacon to this dish. About 50g finely sliced dry-cured streaky bacon is ideal. Fry it with the onion. You could also copy the French way of adding lettuce. Use a robust lettuce such as escarole or radicchio, shred it and add it with the peas.

POSH MUSHY PEAS.
I've had to ape this from memory, since many moons ago it was on a television show Nigella Lawson made. I've not discovered it in any of her books, of which I'm quite an avid reader. Try a mound of it next to something like skate or one of the sole family. It's heavenly.

This dish is not to be confused with real mushy peas, which are made using dried peas. This version is fun, and only slightly evocative of the chippy. In fact, my local chip shop has taken to serving something similar instead of the 'proper' lurid, tinned variety. Which is a bit misguided. Sometimes only the worst will do.

For 4 people you need:
★ 2 garlic cloves, peeled
★ 300g frozen peas
★ 3–4 sage or mint leaves
★ 1 tablespoon butter
★ 1 tablespoon crème fraîche
★ salt

Bring a pan of salted water to a rolling boil, add the whole garlic cloves and blanch them for about 5 minutes. Add the peas and the sage or mint leaves and simmer for a couple of minutes. Drain thoroughly. If you have a food processor, tip the peas into it with the butter and crème fraîche. Blitz until you have a rough purée. Alternatively, you can mash them in the pan like spuds although, peas being on the diminutive side, they tend to give the masher the slip. The back of a spoon or fork might be more effective. Season to taste and serve.

LENTIL AND VINAIGRETTE SALAD.

Try this with chicken or sausages. You can use tinned lentils, if you like, but make sure you wash them first in case they are briny. If you cook the lentils yourself and dress them whilst warm, it brings something extra to the taste, as they often have a smoky taste that is missing from tins.

For 4 people you need:
- ★ 3 garlic cloves, chopped
- ★ 3 tablespoons extra virgin olive oil
- ★ 1 tablespoon white or red wine vinegar
- ★ 2 tablespoons Dijon mustard
- ★ 400g tin of brown or green lentils, or 200g raw lentils, cooked until just tender (see page 191)
- ★ 1 red onion or 2 shallots, finely diced
- ★ a handful of roughly chopped flat-leaf parsley
- ★ salt and freshly ground black pepper

The best way to start the dressing is to pound the garlic in a pestle and mortar, then mix in the oil so that you have a kind of paste. Add this, the vinegar and the mustard to the lentils. Then add the onion or shallots and the parsley and season to your liking. You might need more oil or vinegar, depending on how sharp you want the lentils to be.

TWO DELI CLASSICS.

The next two items are, strictly speaking, salads. Coleslaw is the more famous of them in this country, but over in France, no *traiteur* worth its salt would be complete without a remoulade.

I used to be a bit of a purist about serving things like coleslaw and remoulade next to hot meat. I thought that mayonnaise-based salads were best served with cold cuts. With hindsight this was silly. Mayonnaise and burgers go well together, so why shouldn't steak and coleslaw? If you haven't tried this combination already, trust me, a rare steak and a really fresh coleslaw (i.e. one not from a plastic tub) is a wonderful thing. The same is true of remoulade, which is also good with grilled fish.

AN EDIBLE COLESLAW.
I think shop-bought coleslaw is revolting – like all the worst salads, it tends to be overdressed. My coleslaw is rather plain. I don't add dried fruit or apple. If the carrots are fresh and young enough, they will provide all the sweetness you need. I've had coleslaw with walnuts thrown in, which works.

This is great with steak and chicken, or even sausages (especially cold ones).

For 4 people you need:
- ★ ½ small white cabbage, cored and shredded
  as finely as possible
- ★ 2 youngish carrots, shredded
- ★ juice of 1 lemon or 1 tablespoon white wine vinegar
- ★ 1 tablespoon light olive oil
- ★ ½ teaspoon salt
- ★ a scant pinch of sugar (optional)
- ★ 1 tablespoon Dijon mustard
- ★ 3–4 tablespoons mayonnaise
  (for home-made, see page 211)
- ★ salt and freshly ground black pepper

You should 'cure' the cabbage and carrots by tossing them with
the lemon juice or vinegar, oil, salt and sugar and letting them
sit together for half an hour. Then dress with the mustard and
mayonnaise and season to taste.

CELERIAC REMOULADE.
This is brilliant with lamb chops, steak or salmon. Celeriac
remoulade is, I suppose, an understated version of coleslaw. Try
to find the smallest celeriac you can get your hands on. You will
probably need only about half of it, unless there are plenty of you.

For 4 people you need:
- ★ about 200g celeriac, peeled and either grated
  or cut into very fine matchsticks
- ★ juice of 1 lemon
- ★ 1 tablespoon light olive oil
- ★ 3 tablespoons mayonnaise
  (for home-made, see page 211)

* 1 tablespoon Dijon mustard
* salt and freshly ground black pepper

The trick here is to 'cure' the celeriac before adding the
remoulade sauce. As soon as you have peeled and cut it, you
must marinate it in the lemon juice, oil, ½ teaspoon of salt and a
pinch of black pepper. This will soften it a little and stop it
discolouring (it can oxidise like an apple). Leave it to cure in this
mixture for about half an hour, then dress it with the mayonnaise
and mustard. Season it to your liking.

VARIATION.
For an interesting variation, dress the celeriac with the anchoïade
on page 161.

Soup.

THE WATCHED POT: SOUP.

When it comes to cooking, there are definitely 'soup people' and 'non-soup people'. Let me make sense of that. Soup people don't make posh, starter-type soups for dinner parties. We've all tried that (some more successfully than others, as Helen Fielding illustrates so beautifully in *Bridget Jones's Diary*). Soup people don't really follow recipes anyway. They just seem to throw their creations together with perfected nonchalance. I shared a flat with a soup person once and she could turn everything, from a sack of lentils to the really sorry-looking lettuce in our fridge, into a satisfying meal.

Having worked in restaurants, I can tell you that chefs are soup and non-soup people as well. Some male chefs think it's a bit girly to be good at soup, which is a bit weird if you ask me (show me a menu without it). I've worked with some chefs who only follow recipes slavishly and others who can do what my flatmate used to. I fall somewhere between the two. I'm a soup person in that I like soup but I'm not all that inventive (I lack the requisite patience to look at a cupboard and translate the contents into soup). I'm a soup person because I make soup but I do that because I can't bring myself to buy it. I hate tinned soup, cup soup, packet soup and all the rest because they are full of rubbish. Soup is supposed to make the kitchen feel as old as time (which is to say, as old as soup). Soup is supposed to make us feel better. You can at least pretend to cure a cold with soup. You can try to atone for overindulgence with the simplicity of soup. But it's a pointless exercise if it contains all the unwelcome ingredients of mass production.

There are all sorts of supposedly posh 'fresh' soups on offer these days, of course, but finding a really good one is tricky. Even the best-intentioned commercial soup maker is working with so much bulk that the things that make a great soup (i.e. time and a short list of good ingredients) can easily be jettisoned in favour of what I call the 'big guns'. The first of these is artificial thickening. Modified starches, or simply over-enthusiastic amounts of flour, make soups gloopy, not rich. Next big gun: overseasoning. Most commercial soup is overseasoned, and the worst culprits hide behind a liberal amount of black pepper, which swamps other tastes. Dried mixed herbs are just as prone to bullying your taste buds. Commercial soup also tends to be puréed to within an inch of its life. Nothing depresses me more than Mediterranean bean soup that turns out to be a purée. I want to see beans, not just pretend I can still taste them.

Make soup. It is easy. It isn't always quick, but it isn't all that involved. To illustrate this, I've trawled my brain for the least involved. Ironically, these can be the tastiest. I talked about thickening, above, but the soups that follow all thicken themselves. Oh, and none are the puréeing kind, although you can whiz them up if you want.

THE KIT.

THE STOCK. One thing that you are welcome to use but absolutely don't need for this chapter is stock. If you like making stocks, use them by all means. If not, follow the method of starting all the recipes by cooking a base of vegetables (usually with onions and garlic) very gently with a little oil and some salt. The salt and the gentle heat tug juices and flavours from the base before any water is added. This is known as 'sweating'.

I was once lucky enough to work for a fascinating chef who believed that sweating the ingredients enough meant that you never needed stock. She was right and I don't use stock for any of the soups in this chapter.

THE POT. You need a large, heavy-bottomed pan with a well-fitting lid. And you need time. Soup improves if you rest it after you have made it. Somehow the flavours deepen. This is particularly true if it's left overnight. Try it if you don't believe me.

A BASIC POTATO SOUP.

If you really think that you're not a soup person, it is worth starting your journey with potatoes. This incredibly simple base can be transformed by the addition of one or two ingredients. It can offer you comfort (make the watercress and nutmeg version on page 177 to see what I mean). And it can be pretty punchy, too. Try adding harissa, as suggested on page 177. Puréed, a potato soup is velvety and sophisticated. Left chunky, it is as rustic as it gets (see the leek version on page 180).

Before you add anything to this soup, however, just try a spoonful on its own. Sometimes the simplest of flavours is enough.

For 4–6 people you need:
- ★ 2 tablespoons olive oil
- ★ 2 onions, chopped
- ★ 2 garlic cloves, chopped
- ★ 1 teaspoon salt
- ★ 3 large, floury potatoes, peeled and roughly diced

Gently heat the oil in a saucepan. Add the onions and garlic and then stir in the salt. Turn the heat down very low and cover the pan with a lid. Walk away for about 10 minutes. The onions, egged on by the salt and the heat, are having a sweat, releasing their vital juices and flavours. After 10 minutes or so, add the potatoes. Half fill a mug with water and add it to the pan. Bring to simmering point, then lower the heat, cover again and allow the ingredients to sweat for another 20 minutes or until the potatoes are really tender. This may take up to half an hour. Just check it every 10 minutes or so to make sure all the liquid hasn't gone and you're not frying the base. If it has dried out, add a little more water. You need to cook it without letting anything catch on the bottom. What you are after is a smoothly creamy-coloured soup, almost the colour of white chocolate.

When the potatoes are tender to the point of falling apart, add more water until you get the consistency you like. About 400ml will probably be just right but it will depend a little on how starchy the potatoes were. You can purée the soup at this point, if you like, or use a potato masher, which is what I do unless I want a really smooth soup for entertaining. You may also want to add more salt. As I said, do try it plain, and then go with one of the following ideas.

THREE JAZZED-UP POTATO SOUPS.

The soups below are all easy variations on the basic potato soup theme. An even easier way to jazz up a potato soup base is to add a herb or two. Chop a generous bunch of parsley, tarragon or chervil and stir it into the soup as you are about to

serve up. Chervil has a particularly fine flavour. Sorrel is sharp
and summery. Chives are just the right side of astringent for the
texture of this soup.

POTATO, WATERCRESS AND NUTMEG SOUP.

At the table you could give people the option of adding grated
Parmesan or Gruyère to this soup; it's deliciously rich that way.
Neither would a sprinkling of dried chillies be a bad idea.

For 4–6 people you need:
- ★ 1 supermarket bag or grocer's bunch of watercress
- ★ 1 quantity of Basic Potato Soup (see page 175), with
  ½ nutmeg grated into it as the ingredients sweat

Remove only the thickest part of the watercress stalks.
Everything else can be chopped as finely or roughly as you like.
Stir the watercress into the soup just as you serve it (you can do
a natty trick here of swirling very finely chopped watercress into
each bowlful, so that the soup is two tone).

POTATO, CORIANDER AND HARISSA SOUP.

Here is another variation of the simple base with herbs and
spices. Harissa is a spice paste from North Africa and the
Middle East. You can buy it in tubes, like tomato purée, from
some delicatessens and supermarkets. I like to make my own,
quite loose version for this soup. If you like spicy pastes, double
the quantities and store it in the fridge, covered with a thin layer
of extra oil. It will keep for about 3 weeks and the oil will pick up
the flavour. You can add it to all sorts of dishes, particularly
grilled meat and fish.

For 4–6 people you need:
* ★ 1 quantity of Basic Potato Soup (see page 175)

For the harissa:
* ★ ½ teaspoon cumin seeds and ½ teaspoon
  caraway seeds (or just 1 teaspoon of either)
* ★ 2 garlic cloves
* ★ 4–5 long red chillies, deseeded
* ★ ½ teaspoon salt
* ★ about 2 tablespoons coriander leaves
* ★ ½ teaspoon paprika (the smoked Spanish
  paprika is good here)
* ★ 50ml extra virgin olive oil

For the harissa, roast the cumin and/or caraway seeds by
warming a frying pan until it is just beginning to show wisps of
smoke, then throwing in the spices. Remove the pan from the
heat immediately, give it a shake and set aside. This helps
unlock the flavour of the spices.

You can blitz the paste in a food processor or chop it by
hand, which gives it a better texture. Lay the garlic and chillies
on a chopping board and sprinkle them with the salt. This helps
the chillies 'bleed' a little as you chop them. Chop the garlic and
chillies until you have a rough-looking paste, then put them in a
bowl. Chop the coriander and add it to the chilli mixture with the
paprika. Pound the seeds in a pestle and mortar and add them
too. Now fold in the oil. If you have time, this paste likes to sit for
a few hours before being eaten.

Stir a small amount of the harissa into each bowl of soup, or
just put a small amount in the middle of each bowlful.

POTATO AND DRIED MUSHROOM SOUP.

You will get equally interesting, but quite different, flavours depending on which mushrooms you use for this. Porcini or shiitake are the best. You can buy dried porcini in small bags, ready sliced. Shiitake are likely to be whole. And if you make this version of potato soup, it is worth soaking the mushrooms before starting on the soup. Although I have said that you don't need stock for these soups, the water that you use to soak the mushrooms makes a fine addition to the pot.

For 4–6 people you need:
- ★ 20g dried mushrooms
- ★ 200ml hot water
- ★ 1 quantity of Basic Potato Soup (see page 175), preferably made using the mushroom-soaking liquor (see method)
- ★ 2 sprigs of thyme or rosemary (optional)
- ★ extra virgin olive oil, to serve

Soak the mushrooms in the water for about 20 minutes, then drain them, reserving the liquor. Use the liquor to cook the soup. Either chop the mushrooms into a rough paste or slice them as finely as you can, then stir them in at the end of the cooking time. If you have a couple of sprigs of thyme or rosemary to hand, chop the leaves and scatter them into the soup with the mushrooms and a drizzle of extra virgin olive oil.

BULKED-UP POTATO SOUPS.

These soups are chunkier and heartier than the ones above. They are perfect for occasions when you want soup as a meal in itself.

LEEK AND POTATO SOUP.

What can you say about leek and potato soup? Only that if you make it yourself, you will beat any bought-in version hands down. Despite its creamy taste, this soup is incredibly low in fat. Don't use anything 'skinnier' than semi-skimmed milk though. There is a limit to how goody-two-shoes you can be when cooking.

For 4–6 people you need:
- ★ 3–4 leeks (about 400g untrimmed weight)
- ★ 2 garlic cloves, chopped
- ★ 100ml milk
- ★ 2 large, floury potatoes, peeled and diced
- ★ 1 teaspoon salt
- ★ 300ml water
- ★ 2 sprigs of tarragon, stripped from the stalk
  and chopped, or ½ teaspoon of the freeze-dried
  version (entirely optional)

Use as much of the leeks as you can. Trim away only the very roughest part of the green top and the little beard on the root. If they are thick stemmed, you may want to peel away the outermost layer like onion skin and discard it. Leeks can be muddy, and the easiest way to wash them is after you have sliced them up. Just put the slices in a colander and run them under a tap. It doesn't matter if they break up a bit.

This soup is very, very straightforward. Braise the leeks and garlic in the milk over a gentle heat until soft, then add the potatoes. Don't worry if the leeks appear to curdle the milk. The soup will come back together. Add the salt and about half the water. Simmer gently until the potatoes are about to fall apart, then add the remaining water. Bring back to simmering point and mash gently. If you want to use the tarragon, add it just before serving. If the soup seems thick, loosen it with more milk or water, then check the seasoning.

VARIATIONS.

★ You can purée this soup and serve it chilled, like vichyssoise (on which it is based). Garnish with crème fraîche, chives and cracked black pepper.

★ You could also add a fillet of smoked haddock to the soup. The easiest way to do this is to put the fillet into a bowl, half an hour ahead of cooking time, and cover it with water from a just-boiled kettle. Cover and leave for about 10 minutes, then drain, reserving the water (use that to make the soup). When the fillet is cool enough to handle, flake it very gently, getting rid of bones and skin. Add the flaked fish to the soup just before it is ready to serve. If you do this, garnish each bowlful with a small knob of unsalted butter.

★ Substitute a smallish cauliflower and an onion for the leeks. As you braise them in the milk, you could add a tiny (be really stingy) pinch of saffron and about ½ teaspoon of dried mint.

POTATO, CABBAGE AND CHORIZO SOUP.

This is the heartiest potato soup of all. Across Europe there are many meat and potato soups (even Irish stew has its roots here), but the Portuguese classic, *caldo verde*, is possibly the best. For true *caldo verde*, you need dried, spicy Portuguese chorizo, but don't go mad looking for it. Spanish will do, as will any French spicy sausage, or the Italian Napoli salami.

The Portuguese use spring greens for this dish but sometimes these are not around either. Savoy cabbage makes a good substitute. This is a great way of using the dark green outer leaves that so many recipes ignore. If you like dark green cabbage, try this soup with kale or the super-trendy cavolo nero so beloved in Italy.

For 4–6 people you need:
★ 100g chorizo, sliced as finely as possible
★ 1 onion, chopped
★ 2 garlic cloves, chopped
★ 1 teaspoon salt
★ 2 medium-sized floury potatoes, peeled and roughly diced
★ 2 heads of spring greens or the outer leaves of a Savoy cabbage, shredded
★ extra virgin olive oil

Chances are there is plenty of good cooking fat lurking within the sausage so, before you start the soup, gently fry the chorizo in a saucepan until crisp. Remove with a slotted spoon and set aside.

Now use the fat to fry the onion. Add it to the pan with the garlic and salt, cover and leave to sweat over a low heat for about 10 minutes, without letting them brown. If it doesn't look as if there is enough fat left from the chorizo to sweat the onion, do complement it with a tablespoon or so of olive oil.

When the onion is pale and soft, add the potatoes with about a mugful of water. Bring to a simmer, then cover and leave the soup for about 20 minutes. Add the cabbage and chorizo, plus just enough water to cover everything (not so much that the ingredients are swimming). Keep simmering until the cabbage is tender, then check the seasoning. I like to attack this soup with a masher before I serve up so that some of the potato and sausage gets a bit smushy (don't purée it!). Garnish with a generous slug of extra virgin olive oil.

One thing to note: if you make this soup in advance, it may need loosening with a splash more water when you reheat it.

FIVE SOUPS WITH PULSES.

One of the greatest things about the explosion of Mediterranean-style eating in the UK was that it put to bed the old notion of beans and lentils as 'hippy food'. That statement is not meant to be an insult to hippies, of course, who were merely attuned to an ancient wisdom: a diet without meat benefits hugely from protein-rich pulses (think of the myriad variations of *dhal*, the Hindi word for pulses in Indian cookery). This is why pulses also have a reputation for being pauper's food. Some of the world's favourite dishes have grown out of the habit of adding beans to a pot where meat was scarce (think of cassoulet or chilli con carne).

Pulses make great soups and stews. Besides being extremely nourishing, they make their own uniquely flavoured stock while they cook. You can use either dried or tinned pulses for all the recipes in this section. At certain times of the year you will find fresh pulses too, but more of that in a minute. You can also mix and match. If lentils don't grab you, make the same soup with chickpeas or black-eyed beans. You could also use fresh pulsey vegetables like peas or broad beans. Just adjust the cooking time accordingly.

AN EASY LENTIL SOUP, THE TURKISH WAY.

Part of me wants to call this 'soup of the day', in an act of homage to my local Turkish café. I have spent many rainy afternoons skulking in this warm and fuggy hideaway over the last decade, and I have ordered soup of the day hundreds of times. The soup has never changed. Not once. Is it an in-joke with the staff? I've never dared to ask. Were the soup to change now, I'd be outraged. It's easy to reproduce at home.

Ideally, you need split red lentils. These will fall apart and turn a pale but earthy yellow colour when cooked. You could use any pulse you like, as long as you adjust the cooking time. Obviously you could use tinned lentils and then it will be very quick. You don't have to include the pearl barley either; it just adds texture, since the grains never seem to get as soft as the lentils.

For 4–6 people you need:
- ★ 200g split red lentils
- ★ 3 tablespoons pearl barley
- ★ 1 litre water
- ★ 3 tablespoons olive oil
- ★ 2 onions, chopped
- ★ 3 garlic cloves, chopped
- ★ 1 teaspoon salt
- ★ 1 tablespoon dried mint
- ★ 1 tablespoon tomato purée
- ★ salt and freshly ground black pepper
- ★ a pinch of dried crushed chilli (optional)

Cook the lentils and barley in the water first. Don't add any salt to the pot. Bring them to a rolling boil and, for the first 15 minutes or so, you may need to skim off some pale, frothy scum

POTATO, CABBAGE AND CHORIZO SOUP, P181.

KEBAB NIGHT, P213.

PIZZA NIGHT, P220.

CHICKEN AND GREEN CURRY, P266.

'THUNDER AND LIGHTNING', P286.

CHOCOLATE SOUFFLÉ CAKE, P301.

from the top. Turn the heat down if they look as if they will boil over. It can happen. The lentils and barley will take anything from 1–1½ hours to cook. If they start to look too dry, add more water. When they are very tender (the lentils will fall apart), set them aside, in their liquor.

Heat the oil in a large saucepan, throw in the onions and garlic and fry for a couple of minutes. Lower the heat, add the salt and cover so they sweat for 10–20 minutes. Don't let them brown. Add the mint and tomato purée and stir them through the onions. Add the lentils with all their cooking liquor and simmer for another 15 minutes or so. Add water if the soup is getting too thick. Season to taste (here's where you add the chilli, if you want it) and serve with plenty of toasted pita bread and olive oil.

VARIATION.
One delicious variation on this soup is to add the leftovers of a roast joint of lamb or a roast chicken to the pot. Throw the meat in, cut into smallish pieces, at the same time as the lentils.

A SIMPLE BEAN SOUP, THE ITALIAN WAY.
The bean you use here is up to you. The mealier kind is best, by which I mean cannellini or borlotti (sometimes sold as pinto beans). The Italians are masters of the bean soup because they truly understand the point of a dish like this. Nothing is meant to leap out at you except the rather gorgeous simplicity of the beans. Which is why a pale cannellini bean soup might be used to showcase something with a bit of oomph, such as a really green and punchy olive oil. It's almost 'mood food'. You want this; you want to feel like one of the elderly people in those silly adverts for olive oil spread. To see what I mean, just try it.

For 4–6 people you need:

★ 2 tablespoons light olive oil
★ 3 garlic cloves, chopped
★ 2 onions, chopped
★ 2 celery sticks, roughly chopped
★ 1 carrot, roughly diced
★ 1 tablespoon tomato purée
★ 1 teaspoon white wine vinegar
★ 2 x 400g tins of beans
★ the leaves from 2 or 3 sprigs of thyme or rosemary
★ good extra virgin olive oil for drizzling
★ salt and freshly ground black pepper

Heat the oil gently in a large pan, then add the garlic, onions,
celery and carrot. Stir a couple of times, lower the heat, then add
a very scant pinch of salt and cover the pan. Leave the vegetables
to sweat for about 10 minutes. After that, add the tomato purée,
vinegar and then the beans and all their liquor. Add enough
water just to cover everything (it should be more like a stew than
a brothy soup). Throw in the herbs, bring the mixture to a simmer
and cook for about half an hour. If you like, mash the soup very
lightly so that some of the beans get a bit smashed up. Season
with salt and pepper to taste. Serve the soup with plenty of extra
virgin olive oil to drizzle over it in the bowl. You could also
garnish it with freshly grated Parmesan cheese.

VARIATIONS.

★ You could flavour the oil for drizzling. Rosemary is best. To about
100ml extra virgin olive oil, you need to add 2 generous sprigs
(or the contents of one of those slightly gauche bags from a
supermarket). Lay the sprigs out on a chopping board and sprinkle

them very lightly with salt. Using the end of a rolling pin or the base of a small pan, bash the rosemary so that it is bruised. Put it into a bowl or jar and cover with the oil. Leave to infuse for at least half an hour before using. If you have pesto or harissa knocking around, a small blob in each bowl will also enhance this soup.

★ Fresh pulses: in late summer you may see fresh borlotti beans in some shops. They are hard to miss, since the pods are splashed with yellow and purple, Jackson Pollock style. You need a kilo to yield just under 200g and they are not cheap, but they are special. You don't need to soak them and you can skip the rapid boiling that is necessary for most dried beans. They will be tender and creamy in less than an hour.

A SPRING BEAN SOUP, THE PECKHAM WAY.

I say spring bean because I associate dried pulses (except lentils) with winter. For this soup I use frozen broad beans. There is no reason not to use peas or runners instead. There is also nothing to say that you need to make it in spring either. In fact, it is a useful way of using up fresh beans that are a little long in the tooth.

For 4–6 people you need:
★ 2 tablespoons olive oil
★ 2 garlic cloves, chopped
★ 1 onion, chopped (red onion is pretty here, but totally optional)
★ 2 celery sticks, chopped
★ 1 carrot, chopped as finely as possible
★ 1 potato, peeled and diced as finely as possible
★ 1 teaspoon salt
★ 250g frozen broad beans
★ 400g tin of tomatoes
★ about 500ml water

Heat the oil gently in a large pan, then throw the garlic, onion, celery, carrot and potato in together. Add the salt, stir thoroughly, then lower the heat, cover and sweat for 10 minutes or so. Stir in the broad beans. Tip the tomatoes into a colander and squish them with your hands until the juice has gone and you have a rough pulp. Add it to the pot. Now add the water, bring to a simmer and cook for about 45 minutes. After that you can keep it going as long as you like. The longer you cook it, the less *al dente* the beans will be. Check the seasoning when it's finished cooking. You will probably need more salt. I attack this soup with a potato masher when it's done, just to give it some cohesiveness. It's really only the potato and some of the beans that get smashed. The rest of the ingredients will slip through the gaps! Don't purée this soup.

VARIATIONS.

★ Try adding a spoonful of pesto to the soup. You can make your own, if you like (see page 27).

★ My favourite addition to this soup is a handful of leaves, wilted in as I take it off the heat. Whole basil leaves are great, as is mint. Young salad leaves such as rocket or baby spinach work wonders. You just throw them in and stir them round. They will wilt before your eyes. But the best addition is the main reason I make it in the spring. If you can get your hands on a couple of fistfuls of wild garlic leaves, the results are outstanding. Wild garlic may be growing near you. If it is, you will smell it. It favours woodland and often grows amongst bluebells. It's a shame that something so abundant in this country is so hard to get hold of for those of us without access to woodland. The trick to buying the stuff is to ask a butcher or fishmonger who deals in game if he or she can get you some.

COR-BLIMEY-GUV'NOR SOUP.

I suppose this is pea soup the Peckham way, as well. I know from my favourite Lindsay Bareham book, *In Celebration of Soup* (Michael Joseph, 1993), that there is a split pea soup known as 'London Particular'. This is the frozen pea version. I don't know if the addition of Worcestershire sauce is traditional or Lindsay's own but it was an inspired move. Don't omit it!

For 4–6 people you need:
★ 1 tablespoon butter
★ 1 tablespoon olive oil
★ 2 onions, roughly chopped
★ 750g frozen peas, thawed
★ 1 tablespoon Worcestershire sauce
★ about 1 litre water from a recently boiled kettle
★ 2–3 slices of stale white bread
★ 3–4 rashers of bacon, cut into strips (optional)
★ salt and freshly ground black pepper

Heat the butter and oil in a large pot. Add the onions and ½ teaspoon of salt, stir briefly, then cover and cook over a low heat for a good 20 minutes, until the onions are very tender. They shouldn't brown, so keep checking on them. If it looks as if they are beginning to catch, lower the heat further and add a couple of tablespoons of water.

When the onions are soft, add the peas, Worcestershire sauce and just enough water from the kettle to cover everything. Bring to a simmer and cook for half an hour or so. After that, add the bread, broken up as small as possible. At this point, the soup can be mashed, like potatoes, but for the best results, blitz it to a smooth purée in a food processor. If, at any point, it starts to look too thick, just add more water. Reheat gently and season to taste.

To garnish with the bacon, fry the strips gently in a little butter until they are very crisp. Sprinkle them over the soup once it is in serving bowls. Another garnish for this soup is a poached egg, which is not as bizarre as you might think. To make the soup very rich, add a big dollop of soured cream or crème fraîche.

CHICKPEA, BACON AND MUSHROOM SOUP.

This is a rich, dark and quite ugly soup, but don't let that put you off. It's extremely hearty, and the bacon gives it a smoky edge. Vegetarians can make it without the meat and it will still be very tasty.

For 4–6 people you need:
- ★ 4 or 5 dried shiitake or porcini mushrooms
- ★ 500ml warm water
- ★ 100g smoked back bacon, cut into thin strips
- ★ 2 tablespoons olive oil
- ★ 1 onion, chopped
- ★ 2 garlic cloves, chopped
- ★ 2 celery sticks, chopped
- ★ 1 carrot, chopped
- ★ 1 teaspoon salt
- ★ 1 teaspoon tomato purée
- ★ 2 bay leaves
- ★ 400g tin of chickpeas

Soak the mushrooms in the water for at least half an hour. When softened, drain, reserving the water, cut the mushrooms into cross-sections and set aside.

In a large pan, fry the bacon gently in the olive oil until it is fully cooked but not crisp. Remove it from the pan with a slotted spoon and set aside. Add the onion, garlic, celery and carrot to the same oil, then add the salt and stir a couple of times. Lower the heat, cover and sweat for about 10 minutes, until the vegetables have softened. Stir in the tomato purée, return the bacon to the pan and add the bay leaves, mushrooms, chickpeas and all their liquor. Strain the mushroom stock through a fine sieve lined with kitchen roll and add just enough of it to cover the contents of the pot (not enough for them to be swimming). Bring to a simmer and cook for a further half an hour or so. Adjust the seasoning and serve.

VARIATION.

To turn this soup into an even heartier meal, you could add pasta. Use about 50g short tubes per person (macaroni and ditalini are good). Cook them separately, then divide them between soup bowls and pour the hot soup on top. Serve with grated Parmesan cheese.

DIY: COOKING DRIED PULSES

Lots of people prefer not to use dried pulses because there is no getting round the fact that, with the exception of some lentils, they need soaking and a lot of cooking. It is true that they take time, but if you have some at your disposal it's not as if you will be lurking over the pot for hours. The logical approach to soaking pulses is to do it either the night before you plan to eat them or through the working day. I'd aim for the night before. Unless you are a horribly organised, perky-in-the-morning-type person, you'll forget. Basically eight hours' soaking, in lots more water than you might think (it should come at least 8cm above the beans), will do. For the recipes in this section, about 200g dried pulses is the same as one 400g tin.

After soaking the beans, drain them, put them in fresh cold water in a high-sided pan and bring to a rolling boil. As soon as this happens, a frothy scum may start to appear on the surface of the water. Scoop it off and discard it. Let the beans boil for about 10 minutes, then drain them and start again. Lots of people don't bother to do this but a good friend from India (where they cook pulses better than anyone) told me that the first boiling draws out whatever it is in beans that has a, let's say, musical effect on some people's insides. It follows that you might as well totally change the water just to ensure it's all gone!

Cover the beans a second time. Once again you want a good 8cm of unsalted cold water. Never season pulses until they are fully cooked – salt in the cooking water will toughen them up and you want them tender. Bring the water to a boil and then almost immediately reduce it to a simmer. Now let them cook gently for anything between 1 and 2 hours. If that sounds vague, it is because the speed at which beans cook depends upon their age. The longer they've been around, the drier they are. Just make sure they are always covered, topping up the water if it goes below the level of the beans. To test if they are done, taste a bean – it should be tender all the way through, and not taste dry or 'mealy'.

Once they are cooked, keep them in their liquor (it should be a good stock by now). You can season it at this stage. I use salt and a really diminutive glug of olive oil. Sometimes I throw in a bay leaf or two. For the recipes in this book, all the pulses are either added to the other ingredients in this state or from a tin.

You can cook pulses without soaking them first, although this is not to be encouraged because they lose nutritional value. Boil a kettle full of water, pour it over the beans and walk away for half an hour – perhaps soak yourself in a hot bath or something. Change the water, covering the beans by at least 8cm, and add a teaspoon of baking powder or bicarbonate of soda. Bring the beans to a rolling boil and boil for about 20 minutes, skimming off any scum. Now change the water again and cook as if you had soaked them all along. Don't do this with red-skinned beans, as it doesn't work so well. Don't do this full stop if you have tins in or if the recipe will allow you to switch to lentils.

Lentils deserve a little section to themselves. They are the low-maintenance pulse – especially the rather trendy Puy lentils you see everywhere now. These will cook in 30–40 minutes, as will any small brown or green lentil. Red lentils will fall apart by the time they are cooked, but in some instances this is what you want. Yellow split peas are best soaked briefly before cooking. An hour will be plenty. Then cook them in plenty of unsalted water until they are tender.

TWO ONION SOUPS.

Having introduced the idea of sweating onions as the base for soup, I thought it would be nice to include a couple of soups where the onions take centre stage. Once again, they are incredibly easy, although they do take longer than some of the other soups. I am still going to tell you that you don't need stock, but do use it if you have some around. Meat stock might just redeem my busked version of French onion soup from its total lack of authenticity.

RED ONION SOUP.

Here is a shockingly boozy soup taught to me by my friend, George Manners, who owns the highly acclaimed Atlas pub in Earls Court, London.

For 4 people you need:
- ★ 200ml good red wine (please don't use plonk)
- ★ 2 bay leaves
- ★ 2 cloves
- ★ 4 sprigs of thyme (optional)
- ★ 1 tablespoon butter
- ★ 2 tablespoons olive oil
- ★ 8 red onions, sliced
- ★ 2 garlic cloves, chopped
- ★ 1 teaspoon salt
- ★ 1 tablespoon tomato purée
- ★ 2 tablespoons balsamic vinegar
- ★ about 1 litre water or stock

Start this soup by pouring the wine into a large pan with the bay, cloves and thyme, if using. Boil it until it reduces by about half, then strain it, reserving the liquid. In the same pot, heat the butter and oil and throw in the onions and garlic. Add the salt, stir all the ingredients together, then lower the heat, and cover the pan. Leave to sweat very gently for at least half an hour. Check from time to time that the onions are not catching and, if they are, add a couple of tablespoons of water.

When the onions are tender, add the tomato purée, balsamic vinegar, reduced wine and the water or stock and cook gently for another half an hour – or longer, if you like, to deepen the flavour.

To make this soup a real treat, serve it over, or with, bruschetta (see page 61) and garnish with grated Parmesan cheese.

BUSKER'S ONION SOUP.

I'm calling this version of onion soup 'busked' because it can be made without stock. Traditional French onion soup requires a slowly simmered beef broth. It follows that this could be described as 'veggie' onion soup. If you've ever been vegetarian, you'll know that sinking feeling you get, particularly in French restaurants, when you realise that even the most verdant of dishes is barbed with the fat or bones or whatever of some poor beastie.

You really *don't* need good beef stock to make French onion soup. It does benefit from a simple stock, however, and I sometimes make one as I go along, by adding all the skin, tops and tails from the onions and garlic to about 3 litres of water with a bay leaf, and simmering it alongside the soup pan while the onions sweat. The skins will make the stock a beautiful coppery brown. If you own something as heinous as Marmite or Bovril, you could add a teaspoon (but no more) to the stock.

For 4 people you need:
- ★ 1 tablespoon butter
- ★ 2 tablespoons olive oil
- ★ 8 onions, sliced
- ★ 4 garlic cloves, chopped
- ★ 1 teaspoon salt
- ★ 2 tablespoons brandy (optional)
- ★ 100ml dry vermouth or white wine
- ★ about 1 litre water or stock
- ★ 8 slices from a French stick or baguette
- ★ 100g Parmesan or Gruyère cheese, grated

Heat the butter and oil in a large pan, then throw in the onions, garlic and salt. Stir everything together, lower the heat and cover. This base needs to sweat for at least half an hour, until the onions are very tender, so make sure the heat is really low and check it from time to time. If the mixture starts to look dry or if it catches, add a couple of spoonfuls of water.

Add the brandy, if using, turn up the heat (stand well back if you're worried about your eyebrows) and if it catches the flame, good. If not, the alcohol burns off anyway, so don't worry. A minute or so later, add the vermouth or wine. Let it bubble hard for about 5 minutes. Then add the water or stock, bring to the boil and simmer for at least 30 minutes – longer won't do any harm at all and may deepen the flavour.

To serve the soup, you can top the bread with the cheese, float it on top of the soup and place under the grill until the cheese is bubbling. It won't take long. Some people, myself included, like to spoon the soup over toast and garnish the bowl with the cheese. I think it's easier to eat that way.

'*Junk*' *food.*

WRAP IT UP: 'JUNK' FOOD.

I'm using junk food as a term of endearment. I love it. It ticks all the right boxes with its overwhelming savouriness when savoury and appallingly brilliant sweetness when sweet. It is unsubtle in the best of ways, which is why when the craving strikes it is so strong. This chapter is about making food to eat with your hands, and giving it a sense of occasion. I think it is important to do so because so many of us turn to this kind of food for the wrong reasons. Too often I hear friends say that they live on takeaways such as pizzas, kebabs, burgers and fish and chips because they don't have time to 'eat properly'. They feel guilty and dissatisfied, which is a shame because, made with a little care, and seen as a treat rather than fuel, this kind of food can be great.

So, in this chapter there are three 'nights': burger night, kebab night and pizza night. All three are easy to put together. You will have noticed that fish and chip night is missing, and this is only because it requires gadgetry. I promised you at the beginning of this book that you wouldn't need deep-fat fryers, ice-cream makers and all that caboodle to cook the recipes, so I had better stick to my guns.

Earlier in the book (page 60, to be precise) I extolled the virtues of eating with your hands. With burgers, kebabs, pizzas, etc, we are talking *both* hands. We don't just pick 'em up, we manhandle them. We hold them steady as we open our mouths wider than might seem well mannered and shove them in. Strange that we eat the most modern, the most processed of foods like utter cavemen.

I love the fact that a burger in a bun or a kebab in pita bread is all things to all people. The seasoning, the condiments, all that part is up to the individual diner. No one gets a dirty look in a pizzeria for not liking anchovies. You don't offend a burger chef by asking him to hold the onions.

I visited my last burger bar many moons ago, however. Let's just say my relationship with them had become scratchy. I hate the way they target children with their advertising. I hate their overwhelming reliance on intensively reared meat. And their coffee sucks. Mine was probably the last generation to grow up without the ubiquitous presence of fast-food chains in our lives. There were no toy promotions on Saturday-morning television. I couldn't pester my parents to take me 'you know where' because it wasn't around. I still remember seeing the first of the big burger bars on London's Leicester Square when I was about eleven or twelve, but it was a long time before they decorated every high street. Burger bars served American food in an American way. This was as foreign and exciting as sushi from a conveyor belt might seem today. More than that, it was a treat.

Is the word 'treat' going to go missing soon? Sometimes I think so. We are intent on devaluing everything to the point where it must be available to everybody all the time. When applied to food, the effects of this are far reaching. The line between farms and factories is blurred. The food these places produce is then processed beyond recognition and loaded with fat, salt and sugar, to compensate for its mediocrity. This is playing havoc with the health of an increasing number of people who eat it too often. And why is it eaten so often? Because it is cheap, easy, ubiquitous and targeted at an impressionable audience – the young. I want nothing to do with the whole vicious circle.

I do, however, want to eat burgers. And luckily, they are very easy to make – child's play, in fact. There is an irony, since involving children in food preparation has an extremely positive effect on their attitude to it. Cooking is easy enough to build up a young person's confidence in the kitchen. On the other hand, it warrants enough time and effort to prevent food being taken for granted. Perhaps it is more prudent to involve children in the preparation of this type of meal than any other.

THE KIT.

SQUEEZY CONDIMENTS. Gawd bless the clever person who decided to put Heinz ketchup, Hellmann's mayonnaise and French's mustard into squeezy plastic bottles. I keep all of these in the fridge, ready for burger night.

PICKLES AND RELISHES. You may not believe me but you are more likely to feel like cooking your own takeaway-style food if you already have the right condiments in. Your selection is really down to personal taste, but I think a jar of gherkins is a great standby for both burgers and kebabs. Sweetcorn relish is never sold in the fast-food chains but for some reason I can't eat burgers without it. You will find a recipe for making your own on page 212. I also love those pickled chillies that Turkish shops sell. They are not hot, but have a sort of semi-kick to them.

BAKING PARCHMENT. I serve all the meals in this chapter on baking parchment (feels more like a takeaway; no washing up!). Baking parchment is one better than greaseproof paper because it is stronger and, to a certain extent, reusable. Nothing, but nothing, sticks to it, so it is great for cooking pizza (see page

221). You may find it sold as baking paper, parchment or silicone paper in supermarkets. There is no difference between the performance of the white or brown (unbleached) version.

BURGER NIGHT.

Here are some recipes for burgers and suggestions for side orders. You can make the occasion as simple or as complicated as you like. I include recipes for relishes (and one for oven chips) for those who want to make them rather than use shop-bought versions. I have nothing against buying in the paraphernalia for burger night. My main reason for making rather than buying the burgers themselves is because they taste better. While we are on that subject, I think it is pointless trying to be too 'worthy' with this kind of cooking. Especially if you are a parent who plans to persuade children that your burger night is better than a trip to a fast-food joint. Think happy meal, not hippy meal! Wholemeal rolls might be less 'evil' than pappy white sesame buns but the devil lurks in details like this. I love making chunky oven chips from scratch for myself but if I think a young audience is likely to compare them unfavourably with the burger-bar version, then I use oven fries. There is not much wrong with them. They are very low in fat and they taste good.

One last thing: it would be dishonest to imply that this kind of food is cheaper to make than to buy, but it needn't be an expensive exercise. To test the following burger recipe I bought enough organic pasture-fed Scottish beef to make four burgers. I did this because it was the most expensive beef I could find. The price came in at just under that of two quarter-pounders from a well-known chain.

A BASIC, NO-NONSENSE HAMBURGER.

For the best burgers, ask your butcher for mince made from rump or chuck steak. Whatever you do, avoid the leanest cuts, since you need some fat in the meat to prevent dryness.

For 4 people you need:
★ 500g minced beef
★ ½ teaspoon salt
★ a scant pinch of black pepper

It doesn't come much easier than hamburgers. Combine the meat, salt and pepper in a bowl and shape the mixture into 4 burgers with your hands. To follow my cooking times below, the burgers should be about 2cm thick. Choose a heavy-based frying pan or a cast-iron griddle and make sure it is searingly hot before you add the burgers. Cook them for about 6 minutes on either side to leave them pink in the middle. If you like really rare burgers, then reduce the time to about 4 minutes. Whatever you do, try and rest the burgers for a few minutes before serving them, as you would a steak (see page 151). Serve in a bun, with whatever accompaniments you like (see pages 208–12).

ALTERNATIVE BURGERS.

The following recipes would not really qualify for burger status if one was going to be pedantic about it. But I wanted to include ideas for people who don't eat beef. So here come my chicken, fish and veggie fillings for your sesame bun!

CHICKEN IN A BUN.

This was the result of a fruitless search for any decent kind of chicken burger. I hate to think what cuts go into your average chicken patty but I couldn't see the virtue in grinding up something as oven ready as chicken breast. This was inspired by a wonderful recipe for flattened chicken in one of the River Café books. I think of it as a sort of chicken schnitzel. Ask your butcher for chicken breast supremes (which means boned out). You want them skinned, as well, for this recipe.

This is the first crumbed recipe you will find in this book. I use instant polenta instead of breadcrumbs for this purpose, across the board. This habit started when I worked with a wheat-intolerant chef, but it stuck. The polenta is a more natural ingredient, it's more versatile, and slightly prettier when fried or grilled!

For 4 people you need:
- ★ 4 chicken breasts, boned and skinned
- ★ 1 tablespoon olive oil
- ★ juice of 1 lemon
- ★ 1 garlic clove, chopped
- ★ 1 teaspoon black pepper
- ★ 1 teaspoon salt
- ★ 4 tablespoons polenta or dried breadcrumbs
- ★ 2 eggs, beaten

Lay the chicken breasts between 2 sheets of baking parchment and, using the heel of a large knife or a rolling pin, flatten them out as much as possible – it's pretty easy.

Now combine the oil, lemon juice, garlic and black pepper and marinate the breasts in this mixture – ideally for 2 hours but this isn't essential if you don't have time. Try and give them at least 30 minutes.

Combine the salt and polenta or breadcrumbs on a large plate and put the beaten eggs in a shallow dish. Coat the breasts in the beaten egg, letting any excess run off, and then in the polenta or breadcrumbs. I like to grill the chicken. You could fry it but it takes slightly longer. Grill under a medium heat for about 15 minutes, turning once, until the coating is golden on both sides. This is easiest if you do it on baking parchment as well. Cut the parchment slightly smaller than the grill pan so that it doesn't stick out and risk catching alight. I like to eat the chicken in a bun with nothing more than Little Gem lettuce and mayonnaise.

VARIATION.

You can tart up the chicken by adding herbs or spices to the marinade. Half a teaspoon of thyme is good, cumin even better. Another option is to turn up the heat a little with a smear of harissa or a shake of tabasco.

VEGETABLE CUTLETS.

I call this a cutlet, which is how it is described in India, where this kind of thing is more common than you might think. I love veggie cutlets and yet I hate veggie burgers, and I can tell you why in three easy words: textured vegetable protein. Could anything sound less appetising?

Note the waxy potato specified in the ingredients list. You need this for holding the patties together. Use a large-ish new crop potato such as Cyprus or late Jerseys.

For 4 people you need:

★ 2 medium-sized waxy potatoes

★ 2 carrots, grated

★ 100g frozen peas, thawed

★ ½ teaspoon ground cumin

★ ½ teaspoon ground ginger

★ 4 tablespoons polenta or dried breadcrumbs

★ 1 tablespoon butter, ghee or olive oil

★ salt and freshly ground black pepper

Boil the potatoes, whole if you can, until they are tender all the way through, then drain and leave to cool. Peel off the skin.

Put about ½ a mugful of water in a small pan, add the carrots and peas and a pinch of salt, and bring to the boil. Cook gently for a good 20 minutes, until they are really soft, then remove from the heat and leave to cool. Add the potatoes to the carrots and peas and mash the mixture thoroughly, but don't be tempted to blitz it in a food processor. Add the spices and season to taste. Leave the mixture to rest in the fridge for 30 minutes, then shape it into 4 patties and coat with the polenta or breadcrumbs (you can freeze the patties at this point, if you like). They are tastiest fried in butter or ghee, but you can also fry them in olive oil. Heat the fat in a heavy-based frying pan, add the patties and fry over a medium to low heat for about 5 minutes on either side, so that the edges are crisp.

Shove these in a bun with ketchup or the Mint and Onion Chutney on page 254. Junk food without bad karma.

A FISH BURGER.
Here is another burger that doesn't feel all that naughty. I have to admit to making the tartare sauce more often than the actual

burger, because I am a huge fan of fish finger sarnies. Try slapping 3 grilled fish fingers between doorstep rounds of white bread with butter and home-made tartare sauce and you might be too.

A word about the fish for this recipe: you could use any white fish, from cod and haddock through to turbot or brill (which would make this a rather expensive burger). With the current crisis in fish stocks, it would be wise to ask a fishmonger for any unusual varieties, such as pollock or whiting. They work just as well and are very tasty.

For 4 people you need:
★ 700g white fish fillets, skinned if possible
★ 3 slices of white bread
★ 1 egg, separated
★ 2 tablespoons milk
★ 4 tablespoons polenta or dried breadcrumbs
★ 1 tablespoon oil
★ salt and freshly ground black pepper

If your fishmonger doesn't skin the fillets, it's fairly easy to do yourself. Lay each fillet skin-side down on a chopping board with the tail end to the left (assuming you're right-handed). Lift up the very end of the tail and slide a good sharp knife between the flesh and the skin. Run the knife carefully along about a third of the fillet in this way. Now if you turn the fillet over and hold it down with one hand, you should be able to tug the rest of the skin gently away with the other. To get rid of any bones, run your index finger carefully along the surface of the fillet. You will feel the ends of the bones. Use tweezers to tug them out.

Making the fish burgers is easy. First, if you're not using polenta, make the bread into crumbs in a food processor, then add the fish and some seasoning and pulse until finely minced. Transfer to a large mixing bowl and fold in the egg white. This is easiest if you beat the white a little first to loosen it up. Shape the mixture into patties about 2cm thick. Lightly whisk the egg yolk and milk together in a shallow dish. Put the polenta or dried breadcrumbs on a large plate. Coat the burgers in the egg mixture first, letting any excess run off, and then in the polenta or crumbs.

Heat the oil in a heavy-based frying pan and add the burgers. They will need about 5 minutes per side over a medium heat. When golden brown and cooked through, serve in a bun with Little Gem lettuce, perhaps slices of tomato, and tartare sauce (see page 210).

VARIATION.

The recipe above is adapted from an Australian one, which included chopped coriander and tasted more like an oriental fishcake. If you would like to try this, substitute 100g ground almonds for the polenta/breadcrumbs and add 2 tablespoons chopped coriander. Season with Thai fish sauce instead of salt, if you have it.

SIDE ORDERS FOR BURGER NIGHT.

With my burgers looked after, I have to have sliced tomatoes, shredded lettuce (it really should be iceberg but I'm a sucker for Cos and Little Gem), slices of onion, mustard and ketchup standing by ready to overstuff the bun with. Here are some optional extras. You want fries with that? You got 'em . . .

OVEN CHIPS.

I'm quite happy buying in oven chips, since they are additive-free and reliable. The original McCain oven chip is just potatoes plus a little vegetable oil (3.8 per cent). I don't know that I can achieve such low-fat fries in my own home. Still, here is my version. They are chunkier and tastier than the ones from a bag.

For 4 people you need:
★ 3 tablespoons butter or vegetable oil
★ 6 large new-crop potatoes, such as
   Cyprus or late Jerseys, peeled if you prefer,
   and cut into thick wedges
★ salt

Preheat the oven to 200°C/Gas Mark 6. Put the butter or oil in a roasting tray and heat it in the oven for 5 minutes. Remove and carefully add the potatoes, spreading them so they are in a single layer. Season with a little salt if you wish, then return to the oven and cook until the potatoes are golden and tender, turning them half way through. They will take anything up to an hour, depending on how thickly you cut them.

DILL SAUCE.
This is my attempt at an American-style burger dressing. I have to say it works well. If you want to make your own mayonnaise, follow the instructions on page 211. I admit that I regularly resort to Hellmann's.

You need:
★ 4 tablespoons mayonnaise
★ 1 tablespoon mustard
★ 2 tablespoons chopped dill
★ 8–9 cocktail gherkins or a couple of large
   gherkins, finely sliced or chopped

Combine all the ingredients and check the seasoning. I find that it never needs salt. If you are using freshly made mayonnaise, be sure to keep the sauce in the fridge until you need it.

TARTARE SAUCE.

I would include this with the fish burger on page 206. There is also something wonderful about tartare sauce with a hamburger, thanks to the tarragon, which complements beef very well. I've yet to find a decent shop-bought version of tartare sauce, if only because most of them are too sharp and skimp on the herbs. That said, you could commandeer a jar of Hellmann's to make a busked version if you don't fancy making mayonnaise. Or, if you have the herbs, capers, gherkins and mustard to hand, you could also make a similar, looser sauce that is just as good using Greek yoghurt or crème fraîche instead of mayo.

You need:
★ 3 tablespoons mayonnaise
★ 1 teaspoon chopped tarragon
★ 1 tablespoon chopped parsley
★ 1 tablespoon capers, roughly chopped
★ 1 tablespoon cocktail gherkins, roughly chopped
★ salt and freshly ground black pepper

I like to keep my tartare sauce quite rough, so I chop the ingredients very sparingly before folding them into the mayonnaise. Whatever you do, don't blitz them in the food processor. It is too brutal. When seasoning, remember that the capers will be salty.

DIY: MAKE YOUR OWN MAYONNAISE.

Here is a very simple recipe for home-made mayonnaise. If you make it in advance, remember that it contains raw egg, so be sure to store it in the fridge in an airtight container and eat it within 2 or 3 days.

You need:
★ 2 egg yolks
★ 1 teaspoon of your favourite mustard
★ 1 teaspoon white wine or cider vinegar, or lemon juice
★ 200ml olive oil (but not virgin)

A food processor is best for this. Start by whizzing the egg yolks with the mustard and vinegar or lemon juice, then add the oil in a steady stream. If you are used to making mayonnaise by hand, you will know that you need to add the oil very slowly – not so with a food processor, where you have to keep up with the high speed of the blades. Add it steadily and confidently. The mayo is ready when the blades leave a visible trail as they cut through it.

To make mayonnaise by hand it is best to get a volunteer to help you. One of you holds the bowl steady and whisks, while the other adds the oil a few drops at a time, following the pace of the whisker.

Season mayonnaise very carefully. If you are making the dill or tartare sauces above, wait until you have added all the other ingredients in those recipes before checking the seasoning. This is especially true where you are adding salty capers or anchovies.

DIY: MAKE YOUR OWN SWEETCORN RELISH.

I think this makes a burger, more so than the dill sauce. When sweetcorn is in season, use it fresh off the cob. The rest of the time use frozen rather than tinned, which is pretty tawdry stuff.

You need:

★ 200g sweetcorn (or 4 fresh cobs)
★ 1 onion, sliced as finely as possible
★ 1 fresh red chilli, deseeded and chopped (optional)
★ 100g sugar (demerara or golden caster, if you have it)
★ ½ teaspoon salt
★ 200ml red or white wine vinegar, or malt vinegar
★ ½ teaspoon mustard powder
★ 1 teaspoon cornflour
★ 2 tablespoons water

If using fresh corn, shuck the kernels off the cobs (this is easiest done by standing each cob upright in a large bowl and running a knife down it, mowing the corn as you go). Blanch fresh or frozen corn in plenty of boiling salted water for about 2 minutes and drain thoroughly. Now combine it with the onion, chilli (if using), sugar, salt and vinegar and bring to the boil. Simmer hard for about 5 minutes, then lower the heat and simmer gently for 20 minutes.

Mix the mustard powder and cornflour with the water to make a paste. Add this paste to the sweetcorn mixture and bring the heat back up. Simmer for about 5 minutes, until the sauce has thickened.

KEBAB NIGHT.

Here is my kebab shop-style feast. It is best left around for
people to build their own fillings for the bread. Save yourself a
heap of washing up and add to the whole kebab-shop feel by
serving all this on baking parchment or greaseproof paper.
People can fill their own pita with slices of lamb and as many
trimmings as they fancy. It also makes ideal barbecue fare.

LEG OF LAMB AND PITA BREAD.

I suppose this is a pretty posh version of a kebab night, thanks
to the cost of a leg of lamb. You could use shoulder instead,
which is fattier but still very tasty and the traditional cut for a
'doner'. An average leg of lamb, weighing 3–3.5kg on the bone,
will easily feed 6 or 7 people. Ask the butcher to bone it for you.

The marinade is like a tapenade, or olive paste. You can
simply season the lamb with salt and pepper but this is delicious.

You need:
★ 1 leg of lamb, boned

For the marinade:
★ 250g pitted black olives
★ 4 anchovy fillets
★ 2 garlic cloves
★ leaves from a sprig of rosemary
★ juice of ½ lemon
★ 2 tablespoons olive oil

Place the leg on a board and trim off any excess fat around the edges. Starting from the least thick point, insert a knife into the cavity where the bone used to be and cut outwards. The leg should now spread on the board in front of you with 2 distinct ends, rather than meeting in the middle, with the 'inside' of the leg facing up. A butcher will do all this for you – ask for the joint to be 'butterflied'. Next, make 6 or 7 slashes across the meat, not to cut it into pieces but to increase the surface area.

Put all the ingredients for the marinade into a food processor and blitz them roughly. If the mixture seems dry, loosen it with a little more oil. Spread the mixture over the meat as evenly as possible and set aside. If you can leave it overnight, that's ideal. But it also works well just left to marinate for a short time, or even spread on the meat as a seasoning and cooked immediately.

A barbecue is perfect for grilling a leg of lamb this way (make sure the embers are really glowing and the flames long gone, or the fat dripping from the lamb will start a fire). Grill it for about 20 minutes on each side for pink meat, 30 minutes if you want it well done. You can also use a heavy-bottomed frying pan or a ridged griddle pan and a hot oven. Preheat the oven to its highest setting. Heat the pan until it is smoking hot. You won't need any fat. If the lamb is too long for the pan you can cut it in half. Place it fatty-side down in the pan and cook over a high heat until the underside has browned dramatically. Turn the meat over and do the same to the other side. Now transfer the leg to a roasting tray (or leave it in the pan if you are using an ovenproof one). Add a drizzle of oil and, if you like, a splash of red wine. Place the meat in the oven and, to serve it very pink, cook it for 20 minutes. Cook it for half an hour if you want it well done. Then allow at least 10 minutes' resting before you slice it.

If you don't fancy tackling a whole leg of lamb, you could ask a
butcher for leg steaks. Sometimes these are sold as leg chops
or 'gigot' of lamb. These have a bone through the middle but it is
easily snipped out with a good pair of scissors. While you're at it,
be sure to break the skin around the edge of these steaks, as it
can tighten and cause them to curl up.

MINCED LAMB KOFTEH.

A quick alternative to the recipe above is this lamb 'burger'.
You'll find minced kebabs, or kofteh, in various guises all over
the Middle and Near East, from Tehran to Athens. This recipe is
Iranian, adapted from Margaret Shaida's book *The Legendary
Cuisine of Persia* (Penguin Books, 1994).

For 4–6 patties you need:
★ 500g minced lamb (you need a fatty
  cut, so ask for shoulder)
★ 1 onion, chopped
★ 1 teaspoon fresh breadcrumbs
★ ½ teaspoon salt
★ ½ teaspoon black pepper
★ ¼ teaspoon turmeric (optional)
★ ¼ teaspoon baking powder

Even though the lamb is minced, it should be kneaded with the
onion to make it cohesive. The best way to do this is with a cake
paddle or dough hook in a food processor. Otherwise use a
normal blade but pulse for a few seconds at a time rather than
leaving it running.

Once you have done this, add all the other ingredients and

mix briefly. Shape the mixture into 4–6 patties, about 2cm thick. This is easiest done with wet hands, so have a bowl of water handy.

Grill the patties, either under the grill or on a ridged griddle pan, for about 5 minutes on each side to leave them only just pink in the middle. Then rest them for at least 5 minutes, just like a steak or burger.

FILLINGS FOR THE PITA BREAD.

I like to have various condiments around when I'm eating out of pita bread. You can buy any number of excellent accompaniments in a deli or supermarket, from olives to those pickled chillies that look as if they should be fiercer than they are. Greek yoghurt, seasoned with mint or embellished with cucumber, makes a good foil for the lamb. You could buy a passable tzatsiki or hummus from the shop, but you'd only be saving yourself the most minimal of effort. Here are both those dishes and a couple of others for you to have a go at.

A QUICK HUMMUS.

Some shop-bought hummus is fine, but it is so easy to make that it is worth doing your own. I have a mild beef with supermarkets for making it with vegetable oil rather than olive oil. I think the latter gives it a better flavour. I sometimes find commercial hummus a bit smooth, too. Making your own gives you more control over the texture.

Tahini is a paste made from crushed sesame seeds. It is best known in this country as a seasoning for hummus but in Middle Eastern cooking it is used in desserts as well as savoury dishes.

You will find it in most supermarkets, healthfood shops and delicatessens. Once it is opened, store it in the fridge. It keeps very well.

You need:
★ 400g tin of chickpeas or 200g dried chickpeas, cooked until very tender (see page 192)
★ 3 garlic cloves, chopped
★ ½ teaspoon salt
★ ½ teaspoon black pepper
★ juice of 1 lemon
★ 3 tablespoons extra virgin olive oil
★ 2 generous tablespoons tahini

You really need a food processor for this. The trick with hummus is to blitz all the ingredients before adding the tahini. This thickens up as soon as it goes near lemon juice, so to get an even paste it's best to let that happen at the end.

Check the seasoning when you have a paste. You may want it sharper or saltier, so adjust the amounts of lemon or salt. You may also want to loosen it with a little more oil, but go easy on this if your oil is strongly flavoured.

TZATSIKI OF SORTS.

I say of sorts, because strictly speaking tzatsiki is a mezze dish or salad. But cucumber, mint and yoghurt turn up across the Near and Far East in various guises. In India it is raita, a cooling foil for chilli-hot dishes. In Turkey it is cacik and might come like a soup. Try smearing it inside pita bread stuffed with lamb or kofteh and you will forgive its inauthentic inclusion in this book.

You need:

- ★ 1 large cucumber or 2 small ones
- ★ ½ teaspoon salt
- ★ 2 garlic cloves, finely chopped
- ★ 450g Greek-style yoghurt (don't use low-fat; it will be too runny)
- ★ ½ teaspoon black pepper
- ★ 1 tablespoon dried mint
- ★ freshly ground black pepper

Peel the cucumber and deseed it by cutting it in half down its length and scooping out the seeds with a spoon. Grate the cucumber on the same blade as you would Cheddar cheese, then squeeze out excess moisture with your hands. Mix the cucumber with all the other ingredients. Taste and adjust the seasoning. This is best kept chilled to add to its overall effect. Now you know why they say 'cool as a cucumber'. If you don't like dairy, the grated cucumber with all the other ingredients apart from the yoghurt makes a good relish on its own.

CHEAT'S CURED RED CABBAGE.

This isn't cured at all but sort of stir-fried and then seasoned. I find truly raw red cabbage a bit starchy.

You need:

- ★ 1 tablespoon olive oil
- ★ 2 garlic cloves, chopped
- ★ ½ small red cabbage, cored and sliced as finely as possible
- ★ 2 tablespoons red wine vinegar
- ★ 1 tablespoon Dijon mustard

★ 2 tablespoons capers (washed if salted), roughly chopped
★ ½ teaspoon sugar
★ a handful of roughly chopped mint or parsley

Heat the oil in a wok or large frying pan and then throw in the garlic. Fry until golden, then add the red cabbage, swiftly followed by the vinegar. Stir and fry for just half a minute before removing from the heat. Now add the mustard, capers, sugar and mint or parsley. You can serve this hot or cold.

CURED CUCUMBER.

Here is something to make if you find large gherkins a little sweet.

You need:
★ 1 large or 2 small cucumbers
★ 1 teaspoon salt
★ 3 tablespoons sherry vinegar or white wine vinegar
★ 1 tablespoon chopped dill

Deseed the cucumber by cutting it in half down its length and scooping out the seeds with a spoon. Now slice the cucumber on a slight diagonal so that you get crescent moon shapes. Sprinkle with the salt, place in a colander and leave for as long as possible – at least half an hour.

Transfer the cucumber to a bowl and toss with the vinegar and chopped dill. You can season this with black pepper, if you like.

PIZZA NIGHT.

I am a snob about pizza. I hate all takeaway versions and I have
yet to come across a large chain of pizzerias that offers anything
really good. It's all too easy to be purist about food once you've
had the 'real thing'. I know pizza is best when cooked in a wood-
burning oven (then eaten on the streets of Naples!) but I also
know it needn't taste bad from an electric oven on a winter's
night in deepest Peckham. Pizza is only really disappointing if
the base is a thick, pappy slab smeared with industrial tomato
paste, phoney mozzarella, hairy anchovies and dried oregano.
Why do so many pizza joints skimp on ingredients like this? I
know of at least one pizza chain that makes a big deal out of the
fact that it imports 'the right dough' from Italy in frozen form.
Quite ridiculous when you consider that the same company then
uses those tinned, pitted black olives that taste of mouthwash.

Much like the larder salads on pages 89–112, the pizza is
supposed to speak to us of simple, inexpensive elegance.
Neapolitan pizza is as much about the taste of local anchovies,
tomatoes and olives as anything else. I'm not pretending for a
minute that I can tell you how to re-create that exactly at home
but, with decent ingredients, you will at least taste something
with a similar intensity.

I'd love to be able to say that there is a good, ready-made
pizza base available to buy but sadly I haven't found one yet. A
couple of the larger supermarket chains have produced their own,
but they are very thick and doughy. I also find it irritating that at
least two brands contain hydrogenated vegetable fats instead of
olive oil. This is why I recommend that you make your own bases.

Foodies are always telling you that baking is a therapeutic

pastime, and making pizza falls into this category. Please note that it isn't necessarily super-fast food the first time you have a go. It will be quicker the next time if you freeze some of the dough. The same goes for the tomato sauces.

PIZZA DOUGH.

Pizza owes much of its unique taste and texture to the nature of the oven in which it is cooked. Whether wood burning or electric, the pizza oven works a bit like an Indian tandoor, in that the cooking space is small and the cooking surface is intensely hot. Thus the base cooks quickly from underneath while the topping is grilled equally speedily from above. This is why it makes such good fast food. You can ape something like this at home. A flat baking sheet (or a specially designed pizza stone) can be preheated in a domestic oven on its maximum setting.

I roll out my pizza dough on baking parchment, which I then slide straight on to the hot baking sheet. It makes the dough easy to move around.

This recipe is very reliable and freezes well, so if you have a good-sized freezer you can make a big batch of dough, roll it out into pizza bases as described in the recipe, and put some aside for another time.

To make 4 pizzas you need:
- ★ 300ml tepid water
- ★ 500g strong white flour (sometimes called bread flour), plus extra for dusting
- ★ 1 teaspoon salt
- ★ 7g sachet of Easyblend dried yeast (very handy to use sachets unless you do a lot of baking)
- ★ 1 tablespoon olive oil

First, make sure the water is definitely tepid, not hot. It should be blood temperature-ish. In a large bowl, combine the flour, salt and yeast and make a well in the centre. In a jug, combine the water and oil. Pour a third of the liquid into the well in the flour and, using a fork, whisk in some flour from around the well until you have the beginnings of a paste or loose batter. Add more of the water and work in more of the flour, and so on and so on, until you have a dough. It should easily come away from the sides of the bowl. Keep working at it if not, and it will happen.

Dust a worktop or a very large chopping board with flour and knead the dough for a good 10 minutes: just push it out away from you with the palm of your hand, then fold it towards you and give it a quarter turn. If you have a food processor with a dough hook you could, of course, use that and let it run for about 5 minutes. When the dough feels smooth and elastic, put it back into the mixing bowl, cover with baking parchment or cling film and let it rest in a warm place for about 45 minutes–1 hour, until doubled in size. Now you need to knock it back; just punch it lightly with your knuckles. Take it from the bowl and roll it out into a sausage shape. Divvy it into 4 pieces and roll them into balls.

Cut 4 large pieces from a roll of baking parchment, each about the size of your baking sheet. Lay the first piece on your worktop and flour it lightly. Now you can roll out your first piece of dough on it. Aim for as thin a base as possible, 23–25cm in diameter. Rolling it into a perfect circle is no mean feat and I've yet to master it. I'm envious when I see practised pizza chefs spinning the dough so nonchalantly between their hands. If you want a round pizza, it's best to place a cake tin, pizza stone or tart tin on top and cut round it with a small knife (use the excess dough to make an extra base or two later). Set your first base aside and go on to the next one. At this point it is possible to freeze the bases. You can lay them in the freezer on the sheets of parchment, stacking them up as you go. A tower of pizza!

TWO RECIPES FOR TOMATO SAUCE.

One of these is easy to make but requires some cooking, while the other is an out-and-out cheat's sauce, but no worse for that. You can use either version of the sauce to smear over a pizza base before cooking. Which sauce you choose is up to you, depending on how fast you want your food.

QUICK TOMATO SAUCE.
This recipe calls for tinned tomatoes. If you have some ripe, flavoursome fresh tomatoes you want to use up, turn the page for my Quicker Tomato Sauce.

For 4 pizzas you need:
★ 2 tablespoons light olive oil
★ 3 garlic cloves, chopped or sliced
★ 3 x 400g tins of peeled plum tomatoes
★ 1 teaspoon salt
★ ½ teaspoon sugar (optional)
★ a handful of flat-leaf parsley, roughly chopped

Use the widest pan you have. Heat the oil in it and add the garlic. Turn the heat very low and allow the garlic to go soft and translucent without browning. This should take about 10 minutes. While this happens, drain the tomatoes in a colander and squish

them with your hands to get rid of all the juice. You will be left
with a pulp. Add this to the pan and stir so that the garlic is
thoroughly mixed in. Add the salt and sugar, then the parsley.
Continue to cook, very gently, for another 15 minutes or so,
until the sauce is reduced and thickened.

If you like, you can make the sauce very smooth by blitzing
it in a food processor. I don't bother.

QUICKER TOMATO SAUCE.

If you are confident that you have ripe, tasty, fresh tomatoes, you
could substitute them for the tinned ones here.

For 4 pizzas you need:
- ★ 1 garlic clove
- ★ 2 tablespoons light olive oil
- ★ 1 tablespoon balsamic vinegar
- ★ 2 x 400g tins of peeled plum tomatoes
- ★ salt

This works best with a pestle and mortar. Pound the garlic with
a pinch of salt until it becomes a paste, then stir in the oil and
vinegar. If you don't have a pestle and mortar, crush the garlic
on a board with the flat of a large knife, then mix with the oil
and vinegar.

Drain the tomatoes in a colander and squish them with your
hands until all the juices are gone and you are left with a pulp.
Add this to the garlic paste and stir thoroughly. Now season
to taste and, if you like, purée the sauce by blitzing it in a
food processor.

THREE PIZZA TOPPINGS.

A base smeared with one of the tomato sauces above is the starting point for these fairly classic Neapolitan pizzas. The two favourites in Naples are the margherita and the napoletana.

MARGHERITA.

This was supposedly invented for Queen Margherita of Savoy, and the addition of mozzarella to the red of the tomatoes and the green of the herbs was a patriotic nod to the *tricolore* of the modern Italian flag.

For each pizza you need:
★ 3 tablespoons Quick or Quicker Tomato Sauce
  (see pages 223–4)
★ ½ ball of mozzarella cheese, chopped or grated
★ 1 tablespoon freshly grated Parmesan or pecorino cheese
★ a very generous drizzle of extra virgin olive oil
★ 1 tablespoon chopped oregano or basil
★ salt and freshly ground black pepper

Preheat the oven to its highest setting, with the baking sheet or pizza stone inside. Spread the tomato sauce over the pizza base, leaving a good inch of crust uncovered at the edge. Sprinkle over the cheeses, then transfer the pizza, on its parchment, to the preheated oven and baking sheet and cook for 10–15 minutes, until the crust has puffed up and browned and all the cheese has melted. Sprinkle over the oil, herbs, salt and pepper and serve immediately.

NAPOLETANA.

Like the margherita, this is a traditional recipe. You must use the best anchovy fillets you can get hold of and good, dry, wrinkly black olives. Adding mozzarella to a napoletana pizza is supposed to be a no-no but who's looking? It tastes great. If you want to do that, simply add the same amount of mozzarella as in the recipe above.

For each pizza you need:
* ★ 3 tablespoons Quick or Quicker Tomato Sauce (see pages 223–4)
* ★ a handful of dried black olives
* ★ 4–5 anchovy fillets
* ★ 1 tablespoon chopped capers
* ★ 1 tablespoon chopped basil or oregano
* ★ a very generous drizzle of extra virgin olive oil
* ★ salt and freshly ground black pepper

Preheat the oven to its highest setting, with the baking sheet or pizza stone inside. Spread the tomato sauce over the pizza base, leaving a good inch of crust uncovered at the edge, then add the olives, anchovies and capers. Transfer the pizza, on its parchment, to the preheated oven and baking sheet and cook for 10–15 minutes, until the crust has puffed up and browned. Sprinkle over the herbs, oil and seasoning (go easy on the salt) and serve immediately.

FIORENTINA.

I'd guess that this is not a traditional pizza. I would say (guessing again) that it is an adaptation of eggs cooked the Florentine way, with spinach and Parmesan. However untraditional, it is my favourite, especially with chilli oil drizzled on the egg.

For each pizza you need:
- ★ 3 tablespoons Quick or Quicker Tomato Sauce (see pages 223–4)
- ★ 1 garlic clove, sliced
- ★ ½ ball of mozzarella cheese, grated
- ★ a handful of baby spinach leaves, washed and drained
- ★ 1 egg
- ★ 1 tablespoon freshly grated Parmesan or pecorino cheese
- ★ ¼ nutmeg, grated (optional)
- ★ salt and freshly ground black pepper

Preheat the oven to its highest setting, with the baking sheet or pizza stone inside. Spread the tomato sauce over the pizza base, leaving a good inch of crust uncovered at the edge. Sprinkle the garlic over the sauce, followed by the mozzarella and spinach leaves. Now, using the back of a spoon, create a hollow in the middle of the sauce and leaves and break in the egg on this spot. Sprinkle everything with the Parmesan or pecorino and the nutmeg, if using. Transfer the pizza, on its parchment, to the preheated oven and baking sheet and cook for 10–15 minutes, until the crust has puffed up and browned and the egg is just set. Season with salt and black pepper.

RAW PIZZA TOPPINGS.
While we are dispensing with any notions of authenticity, I should tell you that my favourite home-made pizzas are those where the topping is not really cooked at all. Try baking a pizza base with nothing but the tomato sauce on it for about 10 minutes, or until the edge is good and crusty. Then add any of the toppings below and serve.

★ Diced buffalo mozzarella, tossed with anchovies, extra virgin olive oil and lots of roughly chopped basil.

★ 3–4 thin slices of Parma ham with lots of rocket and shaved Parmesan.

★ A generous handful of baby spinach with basil leaves and pine nuts tossed through it, plus slices of Parma ham or (even better) speck.

★ A very generous smear of ricotta cheese, plus thinly sliced red onion, chopped black olives, mint leaves, olive oil and lemon juice.

★ Very thinly sliced raw field mushrooms, with a squeeze of lemon juice and lots of freshly ground black pepper.

★ Marinated artichoke hearts (look for ones in olive oil rather than vegetable oil) and dried crushed chilli.

ALTERNATIVE PIZZA BASES.

If you balk at the idea of making pizza dough (and cooking it), these ideas might be for you, but that is not the only reason I include them. They make wonderful, homely meals and their charms would not be entirely lost on an Italian household.

BRUSCHETTA.

All of the pizza toppings above would work perfectly well on outsize slices of bruschetta (grilled bread rubbed with olive oil and garlic). For making bruschetta, see page 61.

PITA BREAD.

Pita bread tastes great with pizza toppings. To make it really good, split the pita open as if you were going to stuff it, then prise it apart completely. Bake the pizza toppings on the extra-thin pieces of pita.

FRENCH BREAD PIZZA.

My mother used to make these for us. They felt very exotic back in the Seventies. This recipe works best if the bread is slightly stale, but it needn't be. The principle is simple: you pull out the innards of the bread and use them in a stuffing, which is then baked inside the crust. You can replace the meat with olives or anchovies, if you like.

For 2 people you need:
- ★ 1 baguette or similar (or 2 mini versions)
- ★ 1 ball of mozzarella cheese, diced
- ★ 2 tablespoons freshly grated Parmesan or pecorino cheese
- ★ 4 slices of Parma ham or salami (or similar), cut into strips
- ★ 2 tomatoes, deseeded and chopped
- ★ a handful of chopped oregano or basil
- ★ ½ teaspoon salt
- ★ 1 egg, beaten
- ★ extra virgin olive oil
- ★ freshly ground black pepper

Preheat the oven to its highest setting. Cut the loaf of bread in half down its length and scoop out the centre to hollow it out. Either chop or pulse (if you have a food processor) the innards of the bread to make rough crumbs. Set them aside in a mixing bowl.

Combine the mozzarella, Parmesan or pecorino, ham and tomatoes with the herbs, salt and some pepper. Check the seasoning and if it is to your liking (more salt?), mix in the egg and breadcrumbs. Now refill the crusts of the bread with the mixture and bake for about 10 minutes, until the filling has just set. It really won't take long. Drizzle the finished bread with a good slug of extra virgin olive oil.

PIZZA PASTY.

This is really an individual pizza pie or, to use the Italian, pizza rustica, which is made with flaky pastry. I use ready-made puff pastry, which you can buy frozen, and it works brilliantly. You could also use pizza dough (see page 221).

If you don't eat meat, the filling is just as good without the ham or salami.

For 2 pasties you need:
★ 200g puff pastry
★ 200g ricotta cheese
★ 50g Parmesan or pecorino cheese, freshly grated
★ ½ teaspoon salt
★ ½ teaspoon black pepper
★ a scant pinch of nutmeg
★ 50g Parma ham or salami (or similar)
★ 2 generous handfuls of rocket or baby spinach, roughly chopped
★ 2 eggs

Preheat the oven to 200°C/Gas Mark 6, with a baking tray inside. If necessary, roll the puff pastry out into 2 sheets about 5mm thick; if using ready rolled, it's fine as it comes. Place the pastry sheets on top of a sheet of baking parchment.

Combine the ricotta, Parmesan or pecorino, salt, pepper, nutmeg, ham and leaves in a mixing bowl. Beat the eggs and add two-thirds of them to the mixture. Fold the eggs through, then spoon the mixture into the centre of the pastry sheets, keeping it well away from the sides. Now bring the sides and ends up to meet in the middle. Press them together, then brush the pasties with the remaining egg.

Remove the hot baking sheet from the oven. Lift the pasties, still on the baking parchment, on to the baking sheet and return to the oven. Bake for about 25 minutes, until golden brown, then allow them to rest for about 5 minutes before serving.

If you like, you could serve the pasties with Quick Tomato Sauce (see page 223) on the side, or with salad and pickles. They are good served cold, too.

Indian.

STAYING IN FOR A CURRY (PART ONE): INDIAN.

Is this a chapter about curry? I suppose it is. Strictly speaking, though, not one of the dishes that follows is a 'curry'. But then, who wants to be strict?

As words go, curry has come a long way. It started life as a misnomer, a symptom of our ignorance about the diversity of cooking on the Subcontinent. A curry used to mean one of two things: a meal in an Indian restaurant, or a stew with curry powder.

Then, in the early Eighties, like a cross between a missionary and a kindly governess, Madhur Jaffrey published a book that changed everything – *Indian Cookery* (BBC Books, 1982). Curry powder was usurped by larders full of innumerable spices. At least, it was in my house. My father was an instant convert. As a teenager, I think I ate more Jaffreyesque feasts than Sunday roasts. My parents bought me that book and a crate of spices for my eighteenth birthday. I spent my college years cooking dhal and biryanis. Both book and crate still have pride of place in my home today.

Though nowadays we may know our Goan from our Gujerati, something deeply rooted in our psyche does not want to let go of 'curry'. The word is globally understood. Curry has become a collective noun, referring to food with a certain kind of spiciness. It's not about chillies, at least not always. It's not even exclusive to India, although for people in the UK, India is the centre of the curry universe. When I say India, I mean the entire Subcontinent

– for so much of the 'Indian' food eaten in the UK comes from Pakistan and Bangladesh. Indian restaurants are still 'curry houses' to many of us. And any food that is seasoned with Indian spices is 'curried'. Given half the chance, some of us will curry anything that hangs around in the kitchen long enough. Scrambled eggs with garam masala or parsnip soup laced with cumin are classics, while curried baked beans are a painful reminder of my student past. Many of us are addicted to spice. Like the chocoholic, when the curryholic is hit by a craving, nothing else will do.

There has never been a better time to crave a curry – thanks to the explosion of interest in the whole spectrum of Indian culture, from food to film. British Indian restaurants are in transition. You can no longer automatically expect identikit flock wallpaper and dimmed lights from your local curry house. The menus are changing with the decor. Many places now specialise in regional cooking. A few London establishments offer an experience more recognisable as *haute cuisine* than the old model of curry as a cheap meal out. However, there is always the takeaway – or, indeed, the supermarket. Some of the bigger stores offer tailor-made meal packs that you simply heat up at home. Iqbal Wahhab, owner of the brilliant, fêted Cinnamon Club restaurant in London, reckons that the supermarkets are giving many catering outlets a run for their money in terms of quality and authenticity – especially the old-fashioned Indian takeaways. I'm sure he would agree, though, that you can still do better at home.

The main reason this chapter is here is, I suppose, down to my father. Weekends spent preparing for Sunday's curry lunch are still great fun whenever I can get home. Smashing and blending spices is like going back to the chemistry sets I loved when I was a boy. The smell of Indian food cooking is one of the most mouthwatering aromas on the planet.

There is something else about home-cooked Indian food that simply can't be beaten by restaurants and takeaways, and I think it must be to do with blending spices in small quantities. I feel like one of those mad wine critics saying this, but the flavours are so distinctive that you can discern each and every one.

Like most Asian cuisine, the traditional Indian meal is a compound affair, with several shared dishes on the table. I've assembled some fairly classic combinations – the most popular amongst my friends. You could combine one or two, or all of them, in one sitting. And, like the spices in the cupboard, you needn't confine any of the following recipes to some kind of themed Indian night. Try aloo gobi with sausages or grilled fish. Shove chicken tikka into a doorstep sandwich with lettuce and tomato. Spread yesterday's dhal on hot buttered toast. Okay, that's an odd one but trust me, it's good. The texture is not unlike hummus.

THE KIT.

DRIED SPICES. The base of each dish in this chapter is made from blends of dried spices, for the sake of simplicity. I recommend that you buy spices by the recipe, i.e. as they are called for. If you are a curryholic, you probably have the basics in already. I use cumin so often that it might as well be ground into my salt and pepper.

Talking of which, I buy spices whole, rather than ground, since they keep their flavour better that way. Buying them at Asian supermarkets, by the bag, will be cheaper than the dinky glass bottles in supermarkets, but the latter do provide you with a neat, airtight way of storing them.

CHEAT'S GHEE. I use a mixture of light (i.e. non virgin) olive oil and butter to cook most of my Indian meals. This is my cheat's ghee (the Indian word for clarified butter), as the two together have a nutty taste. By all means use just vegetable oil or butter, whatever. And if you find ghee, then use that instead.

SPICE GRINDER. Keeping spices whole means that you will need a spice grinder (some people swear by coffee grinders) or a pestle and mortar, which is what I use. I find pounding away at various seeds and pods incredibly therapeutic.

THE TIKKA FAMILY.

Tikka is really a kebab, seasoned and tenderised in a marinade of yoghurt and spices before it is cooked fast in the intense heat of a tandoor oven. Legend has it that Britain's favourite Indian dish was invented on the spot (the spot being somewhere in the Midlands) for a customer who was dismayed to find that he had ordered a dish with no sauce.

Made well, there is nothing wrong with Anglo-Indian food, and it is fast becoming a recognised cuisine all of its own. Some of the new, hip versions of curry houses are beginning to put their own spin on such dishes. I have recently eaten wood pigeon tikka. It was amazing.

Here are some home-made, well and truly Anglo-Indian versions of both tikka and masala. I cannot say either is definitive, but then variety is the (ahem) spice of life.

(SORT OF) CHICKEN TIKKA.

This is inspired by Vivek Singh's recipe in *The Cinnamon Club Cookbook* (Absolute Press, 2003). Be aware that it will not be a lurid red colour. The commercial versions of chicken tikka often use red food dyes. I can't fathom why, since paprika will provide a gentler, more appetising hue. I use Spanish smoked paprika, which compensates for the lack of a tandoor oven in my kitchen. It gives food a slightly barbecued taste.

You could skewer the meat and barbecue it, then serve it like a kebab, but I cook the chicken breast whole, very quickly, in a searingly hot oven. I think this keeps it juicier. Then I rest it and slice it before serving. The meat is really tender and tasty.

For 2 people you need:
- ★ 2 boneless chicken breasts, skin on
- ★ ½ teaspoon salt
- ★ ½ teaspoon black pepper (or cayenne pepper)
- ★ 2 tablespoons lemon juice
- ★ 2cm piece of fresh ginger, finely chopped
- ★ 2 garlic cloves, finely chopped
- ★ ½ teaspoon cumin seeds, ground
- ★ ½ teaspoon coriander seeds, ground
- ★ 1 teaspoon hot smoked paprika
- ★ 1 tablespoon yoghurt
- ★ 2 tablespoons light olive oil

Pierce each chicken breast in 3 or 4 places with a sharp fork or skewer. Rub the salt and pepper over the meat, add the lemon juice and toss the meat in it a couple of times. Mix together all the remaining ingredients, add them to the chicken and toss again. Chill the marinated chicken for as long as you can. A day or a night is ideal, but a couple of hours is better than nothing.

Preheat the oven to its highest setting. Heat a ridged griddle or heavy-based frying pan and fry the chicken breasts, skin-side down, for about 3 minutes over a medium-high heat. Turn them over and season the skin side with a little extra salt. Fry for a couple of minutes, then transfer to a roasting tray lined with baking parchment. Cook the chicken in the oven for 10–15 minutes, until it is done all the way through. Rest it for a good 5 minutes before slicing and serving it. Be sure to accompany it with the Mint and Onion Chutney on page 254.

WANT YOUR TIKKA WITH MASALA?

Here is the 'gravy' that was supposedly invented in the Midlands for chicken tikka (see above). For the 'real' thing, follow the chicken tikka recipe and serve it with this sauce. The same goes for the aubergine tikka over the page.

Legend has it that the original recipe for the sauce called for tinned cream of tomato soup. I use a carton of passata (sieved tomatoes) instead.

For 2 people you need:
★ 2 tablespoons butter
★ 1 onion, finely sliced
★ 2 garlic cloves, finely sliced
★ ½ teaspoon salt
★ 200ml passata (sieved tomatoes)
★ 1 tablespoon thick yoghurt
★ 100ml double cream
★ ½ teaspoon garam masala
★ a handful of coriander leaves (optional)

Heat the butter in a pan, add the onion and garlic and fry until softened. Add the salt, stir briefly, then cover and cook gently for about 10 minutes. Add the passata and cook for another 5 minutes or so. Stir in the yoghurt and cream, the garam masala and the coriander, if using.

If serving with the chicken, gently turn the cooked chicken pieces in the sauce, or pour the sauce on to plates and lay the pieces on top, if you want 'cute'.

AUBERGINE TIKKA.

During my years as an ardent vegetarian, I discovered a kind of underground network of non-meat-eating foodies. We would meet in secret and discuss the misdemeanours of well-meaning but essentially carnivorous people who thought that all we could eat was aubergine. Everyone had their own 'fear of aubergine' story. The dish I dreaded was the vegetarian kebab, that stalwart of barbecues. Carbonised peppers, onions and courgettes on the same skewer as triumphantly *al dente* aubergine. Why?

Now don't get me wrong, the aubergine is a splendid thing. But it is easily mistreated. It has an alarmingly sponge-like tendency to mop up whatever surrounds it, as you will know if you have ever thrown it nonchalantly into a stew or casserole. It also takes a surprisingly long time to cook. And, undercooked, it is evil. Nearly all good aubergine recipes require it to be fried, grilled or roasted before it goes anywhere near anything else. This ensures that it is the tender, velvety creature it should be and stops that greedy sponging. This is why spearing it with other vegetables is like booby-trapping a kebab. Everything else will be done to a crisp by the time the aubergine is yielding. You are far better off roasting the aubergine slowly. It needn't be lonely in the oven – here is my 'veggie tikka', where everything is roasted together. You can fold it into the masala sauce on page 240, just like chicken, if you like. Or you can serve it plain, as a side dish. It is great at room temperature, and shoved into pita or naan bread with a good smear of yoghurt.

For 2 people you need:
★ 2 garlic cloves, peeled
★ 1cm piece of fresh ginger (optional)
★ ½ teaspoon salt
★ ½ teaspoon cumin seeds, ground
★ ½ teaspoon coriander seeds, ground
★ 1 tablespoon paprika (smoked is good)
★ 3 tablespoons light olive oil
★ 2 tablespoons lemon juice
★ 1 medium-sized aubergine, cut into 2–3cm dice
★ 1 red pepper, cut into similar-sized pieces
★ 1 onion (red is good here), cut into wedges

Preheat the oven to 180°C/Gas Mark 4. Grate the garlic and ginger, if using, as finely as you can into a large mixing bowl and add all the other spices, plus the oil and lemon juice. Mix thoroughly, then toss the cut vegetables in the mixture, making sure they are all well coated.

Transfer everything to a roasting tray big enough to hold the vegetables in a single layer. Roast for about 40 minutes, turning the vegetables very gently with a palette knife or fish slice once or twice during this time. When they are tender, check the seasoning before serving up.

LAMB WITH YOGHURT AND SPICES...

. . . and absolutely nothing else. I have to include this recipe here because it tastes incredible. It is adapted from Madhur Jaffrey's first cookbook. Because many Kashmiri Hindus avoid onions and garlic, they spice their dishes with dry ingredients only, so this really is a store-cupboard meal.

For 4 people you need:
* ★ 2 tablespoons butter
* ★ 2 tablespoons olive oil
* ★ about 1kg shoulder of lamb, boned and cut into large dice
* ★ 1 cinnamon stick or 1 teaspoon ground cinnamon
* ★ 4 cloves
* ★ 2 teaspoons salt
* ★ 2 tablespoons mild paprika (if you have smoked paprika, it works well here, too)
* ★ ½ teaspoon dried crushed chilli (optional)
* ★ 450g yoghurt (Greek is best)
* ★ 1 tablespoon ground fennel seeds
* ★ 1 teaspoon ground ginger
* ★ about 800ml water
* ★ ½ teaspoon garam masala

Heat the butter and oil in a large, heavy-based pan, add the lamb and brown it all over. Remove from the pan and set aside, leaving as much fat in the pan as possible. Add the cinnamon and cloves and let them fizz for a few seconds. Then return the meat to the pot with the salt and stir it through. Stir in the paprika and the dried chilli, if using. Now add the yoghurt and cook it quite hard over a high heat, until all the liquid has evaporated. Add the fennel and ginger, then the water, and simmer quite rapidly, uncovered, for half an hour. Then lower the heat, cover and cook for at least another hour. The meat should be so tender it could fall apart. Keep checking on it to make sure there is always some liquid left. This dish thickens and becomes quite glossy as it cooks. Add the garam masala and check the seasoning once the lamb is ready.

I like to serve this with a flatbread, such as pita or naan, and plain wilted spinach. More fresh yoghurt adds an interesting note to the plate. It is good with rice as well.

A (KIND OF) PRAWN KORMA.

The korma we eat in the UK is a real hybrid, like tikka masala. In fact it bears little resemblance to anything you find on the Subcontinent. Cooking meat or fish in mild, buttery sauces with ingredients such as almonds and yoghurt is fairly widespread in northern India, especially on high days and holidays. But such dishes are not necessarily sweet, which we seem to expect of our kormas. There are Malay kormas, made with coconut instead of yoghurt. The anglicised dish sometimes contains both. For better or worse, the Brit-korma has become the curry of choice for those who don't like their food too spicy. There is nothing wrong with that, but it shouldn't be overly bland or sweet, which just makes it sickly.

I've tried to give my korma a naturally sweet edge by cooking the onions slowly until they start to break down. You could make a quicker, harsher version by frying them briefly, on a high flame. I think seafood is spot-on in a korma sauce like this one, which is why I suggest prawns. White fish is great, too, and of course chicken korma is a classic. Use thigh rather than breast meat for extra flavour.

For 2 people you need:
- ★ 2 tablespoons light olive oil
- ★ 1 onion, finely sliced or chopped
- ★ 2 garlic cloves, sliced
- ★ ½ teaspoon salt
- ★ ½ teaspoon fennel seeds
- ★ 2 cardamom pods
- ★ 2 cloves
- ★ ½ teaspoon ground ginger (or you can use finely chopped fresh ginger)
- ★ ½ teaspoon ground cinnamon
- ★ a pinch of grated nutmeg
- ★ 200g cooked peeled prawns (thawed if using frozen)
- ★ 2 tablespoons yoghurt
- ★ 2 tablespoons ground almonds (or desiccated coconut, or half and half)
- ★ 125ml water

Heat the oil in a saucepan, add the onion and garlic and stir them thoroughly. Add the salt and 4 tablespoons of water, then lower the heat, cover the pan and cook for at least 20 minutes, until the onion is soft and sweet. Check regularly and, if it looks as if it is going to brown, either reduce the heat further or add more water.

Crush the fennel seeds, cardamom pods and cloves in a pestle and mortar or a spice grinder and add them to the onion with the ginger, cinnamon and nutmeg. Fry for a couple of minutes, then add the prawns. Coat them well with the seasonings and add the yoghurt, almonds and water. Simmer for 5–10 minutes, until the sauce has thickened to your liking. At this point check the seasoning. Your korma is ready!

SPICY POTATOES AND CAULIFLOWER (ALOO GOBI).

This is my version of one of those vegetable dishes that you seem to find on every Indian menu. New potatoes, with their waxy texture, are great for braising this way. I love it hot or cold (I might even prefer it cold), which makes it a great alternative to potato salad once the barbecue season gets under way. Don't be afraid to pair it with something as unlikely as sausages. The results are surprisingly delicious.

Last time I ate this dish in India, it contained some delicate leafy greens. I asked what they were and the answer was cauliflower! All my life I have thrown away these leaves, but now I add them to my aloo gobi. If your cauliflower leaves look healthy, discard the outer, thick-stemmed ones and any that have yellowed. Remove the inner leaves from their stalks, and slice them like a cabbage. Add them to the pot with the cauliflower, and let them wilt.

For 2 people you need:
- ★ 1 tablespoon light olive oil
- ★ 1 tablespoon butter
- ★ ½ teaspoon cumin seeds
- ★ 1–2 green chillies – if you like your food hot, don't deseed them, just slice them into fine cross-sections
- ★ 1cm piece of fresh ginger, chopped

- ★ 2 garlic cloves, chopped
- ★ ¼ teaspoon turmeric
- ★ ½ teaspoon garam masala
- ★ 1 small cauliflower or ½ large one, cut into bite-sized florets
- ★ 200g new potatoes, roughly diced
- ★ 1 teaspoon tomato purée
- ★ about 100ml hot water (or vegetable stock)
- ★ a handful of chopped coriander leaves
- ★ salt

Heat the oil and butter in a non-stick pan (you can make this in a wok but you might need to improvise a lid). Add the cumin seeds and allow them to fizz for 30 seconds. Lower the heat and add the chillies, ginger and garlic. Fry them for 30 seconds, then add the turmeric, garam masala and a pinch of salt.

Add the cauliflower and potatoes and stir until they are coated with the spices. Add the tomato purée and about two-thirds of the hot water. Stir again, bring to a gentle simmer, then cover and cook for about 15 minutes. Check half way through to make sure the mixture is not drying out, and add the rest of the water if it is. The dish is ready when the potatoes are tender. Serve garnished generously with the coriander. A good dollop of yoghurt on the side is unbeatable, too.

PEAS BRAISED WITH INDIAN CHEESE (MUTTOR PANEER).

You can buy paneer cheese in supermarkets these days, but it is incredibly quick and easy to make as well, so there is a recipe for the adventurous on page 111.

I've based this dish entirely on the one you find in curry houses up and down the country. And I have included nutmeg in the spice blend because peas and nutmeg are a little-known match made in heaven. I've kept the spicing quite mild, but you don't have to. You can also convert it to an ersatz version of palak (spinach) paneer by substituting the same weight of frozen spinach for the peas. Thaw it before using.

For 2 people you need:
★ 1 tablespoon light olive oil
★ 1 tablespoon butter
★ 1 onion, chopped
★ 2 garlic cloves, chopped
★ ½ teaspoon salt
★ 1cm piece of fresh ginger, chopped
★ ½ teaspoon turmeric
★ ½ teaspoon coriander seeds, ground
★ ½ teaspoon ground cinnamon
★ a pinch of turmeric
★ about ¼ nutmeg, grated
★ 100ml passata (sieved tomatoes)
★ 200ml water
★ 200g peas
★ 100g paneer cheese, cut into small cubes or roughly crumbled
★ freshly ground black pepper
★ coriander leaves, to garnish (optional)

Heat the oil and butter in a saucepan, add the onion, garlic, salt and all the spices, and stir a couple of times. Cover the pan, lower the heat and allow everything to sweat for about 10 minutes. Add the passata, water and peas, bring to a simmer and cook fairly gently for about 15 minutes, until the sauce has thickened slightly and the peas are very tender. Season to taste. If you are using diced, shop-bought paneer, add it now and cook for another 5 minutes. If using home-made, it is best simply crumbled over the top of the finished dish. You could garnish all this generously with coriander leaves.

SPINACH AND MUSHROOMS WITH FENUGREEK.

Here is a very quick vegetable dish. It is quite dark and earthy, and works best with frozen spinach.

Fenugreek is sometimes sold as *methi* in Indian shops. More often than not, it is what gives curry powder its unmistakable taste. The whole seeds are pretty tough. Try to use ground fenugreek or dried crushed leaves for this recipe.

For 2 people you need:
* ★ 1 tablespoon light olive oil
* ★ 1 tablespoon butter
* ★ 1 onion, chopped
* ★ 2 garlic cloves, chopped
* ★ ½ teaspoon ground fenugreek
* ★ ½ teaspoon cumin seeds, ground
* ★ ½ teaspoon dried crushed chilli (optional)
* ★ 4–6 large black field mushrooms, sliced
* ★ juice of ½ lemon
* ★ ½ teaspoon salt
* ★ 200g frozen spinach, thawed
* ★ 1 tablespoon tomato purée
* ★ 100ml double cream (you could use yoghurt, but not low-fat)

You can make this in a wok, if you like. Heat the oil and butter, add the onion, garlic and spices and fry quite hard until they are beginning to brown slightly. Add the mushrooms, lemon juice and salt, and fry until the mushrooms have wilted. Add the spinach, tomato purée and cream and cook for a couple more minutes, until everything has warmed through. Check the seasoning and serve.

As un-Indian as it may seem, this dish is very good with a poached fillet of smoked fish such as haddock.

A VERY QUICK TARKA DHAL.

Dhal, roughly translated, means any pulse dish. Chickpeas are *channa dhal*, mung beans *moong dhal* and so on. A pulse dish, varying from something as runny as a soup to a thick stew, is obligatory for a curry night, so here is arguably the most famous. It is also one of the simplest to cook. My version is made with split red lentils, which fall apart very quickly so that the dhal becomes a fairly smooth purée. You can eat it loose or let it thicken up by cooking it for longer. It thickens as it cools as well and, eaten cold, can be spread on toast, like hummus. It is delicious that way, trust me.

You could make a more textured version of this just as quickly by using Puy lentils, or the tinned pulse of your choice.

For 2 people you need:
- ★ 100g split red lentils (or similar)
- ★ 500ml water
- ★ 2 slices of fresh ginger
- ★ 1 bay leaf (or 4–5 curry leaves)

- ★ 1 dried or fresh chilli
- ★ 1 tablespoon butter
- ★ 1 tablespoon light olive oil
- ★ 1 teaspoon cumin seeds
- ★ 4 garlic cloves, sliced
- ★ salt
- ★ coriander leaves, to garnish (optional)

Put the lentils and water in a pan with the ginger slices, bay leaf and whole chilli. Bring to the boil and cook rapidly for 10 minutes, skimming off any scum that comes to the surface. Lower the heat and gently simmer the lentils until they are tender and start to lose their shape. This could take as little as half an hour; it really depends how long they have been around (older dried pulses take longer to cook than young ones). You can add more water if the lentils get at all dry. Basically, dhal can be as thick or as brothy as you like. Be aware that the thicker dhal gets, the more it likes to stick to the bottom of your pan. Stir it regularly.

When the lentils are done to your liking, take them off the heat, remove the ginger, chilli and bay leaf and discard them. In a small wok or frying pan, heat the butter and oil. When it is fizzing nicely, add the cumin seeds and allow them to fry rapidly for a couple of minutes. Add the garlic and fry until it starts to go golden brown. (If you eat a lot of Indian meals out, you may have come across really caramelised garlic on top of your dhal. If you want that, just keep going for an extra minute or two.) Now season the lentils with salt to taste and pour the garlic over them, butter and all. You can garnish this with coriander leaves. Mint and parsley are also good.

TRIMMINGS FOR A CURRY NIGHT.

You could eat all the above as single meals, or create a spread
for a hungry mob of friends and family. If the latter, you've got to
have a few trimmings around. These could be shop-bought
(good yoghurt, mango chutney and lime pickle; not to mention
poppadoms . . .), or you could have a go at some of the
following suggestions.

I've included a pilau rice in the trimmings, although most of
the time I am happy to eat any of the above with plain steamed
rice. 'Plain' seems an insulting way to refer to basmati rice, with
its fine flavour. For a guide to steaming basmati, see page 135.

AN EASY PILAU.

Here, then, is rice with bells and whistles. You could simplify
the mix of spices. For example, cardamom alone makes a
good pilau. You could also omit the dried fruit or augment it
with a similar weight in pine nuts, flaked almonds or pistachios.

For 2 people you need:
★ 250ml vegetable oil
★ 1 shallot or onion, very finely sliced
★ ½ cinnamon stick
★ 2 cloves
★ 4 or 5 cardamom pods, just cracked slightly
★ 2 small dried chillies (optional)
★ 150g basmati rice
★ 50g raisins or sultanas
★ a pinch of saffron, soaking in a tablespoon
  of warm water

* 300ml water
* 1 tablespoon butter
* salt

Heat the vegetable oil in a wok or frying pan and, when it is pretty hot, throw in a slice of shallot or onion. If it fizzes nicely, add the rest and cook over a medium heat until it turns a deep golden brown. Remove with a slotted spoon and leave to drain on plenty of kitchen paper.

Transfer 2 tablespoons of the vegetable oil to a saucepan with a tight-fitting lid. Leave the rest of the oil somewhere safe to cool (you will be able to use it again, and its slightly oniony taste makes it a good cooking oil to have around). Gently heat the 2 tablespoons of oil, add the spices and cook for a minute or so. Add the rice and allow it to toast just slightly, stirring it through the oil and spices the whole time. Add the raisins or sultanas, saffron infusion and water. Raise the heat a bit, so the water comes to simmering point, then put the lid on the pan and lower the heat as far as it will go. You are going to steam the rice with this small amount of water. It will cook by absorption and the water should simmer really gently. Let the pilau cook, totally undisturbed, for about 15 minutes. After that, take it off the heat and leave to rest for 5 minutes. Stir in the butter and any seasoning. Do this gently with a fork, so that you can fluff the rice a little. Serve with the onion scattered all over the top.

FOUR INDIAN CHUTNEYS.

Here are a handful of relishes or, to use the Indian word,
chutneys. We tend to think of chutneys as preserves, but in fact
chutney is a very broad term. A freshly chopped 'salad' like a
raita or mint and onion 'chutney' (see below) is just as likely to
grace an Indian table as the slowly prepared lime pickles and
mango chutneys you get with poppadoms in a restaurant. Talking
of which, you can now buy great poppadoms, either for cooking
yourself or ready for the table. I think the plain ones are best.
The other, rather highly flavoured types just fight with the relishes.

MINT AND ONION CHUTNEY.
This is so easy to prepare that it doesn't warrant a list of
ingredients. My local curry house serves it with poppadoms
and the two together are very moreish.

I've nicked a trick off a Spanish friend for this, which will
transform an onion from pungent to cooling, yet somehow
without depriving it of flavour. Slice a medium onion as thinly as
possible and just cover it with milk. Leave it in a cool place for a
good hour, longer if possible. When you are ready to eat, simply
drain off the milk. Season the onion with a handful of chopped
mint, a scant pinch of salt and, if you like, an even scanter pinch
of black pepper.

You can use dried mint for this, if you prefer. Add it to the
onion with the milk, though, and allow them to steep together.

COCONUT CHUTNEY.
This is a cheat's version of a southern Indian relish. You will need
a fresh coconut or, at least, roast dried coconut shavings

(available from healthfood shops) rather than the desiccated variety. You could grate a whole coconut for this. Use as much as the recipe requires and freeze the rest. It will come in handy next time.

You need:
★ a handful of coriander leaves
★ a handful of mint leaves
★ 2 tablespoons grated fresh coconut
★ ½ teaspoon salt
★ 1 teaspoon mustard seeds
★ 3–4 curry leaves (optional)
★ 1 teaspoon light olive oil
★ 1 tablespoon yoghurt
★ 1 tablespoon lime juice
★ ½ teaspoon sugar (optional)
★ dried crushed chilli, to taste (optional)

The easiest way to make this is to chop the coriander and mint a little, then combine them with the coconut and the salt on the chopping board and continue to chop. The salt will make the herbs bleed a bit, which helps the flavours infuse. You can, of course, blitz this relish in a food processor, but it will be a bit smooth and luridly green.

Once the relish is chopped, heat a small frying pan and dry-roast the mustard seeds in it. They will pop, so you might want to cover them with a lid. Don't roast them for more than a minute. Transfer them to a pestle and mortar, add the curry leaves (if using) and the oil, and pound them to a rough powder. Mix with the coconut and herbs, together with the yoghurt, lime juice, sugar and chilli, if using. Now loosen it to a dipping consistency, if you like, by adding a couple of tablespoons of water. I usually do this.

This chutney can be used as a salad dressing as well. It is good thrown around a bowlful of very crunchy French beans, mangetout or sugarsnap peas.

MANGO CHUTNEY.

Seen by many as *the* chutney for Indian food, this is a curry house standard. I like mango chutney so much that I pair it with some very western dishes. Sausages taste great with mango chutney and so does really crumbly cheese like Lancashire or feta. Hummus and mango chutney sandwiches may sound odd, but try one and you might just find yourself hooked.

I use underripe mangoes for my chutney because no Indian in their right mind would pass up the opportunity to devour one that was ready to eat on the spot.

You need:
★ 1kg mangoes
★ ½ teaspoon salt
★ 200g granulated sugar
★ 300ml red or white wine vinegar
★ 2 onions, chopped
★ 1 red chilli, deseeded and sliced (optional)

Peel the mangoes, cut the flesh off the stone and dice it roughly. Sprinkle with the salt and set aside.

Gently heat the sugar and vinegar in a pan until the sugar has dissolved completely. Add the onions, mangoes and chilli, if using, and bring to a rolling boil for a couple of minutes. Reduce to a simmer and cook, uncovered, for 1 hour, stirring occasionally. The chutney will thicken and is ready when the spoon leaves a clear trail in its wake if you pull it across the bottom of the pan. Pour into sterilised jars (to sterilise them, either wash in hot soapy water and dry in a very low oven or put them through a hot cycle of the dishwasher). Seal and store in a cool place. The chutney should be ready to eat within about 2 weeks.

LIME PICKLE.

This is salty-sharp and, when made commercially, it can be hot enough to blow your head off. You can make a milder version, if you like. You don't have to keep this pickle in a jar, either. It is one of the few types of chutney that can be kept in a plastic or Tupperware container.

For a 1.5 litre pickling jar you need:
★ 8 limes, cut into quarters
★ 3–4 green chillies, split open (optional)
★ 1 tablespoon mustard seeds
★ 1 teaspoon curry leaves (optional)
★ ½ teaspoon turmeric
★ 2 tablespoons salt
★ 250ml lime juice (I use bottled)

Put the limes into a small saucepan, cover them with water and bring to a rolling boil. Boil for 1 minute, then drain, cover with fresh water and bring to the boil again. Simmer for 30 minutes, adding the chillies, if using, for the last 5 minutes. Drain and set aside in a large mixing bowl.

Heat a wok or frying pan, throw in the mustard seeds and dry-roast for a minute or so (cover them with a lid, if you can, as they will start to pop). Grind them to a rough powder with the curry leaves, if using. Add the turmeric, salt and lime juice and combine this mixture thoroughly with the limes. Store in a sterilised jar or plastic container for a week before using. Keep in the fridge once opened.

INSTANT SALTY LEMON CHUTNEY.

This is a quick and easy take on Indian lime pickle. Not everyone is keen on lime pickle, which is formidably hot, sharp and salty. My version is based on Middle Eastern salted lemons, now available in many Western shops (Belazu make a very user-friendly version with small fruit). Making this chutney gives you the almost olivey, brined taste of lime pickle without the fireworks. You could always throw in a chilli to add some pyrotechnics, if you like.

You need:
★ 2 medium-sized salted lemons
★ 2 red onions, finely sliced
★ ½ teaspoon cumin seeds, dry-roasted in a frying pan, then ground
★ 2 tablespoons red or white wine vinegar
★ 2–3 dried curry leaves, roughly shredded (optional)
★ ½ teaspoon sugar
★ a handful of coriander leaves (optional)

Cut the lemons in half and scoop out all the flesh, taking as much of the pith as possible with it. It is the skin you are after. It will be soft, sharp and salty. Cut the skin into slices and toss it with all the other ingredients. If you are adding the coriander, just sprinkle it over the top as a garnish rather than folding it in.

Thai.

STAYING IN FOR A CURRY (PART TWO): THAI.

I will never forget my first Thai curry. It was in 1990, in Hong Kong, where I was working. I was about to visit Thailand for the first time and thought I'd better 'research' the food. In those days, Hong Kong was served by the world's most insane airport. Kai Tak, as it was known, means 'flat place' in Cantonese – a testimony to the amphitheatre of high-rise blocks and skyscrapers that surrounded the terminal. The runway was really a glorified jetty from which Jumbos would hurl themselves at the famously busy harbour.

A gaggle of Thai cafés lined the streets just north of Kai Tak, their neon signs in direct competition with the landing lights. If you so desired, you could sit and gawp at descending undercarriages, as wake turbulence shook the tables and chairs on the street. This was supposed to be half the fun of eating there (Hong Kong does that sort of thing to people). The night of my first Thai curry, however, I was too busy having my head blown off by the shocking intensity of my meal to notice the planes. This was in the days before we had many Thai restaurants in the UK, which seems unimaginable now that they are everywhere. The taste of lemongrass, kaffir lime, sweet basil and galangal was entirely new to me.

I've thrown a handful of Thai-style curries into this book partly because of their popularity but also because you simply must have a go at making your own. Ready-made versions (and sadly, lots of restaurant versions) are nothing like the real thing.

A Thai curry is almost a stir-fry. In fact, a wok is the best thing to use when making one. The most popular Thai curries in the UK come from the south of the country and are made with coconut milk. The main ingredients are fried with a wet 'paste' of fresh chillies, fermented shrimps, garlic and herbs, rather than dried spices. Then the paste is loosened with the coconut milk and seasoned further with a fair bit of greenery (usually coriander leaves or Thai basil). These curries can be made in minutes, as can stir-fries. So why do we buy them in? Mainly because we labour under the misapprehension that the ingredients, many of which are exclusive to Southeast Asian cookery, are hard to get hold of. This is no longer true. Making a curry paste is, weirdly, considered to be labour-intensive, but it isn't, especially if you own a food processor.

There are also some excellent prepared pastes on the market these days. In fact, I recommend seeking one out if you do not eat this kind of food very often. Home-made pastes do not keep for long. This is not one of those cookbooks that exhort you to stock up your fridge with endless, highly perishable concoctions – the kind you use once and then watch go mouldy.

Purists, please note that this chapter is not about the authentic reproduction of Thai food in the home. Most Thais would not sit down for 'a curry', as we might here. The curries that follow would form part of a spread made up of several small, contrasting dishes, eaten around a pile of sticky rice.

THE KIT.

THAI CURRY PASTES. Thai curries are sort of colour-coded. Red, green and yellow curries are named after the pastes used to start them. Which paste you like is really a case of trial and error. Yellow (or Penang-style) paste tends to be the mildest, then green, then red. Some people will tell you that certain meats or fish go with certain pastes, but at home you needn't really worry about this. I use a red curry paste for nearly all my Thai curries. And I buy a Thai brand called Namjai. It comes in handy 400g plastic tubs (there are smaller ones, too), the ingredients are authentic and it keeps in the fridge for months. Namjai also makes green and yellow pastes, plus vegetarian versions without shrimp paste.

Another brand to look out for is Solomon's. The ingredients are spot-on. These pastes come in jars and half a jar will easily make enough curry for four people. They will keep for three months once opened. If, like me, you know you are capable of neglecting opened jars and watching the use-by date sail by, transfer the paste to a small freezer bag and freeze it. Or try making the curry in bulk and freezing whatever you don't eat.

THAI FISH SAUCE AND SHRIMP PASTE. The saltiness of Thai cooking almost invariably comes from these two items. Fish sauce is to Thailand what soy sauce is to China. It is now widely available in supermarkets under its Thai name, *nam pla* (or in a similar Vietnamese version called *nuoc nam*). It doesn't make food taste fishy, but it does smell slightly odd the first time you use it. Squeamish types (or vegetarians, or both) can use soy sauce instead, but a certain Thai-esque *je ne sais quoi* will be missing from your dinner. Shrimp paste is more pungent and I must admit that I tend to cheat by using *nam pla* when it is called for in recipes.

KAFFIR LIME LEAVES. If you bit into a lime leaf, the taste would scream 'Thai food!' at you. Some supermarkets stock them, but your best bet is an oriental food shop. My nearest one sells handy little packs of them, frozen. They keep brilliantly. Avoid dried lime leaves, which have no real flavour.

THAI BASIL. This is another slightly tricky herb to get hold of. It isn't the same as the Italian variety, more like a pungent mint. Some people say it tastes like a cross between mint and tarragon. You are most likely to find Thai basil in an oriental supermarket. I buy it on the branch, strip the leaves off and freeze them.

LEMONGRASS. This is a long stalk with a fragrant, lemony taste. It is only used in this book as part of home-made curry pastes (see page 271). It can be frozen, if you want to buy a bundle. Don't bother with the dried stuff.

GALANGAL. This rhizome is a near relative to ginger, only harsher and woodier. Again, it tends to be part of curry pastes.

COCONUT MILK. 'Milk' is a bit of a misnomer, since in Thai cookery it does not refer to the liquid from the centre of coconuts. Instead it is a cream made from the shaved white flesh and water. As well as the standard 400ml tins, you can find little half-sized versions, handy if you are cooking for one or two people.

RICE. The perfect accompaniment to a good Thai curry would be a Thai brand of jasmine rice. Although jasmine rice is stickier than its close cousin, basmati, the two taste quite similar. You could use basmati rice wherever you see instructions for cooking jasmine rice. Instructions for cooking long grain rice are on page 135.

PRAWNS AND RED CURRY.

I love my Thai curries with fish more than anything. Instead of the prawns in this recipe, you could use squid, mussels, scallops or more robust seafood such as tuna or snapper. Mackerel also works in Thai curries, as its gaminess matches the spices. Either fillets or steaks are fine, whichever fish you use.

For 2 people you need:
★ 250g fresh or frozen cooked peeled prawns
★ 2 tablespoons vegetable oil
★ 1 generous tablespoon red curry paste
★ 400ml tin of coconut milk
★ 1 tablespoon Thai fish sauce
★ ½ teaspoon sugar
★ juice of ½ lime (or 1 tablespoon bottled lime juice)
★ 3 lime leaves (or grated zest of 1 lime)
★ 3 spring onions, sliced on the diagonal
★ a handful of Thai basil or coriander leaves

If using frozen prawns, thaw them completely and squeeze any excess moisture from them (see page 125). Heat the oil in a wok, add the prawns and fry for a minute or so over a fairly high heat, then add the curry paste. If it is very stiff, add a splash of water or a little of the coconut milk. Stir and fry for a couple of minutes, until the paste has coated the prawns, then pour in the coconut milk. Immediately half fill the tin with water and add that. Now add the fish sauce, sugar, lime juice and lime leaves. Simmer for 2–3 minutes. Now taste it. It should be a mixture of hot, salty and sweet. If you think it needs more of anything, add it now. As you serve the curry, throw in the slices of spring onion and the basil or coriander.

CHICKEN AND GREEN CURRY.

My sister loves to make this. She always uses chicken thighs for their superior flavour, but they take a little longer to cook than some cuts. Feel free to use small slivers of chicken breast if you are short of time. You could substitute another meat instead. Duck goes nicely with Thai curry, as does pork.

For 2 people you need:
★ 2 tablespoons vegetable oil
★ 6 chicken thighs
★ 1 generous tablespoon green curry paste
★ 400ml tin of coconut milk
★ 1 tablespoon Thai fish sauce
★ ½ teaspoon sugar
★ juice of ½ lime (or 1 tablespoon bottled lime juice)
★ 3 lime leaves (or grated zest of 1 lime)
★ 1 small tin (about 200g) bamboo shoots, drained (optional)
★ 3 spring onions, sliced on the diagonal
★ a handful of Thai basil or coriander leaves

Heat the oil in a wok, add the chicken thighs and brown them all over. Remove and set aside. Add the curry paste to the wok with a couple of tablespoons of the coconut milk, then stir and fry until the paste has loosened. Return the chicken pieces to the pan with the fish sauce, lime juice, sugar and lime leaves. Add the remaining coconut milk, then immediately half fill the tin with water and add this to the wok. Simmer for about 20 minutes, until the chicken pieces are cooked through. Add the bamboo shoots, if using, and heat them through. Now taste and adjust the seasoning if you want the curry sweeter, hotter, saltier . . . Add the spring onions and basil or coriander as you serve up.

THAI CHICKPEA CURRY.

It is very unusual to find pulses in Thai food. This recipe comes from the kitchen of a Wat (Buddhist temple). I've adapted it from Vatcharin Bhumichitr's book, *Thai Vegetarian Cooking* (Pavilion Books, 1991). If you don't like Indian curry powder, by all means use a Thai paste instead.

For 2 people you need:
★ 3 garlic cloves, chopped
★ 1cm piece of fresh ginger, chopped
★ ½ teaspoon black pepper
★ 2 tablespoons vegetable oil
★ 1 medium-sized waxy potato, peeled and roughly diced
★ 1 tablespoon Madras curry powder
★ 400g tin of coconut milk
★ 400g tin of chickpeas, drained
★ 2 tomatoes, cut into eighths
★ 1 tablespoon soy sauce
★ ½ teaspoon salt
★ ½ teaspoon sugar
★ a handful of Thai basil or coriander leaves

Pound or blitz the garlic, ginger and black pepper to a rough paste. Heat the oil in a wok, add the paste and fry for a couple of minutes over a medium heat. Add the potato and curry powder and stir thoroughly. Add the coconut milk and chickpeas and bring everything to a simmer. When the potato is just about tender, add the tomato wedges, soy sauce, salt and sugar. Cook for another 5 minutes or so, then add the basil or coriander leaves and serve.

THAI VEGETABLE CURRIES.

As with Indian food, the possibilities for Thai vegetable curries are fairly limitless. There is a famous dish from Chiang Mai in northern Thailand called *gaeng ho*. Literally translated, it means 'thrown-together vegetables'. I wonder if our phrase 'gung-ho' comes from this expression. Whether it does or not, gung-ho is the approach to take with this kind of dish. I tend to work with groups of three or four vegetables, depending on the weather, the season, and the mood I'm in. Here are two quite different examples.

For a barely cooked, summery version for 2 people, you need:
★ 3 spring onions, sliced
★ 2 courgettes, thinly sliced on the diagonal
★ 100g bean sprouts
★ a handful of mangetout or sugarsnap peas

For a warm, autumnal version for 2 people, you need:
★ 100g shallots, peeled but left whole
★ 2 red peppers, cut into slivers

* ★ about 200g pumpkin or butternut squash,
  peeled and roughly diced
* ★ 3 or 4 large field mushrooms, thinly sliced

Plus (for either version):
* ★ 2 tablespoons vegetable oil
* ★ 1 generous tablespoon red or green curry paste
* ★ 400ml tin of coconut milk
* ★ 1 tablespoon Thai fish sauce or soy sauce
* ★ ½ teaspoon sugar
* ★ juice of ½ lime (or 1 tablespoon bottled lime juice)
* ★ 3 lime leaves (or grated zest of 1 lime)
* ★ a handful of Thai basil or coriander leaves

Heat the oil in a wok, add the vegetables for either the summery
or the autumnal version and stir-fry over a high heat for a minute
or so. Add the curry paste and a couple of tablespoons of the
coconut milk and stir and fry until all the vegetables are coated
with the paste. Add the remaining coconut milk, then
immediately half fill the tin with water. Add the water to the pan,
together with the fish sauce or soy sauce, the sugar, lime juice
and lime leaves. Simmer until the vegetables are just about
tender and check the seasoning. Throw the basil or coriander
over the curry as you serve it.

ABDUL'S JUNGLE CURRY.

Abdul is not Thai but Malaysian. However, he did teach me this
very busked 'camping holiday' meal, which I grew extremely
fond of while trekking through a rainforest. (It was a strange,

masochistic kind of camping holiday, involving a lot of insects and sleep deprivation.) The 'curry' is made almost entirely from tinned food. The base is a version of tinned mackerel you can find in oriental supermarkets, where the fish has been fried and preserved in a *sambal* (chilli and garlic paste). The best brand to look out for is Giti. Some Western producers sell mackerel in spicy tomato sauce, which makes a good substitute.

Abdul pairs his mackerel with either bamboo shoots or a tinned Chinese green that I've never managed to get hold of over here. You don't have to stick rigidly to tins, and in fact I don't. I often throw in broccoli, spring onions, fresh Chinese greens or bean sprouts. You could omit the vegetables and pair the curry with a side dish of stir-fried vegetables.

I suppose I'd better tell you this, as a sort of cautionary footnote. I once waxed so lyrically about Abdul's jungle curry to some Thai friends that they let me make it for them. They thought it was a disgrace to oriental cooking – but it didn't stop them eating it.

For 2 people you need:
★ 1 tablespoon vegetable oil
★ 1 onion, sliced
★ 125g tin of mackerel in spicy sauce
★ 1 small tin (about 200g) bamboo shoots, drained
★ 400ml tin of coconut milk
★ 1 tablespoon Thai fish sauce or soy sauce

Heat the oil in a wok, add the onion and fry it hard for about a minute. (Add fresh vegetables at this point if you are using any.) Add all the rest of the ingredients and bring to a simmer. You literally just need to warm the fish through. You can adjust the seasoning if you wish, and loosen the sauce by adding a little water. The sauce can be as rich or brothy as you like. There, that should spice up any campfire singalong.

DIY: MAKE YOUR OWN CURRY PASTE.

At the risk of oversimplifying, the basic difference between a red and a green curry paste is the type of chilli used. Red pastes use dried red chillies and green pastes fresh green ones. Here is a recipe for red curry paste. To make a green paste, replace the dried chilli with fresh green chillies.

Vegetarians note: most Thai pastes contain shrimp. You can buy veggie brands such as Solomon's, or you can make your own using the recipe below. Substitute soy sauce for the shrimp paste/Thai fish sauce.

You need:
* ★ 2 tablespoons dried crushed chilli
* ★ 6 garlic cloves, chopped
* ★ 1 onion, chopped
* ★ A 2cm piece of galangal, peeled and chopped
  (use ginger if you can't get any galangal)
* ★ 2 lemongrass stalks, tough outer skin removed,
  tender inner stem sliced
* ★ 3 lime leaves
* ★ roots of a bunch of coriander, washed
* ★ ½ teaspoon shrimp paste or 2 tablespoons Thai fish sauce
* ★ ½ teaspoon cumin seeds
* ★ ½ teaspoon coriander seeds
* ★ ½ teaspoon turmeric

Put all the ingredients in a food processor and blitz until you have a rough paste. If it seems dry, add 4 or 5 tablespoons of water. Keep in the fridge and use within 3 weeks. This will make enough for 2 or 3 curries, each serving up to 4 people.

DIY: MAKE YOUR OWN COCONUT MILK.

As you will know if you cook lots of South Asian food, in culinary terms coconut milk is not the liquid inside a coconut but the cream extracted from its flesh. There is something quite therapeutic about producing your own, although given the generally excellent quality of the tinned stuff, this would only be for fun. Having said that, DIY coconut milk doesn't taste like the tinned version. It is slightly thinner, sweeter and not as pretty. You could go all-out Thai and get a wooden 'rabbit' (the bench-shaped grater used to extract the juice from coconut flesh), but I couldn't tell you where to start looking for one.

You can buy freshly grated coconut from some oriental shops, but if you want to do the whole thing from scratch, you will need a ripe coconut.

You need:
★ a fully matured (i.e. brown-husked) coconut
★ 250ml water

Make a hole in the little black 'eye' of the coconut with a skewer or screwdriver and drain off the liquid (you can drink this). Then bash the nut with a hammer – it usually breaks neatly in half. The easiest way to get the flesh out of the coconut minus the thin brown skin is to scrape it out using the sharpest-edged dessertspoon you have. If this is tricky, prise the flesh from the shell and peel away the brown bit with a potato peeler. Now you can grate the white meat or, better still, blitz it in a food processor. Add the water and stir it into the pulp. Place a sieve over a bowl and line the sieve with a large piece of muslin. Pour in the coconut mixture, bring up the ends of the muslin to make a bag and wring it out over the bowl. If there doesn't seem to be enough coconut milk (most recipes in this book call for about 400ml), add a little more water to the squeezed pulp and press it through the muslin again.

'Afters'.

INDULGING A SWEET TOOTH: 'AFTERS'.

There are two things I crave at the end of every meal. One is strong coffee (I'm an espresso addict) and the other is sweetness. I don't think I have a particularly sweet tooth, more like a mild obsession with certain combinations of flavours. We all have our favourites. It might be chips and ketchup or steak and mustard for some, but if I crave a strong coffee I've usually got to have something sweet with it. And to illustrate the point further, sweet coffee is not the solution.

My bitter-sweet tooth doesn't really get indulged all that often. Like most people, I tend to eat puds only when I'm out for a meal or if I'm entertaining. I certainly never make them unless I'm entertaining, and in the past I've found producing a sweet course a real chore.

This chapter isn't really about making pudding so much as throwing it together fairly effortlessly. Because producing a sweet course is so tied up with entertaining I think that a lot of people are nervous about inviting friends for dinner. They feel duty bound to provide 'afters' of some sort. Ever noticed how apologetic we are when we serve up a pudding or dessert that we've bought in? As if somehow failing to bake shows us up as a failure. It's a nonsense, but here is a familiar dinner party scenario: post main course, out comes the frozen cheesecake, or something else in a box, along with, if not an apology, at least an attempt to convince everyone that the host is being kitsch on purpose (Arctic roll, anyone?).

I love to invite people over on the spur of the moment, without planning an entire menu like some kind of military manoeuvre, and that usually means skipping home-made pud. Of course, there are plenty of good things you can buy in without resorting to the kitsch stuff, if that is not your bag (I know it isn't mine). In summer, soft fruits with a glug of cream have dessert writ large all over them. As does anything tropical, if you find it in good enough nick. There are less obvious examples, too. Any stone fruit, from summery peaches to autumnal plums, becomes a real indulgence when halved and roasted with a sprinkling of sugar.

But if you fancy something a little more, well, *fancy*, then what about raiding a good pâtisserie or baker's? This kind of thing wouldn't be seen as 'cheating' on the Continent. You don't even need a baker's, do you? There is always ice cream. Shop-bought ice cream has come a long way in the past twenty years or so (unlike Arctic roll).

So, what follows is my busker's guide to the dessert course. There are a fair few recipes that simply require combining bought-in items. And there are a few lazy puds that can be made well in advance, if you prefer – puddings that could be described as baked and *almost* made from scratch. I tend to keep a stash of some or all of the following items around, so that 'afters' is always a breeze.

THE KIT.

GOOD ICE CREAM. By good ice cream I mean one that has as short a list of ingredients as possible. Cream (and milk), sugar, eggs and real flavourings are all that you find in most home-made ice creams. There are several brilliant makes around these days, and many are available in supermarkets.

GOOD CHOCOLATE. By good I mean one that has at least 70 per cent cocoa solids. This makes it dark and bitter enough for cooking with and scary enough to stop me guzzling an entire bar in one sitting. Just you try it. Real dark chocolate is so bitter it kicks like espresso coffee.

I use Green & Black's in all my chocolate cookery, not least because they make a dark chocolate with a whopping great 72 per cent cocoa solids, and a milk chocolate that is slightly less anaemic than most.

FROZEN FRUIT. Frozen summer berries are up there with frozen peas as one of my addictions. I always keep them knocking about. I find that, outside the soft fruit season, they are distinctly preferable to imports of the 'fresh' stuff.

DRIED FRUIT AND NUTS. I have a bit of a thing about Agen prunes from France. Naturally fat and juicy, they never need soaking. Apricots are a different matter. The best are from the Hunza valley in Pakistan. They still have their stone in and need soaking before use. You can also buy ready-to-eat dried apricots, but watch out for those preserved with sulphur dioxide. For smaller dried fruits like currants and raisins, I have to admit I'm a sucker for the supermarkets' 'luxury' mixes, because you get such a variety.

Some of the baking in this chapter calls for ground almonds or hazelnuts. It is worth keeping a supply of nuts in stock, but ready-ground ones have a shorter shelf life and less flavour. I buy whole blanched nuts and grind them to order in a food processor. Once you have opened packets of nuts, they should be kept as airtight as possible in your coolest, darkest cupboard. Try to keep nuts in small quantities, as their taste deteriorates with time.

PUDDING BOOZE. Two drinks that I wouldn't actually drink make excellent cooking ingredients. For its almond-essence-type kick, I use Amaretto. For just about everything else, I go for Madeira wine or, failing that, a marsala or sweet sherry.

BUTTER. I would recommend keeping unsalted butter handy for baking. Because I do a lot of baking, I tend to have a few packets lurking in the freezer. My favourite is the French *beurre doux* (literally 'sweet butter'). It has an intense, almost cultured, yoghurt taste to it.

SUGAR, SYRUP AND HONEY. Caster sugar is the best all-rounder for baking. If possible, buy the less refined ('golden') version – for its flavour as much as anything. Talking of golden, Lyle's have made golden syrup a lot less messy than it used to be by selling it in a snazzy squeezy bottle. I miss the pretty green tins but my last one is currently doing a good job as a pencil holder by the phone.

With honey, the best type to use for baking is runny. I try to source local honey. There is a theory that honey from your local bees helps reduce your sniffles if you suffer from hay fever. It's worth a try. Besides, with such a huge choice of honey produced in this country, I find it irritating that it is so hard to get the British stuff in supermarkets.

VANILLA. I'm not as big on vanilla as some bakers, as I think it can dominate other flavours. I prefer the taste of vanilla pods to that of vanilla extract but rather than scraping the seeds out of the pods you could just make yourself a stash of vanilla sugar. Commandeer an airtight container (a jar with a rubber seal is good). Spilt open two vanilla pods for 1kg of caster sugar and just put them in the jar, pour the sugar over them and seal the jar. They will lace the sugar with just the right amount of vanilla flavour in about three days. After that, simply top up the sugar whenever it is running low. The same pods will last for several months.

BAKING EQUIPMENT. All the baking recipes in this chapter call for standard-sized tins and trays – mainly a round 20cm cake tin and a 28 x 18cm rectangular baking tray. You will easily feed six to eight people from one of these. I think the best round cake tins are the springform type. Many are so non-stick these days that they don't need lining with baking parchment before use. Keep them well away from dishwashers, which will spoil them. I've recently discovered the roll-up, squishy-squashy baking sheets, which are great for baking biscuits on, especially if you are short of storage space.

PLAYING WITH ICE CREAM.

This is not a chapter about making ice cream. I'm suspicious of cookbooks that require you to own a ton of gadgetry. The fact is that most people, myself included, don't have ice-cream makers.

This is why I always have a tub or two of good-quality ice cream in the freezer. More often than not I keep vanilla – not because I'm horribly unadventurous but because it is a useful foil for a number of things that are fun to make (quickly) to go with it. These are the things I might attempt with limited time and/or resources.

'DROWNED' ICE CREAM WITH COFFEE (AFFOGATO).

This most basic of all ice-cream-based desserts is one of the best. Not surprisingly, the idea comes from Italy, where both coffee and ice cream are generally excellent. You need espresso-strength coffee (I make mine in a stovetop Moka pot). The idea is to pour hot espresso over cold vanilla ice cream. Try to have the ice cream freezer-hard so that it doesn't melt into the coffee too fast. I put it in tumblers ready for serving and leave them in the freezer for half an hour or so before pouring the coffee over the top.

'DROWNED' ICE CREAM WITH BOOZE.

Following the same principle as pairing ice cream with coffee, a racier alternative is to drown the ice cream with booze. You don't need to heat up the booze of your choice but you could, I suppose. My favourite drink to pour over vanilla ice cream is Kahlua – you could also use Tia Maria or Baileys.

One variation of this that I am very fond of is good for lazy entertaining around Christmastime (although it needn't be restricted to then). Serve individual portions of vanilla ice cream in a frozen tumbler with shots of sloe or damson gin poured over as generously as you dare.

ICE CREAM WITH COFFEE GRANITA.

Only slightly more effort is involved in this beautiful recipe for a coffee-flavoured granita (a rough, granular water ice), from Claudia Roden's book *The Food of Italy* (Chatto & Windus, 1989). You need an ice-cube tray and about 500ml strong black coffee. Sweeten the coffee with a heaped tablespoon of caster sugar, then freeze it in the ice-cube tray. Using a food processor, blitz as many coffee ice cubes as you want just as you serve up. Only just smash the cubes, though; the ice shouldn't be too smooth. Spoon it round vanilla ice cream and serve as quickly as possible.

ICE CREAM WITH BITTER CHOCOLATE SAUCE.

A swift hop, skip and jump from dousing vanilla ice cream in coffee brings us to a rich and very dark chocolate sauce. You could use milk chocolate instead, if you prefer, but choose a good-quality one so it won't be too sweet.

For 2–4 people you need:
- ★ 100g dark chocolate
- ★ 3 tablespoons strong black coffee
- ★ 2 tablespoons rum or brandy (near enough to a barman's 'shot')
- ★ 50g golden caster sugar

Simply warm all the ingredients in a thick-bottomed pan over a low heat. Don't stir the sauce too much, as dark chocolate can misbehave if it is overworked. This is wonderful served warm over vanilla ice cream.

If you have a microwave, by all means use it to melt chocolate sauces. Zap the sauce for 30 seconds at a time on a high setting, and stir only briefly between zaps.

ICE CREAM WITH BUTTERSCOTCH SAUCE.

Try this sauce with a bowl of vanilla ice cream and some sliced bananas or a sprinkling of chopped mixed nuts . . . or both! You will feel about ten again. I add lemon zest to my butterscotch because lemon oil is in the traditional recipe for the sweets. You could use orange peel or lime as a variation. It will alter the flavour in a subtle way.

For 4 people you need:

* ★ 50g butter (salted butter is best for this sauce)
* ★ 100g golden caster sugar
* ★ 150g golden syrup
* ★ a sliver of lemon zest, removed from the lemon with a vegetable peeler (optional)
* ★ ½ teaspoon vanilla extract, or seeds scraped from ½ vanilla pod
* ★ 100ml double cream

Melt the butter very gently in a saucepan, then add the sugar, golden syrup and lemon zest, if using. Cook really gently until everything has melted and the sugar has dissolved. Raise the heat slightly and simmer for 5 minutes. Remove the pan from the heat and stir in the vanilla and cream. Serve the sauce warm over vanilla ice cream. It keeps in the fridge for about a month; simply reheat gently to serve.

ICE CREAM WITH TINNED PLUM SAUCE.

I'm not a huge fan of tinned fruit. So much of it loses any character it had when fresh. Dried fruit has tons more flavour. However, tinned plums are a new discovery for me. I thought they would be awful, but I was pleasantly surprised by their intense, slightly perfumed plumminess.

For 4 people you need:

* ★ 1 tin of plums in syrup
* ★ juice of 1 lemon
* ★ a shot of vodka

Drain the plums, reserving the syrup. You will probably need to stone them – this is one convenience food that comes with a bit of labour! Pop the stoned plums into a food processor with the lemon juice and vodka and blitz until smooth. Now loosen to the desired consistency with the reserved syrup. Pour the sauce into a pan and heat through gently before serving with ice cream.

VARIATION.

To give the sauce a slightly different kick, you could omit the vodka and replace it with a 1cm cube of fresh ginger, finely chopped, or a piece of stem ginger. This will make it a real winter warmer, even with ice cream.

ICE CREAM 'BRÛLÉE'.

So easy it's cheeky. Which makes it perfect for this book. You need to make caramel, which is almost effortless. Having said that, you must proceed with caution to avoid ruining a saucepan or burning yourself.

You need:
★ 200g golden caster sugar
★ 50ml water

Grease a flat baking sheet and line it with baking parchment. Heat the sugar and water fairly gently in a thick-bottomed saucepan, stirring occasionally, until the sugar dissolves.
Raise the heat and let the mixture bubble, without stirring, until it starts to colour. As soon as it is golden brown and viscous, it is caramel. You can keep cooking it until it is quite dark and bitter, if you like, but be careful it doesn't burn. When you like the look of your caramel, pour it on to the parchment and allow it to spread and cool. Don't touch it while it is hot.
   Once the caramel is cold and set, you can do one of two

things: either break it into shards and stick it into ice cream at artistic angles (oh, why not?) or blitz it on the pulse setting in a food processor so that you can sprinkle it over vanilla ice cream. Either way is good.

PRALINE ICE CREAM.

As a variation on the above, you can make praline and serve it with ice cream in the same way. Roast 200g blanched almonds in a moderate oven for about 10 minutes, until they are completely brittle. Add them to the finished caramel just before you pour it on to the parchment. Break it up or blitz it as before.

'THUNDER AND LIGHTNING'.

A very old-fashioned English nursery-type dessert that somehow fits this chapter like a glove. Do not be deterred by the bizarre mix of ingredients. This is hardly a recipe, more a gathering of sweet things. Modern versions use honey, although traditionally it was black treacle. You could try either, or even use golden syrup.

I have been known to buy meringues for this. Many supermarkets sell them. It does seem a shame to spend time making meringue only to smash it up. However, one thing that will be missing from most shop-bought versions is that oh-so-slightly-gooey bit in the middle. For that reason alone (and not in any way earnestly), I include instructions for meringues opposite.

When it comes to dishing up, if there are more than a couple of you present, it is fun to plonk each element of thunder and lightning on the table and let everyone 'build their own'.

You need:

★ vanilla ice cream
★ a tub of clotted cream
★ a jar of runny honey, or a tin of black treacle or golden syrup
★ a bowl of broken meringues

The ice cream should be soft so that those who wish can stir everything together, so take it out of the freezer a good half hour before serving. It's easy to forget to do that bit! Here is a recipe for meringues that will make plenty for a party of four.

You need:

★ 2 egg whites
★ 100g golden caster sugar
★ ¼ teaspoon baking powder

Preheat the oven to 150°C/Gas Mark 2 and line a baking sheet with baking parchment. Whisk the egg whites until they form soft peaks, then beat in the caster sugar, 1 tablespoon at a time. Allow a good 30 seconds between each spoonful. When all the sugar has been incorporated, add the baking powder and keep beating. The meringue is ready to cook when it is stiff and resembles a rather glossy shaving foam.

Spoon or pipe the meringue on to the baking sheet. You can do this any way you like. If I know I'm going to break it up I just use a spatula and smear it all over the baking sheet. Put the meringue into the oven and immediately lower the heat to 140°C/Gas Mark 1. Bake for 2 hours, then turn the oven off and leave the meringue inside until it, and the oven, have completely cooled. Hopefully some gooeyness will have remained in the very middle.

SIDE ORDERS FOR ICE CREAM.

I am more than happy to buy in ice cream and pair it with a bit of simple baking on my part. Cookies and ice cream is the obvious starting point; it is a classic American combination. Below is a recipe for an easy cookie, with some other ideas from over the pond to follow.

A SIMPLE CHOCOLATE CHIP COOKIE.

A cookie is not a biscuit. I'm adamant about that. Like a good macaroon, a cookie should be a bit sad and gooey in the middle. If you like cookies with ice cream, try them with ice-cold milk one night. Whereas we Brits put the kettle on at the first sign of a crisis, Americans do cookies and milk.

When I think of cookies, I think of chocolate chips. I've yet to find really good chocolate in true chip form, so I usually contrive them from a conventional bar. Here is a catch-all recipe, for which you could choose the most grown-up (bitter) or kiddish (white) chocolate.

If you make conventional-sized cookies rather than giant American ones, this recipe produces about 20. This means that any that don't get eaten by guests will scream 'Eat me!' from the tin every time you wander into the kitchen. If you share my total lack of willpower, freeze half the dough.

You need:
- ★ 100g bitter, milk or white chocolate, broken up
  (or use chocolate buttons)
- ★ 100g soft butter
- ★ 100g soft brown sugar

- ★ 100g golden caster sugar
- ★ 1 egg
- ★ 100g plain flour
- ★ ½ teaspoon baking powder

If you plan to use a broken-up bar of chocolate, get it good and cold by leaving it in the fridge for a while. Then you can 'pulse' it in a food processor until it is as smashed up as you like. Without a food processor, wrap the chocolate in a good poly bag, wrap the bag in a tea towel and 'whump' it with the end of a rolling pin (note: this mild violence, like chocolate, is very good for a broken heart).

Preheat the oven to 180°C/Gas Mark 4. Cream the butter and sugars together until soft and fluffy, then beat in the egg. Sift the flour with the baking powder and fold it in. Finally fold in the chocolate pieces. Using a tablespoon as a size guide, dollop the mixture on to a baking tray lined with baking parchment. This will make big American-style cookies. Space them well, as the mixture really spreads (on my largest baking tray I only managed 5 dollops). You could use a teaspoon for a more conventional biscuit size but halve the cooking time.

Bake large cookies in the oven for 10 minutes. This time may seem very short, but remember that they cook slightly as they rest and cool down. You can remove the cookies from the oven while they still look a bit underdone. Leave them on the parchment for at least 5 minutes before transferring to a wire rack to cool.

VERY QUICK BROWNIES.
Ice cream and brownies. What can you say?

I often forget to have nuts in my larder but there is always dried fruit, which I buy in rash moments of healthfood mania and never eat. So I was delighted to find this recipe for brownies using both. To make the more traditional version, replace the fruit with the same weight of nuts of your choice. Walnuts and pecans are the usual suspects, but you could go for hazelnuts or almonds.

For a 28 x 18cm baking tray you need:
★ 100g bitter chocolate
★ 100g unsalted butter
★ 2 eggs
★ 75g golden caster sugar
★ 100g self-raising flour
★ 50g dried prunes or apricots, roughly chopped
★ 50g walnuts or pecans, chopped
★ cocoa powder or icing sugar for dusting

Preheat the oven to 180°C/Gas Mark 4. Line a 28 x 18cm baking tray with baking parchment. Melt the chocolate and butter in a bowl set over a pan of simmering water or in a microwave. Meanwhile, beat the eggs and sugar together in a large bowl until pale and thick. Fold the melted chocolate into the egg mixture, then fold in the flour and the fruit and nuts. Pour into the lined tray and bake for about 20 minutes, until a thin crust has appeared on top (the centre should still feel a little soft). Leave to cool in the tin, then cut into squares and dust with cocoa powder or icing sugar.

ROCKY ROAD.
I love the name of this. It is descriptive and surreal all at once. If you have been to the States you may have eaten rocky-road-

flavoured ice cream. My friend, Amy Lamé (broadcaster, New Jersey gal and expert in American culinaria), tells me that nine out of ten Americans would actually describe rocky road as a flavour of ice cream. Until she came to London she had never heard of it eaten in its own right. This recipe is, however, adapted from one by Nigella Lawson, who suggests folding it into vanilla ice cream. You can also serve it, like I do, on the side. I've used milk chocolate but you could make it with dark, which would give a slightly more adult feel.

You can vary the nuts in rocky road without worrying too much about authenticity (although true R.R. is, I think, made with brazils). I use hazelnuts because they are roughly the same size as mini marshmallows. If you can't find mini marshmallows, don't be put off this recipe. Go for regular-sized ones.

For 4 people you need:
★ 100g skinned hazelnuts
★ 100g mini marshmallows
★ 250g good-quality milk chocolate

Line a baking tray with baking parchment. Empty the hazelnuts and marshmallows into a mixing bowl. Melt the chocolate in a bowl set over a pan of simmering water or in a microwave, then, while it is warm and runny, mix it with the other ingredients. As swiftly as you can, spoon it on to the baking parchment in little dollops and allow to cool. Avoid using the fridge unless you are short of time, as the chocolate will lose its sheen that way.

SOMETHING 'SMOREISH'.
Like rocky road, I love the descriptive name of this biscuit – so called because eating it will undoubtedly make you crave

'some more'. Amy (see above) reminded me of smores while we were discussing the finer points of rocky road ice cream. I do hope she won't mind me fiddling around with her dessert heritage. True smores are the stuff of nights around summer campfires. Marshmallow and chocolate are sandwiched between 2 Graham crackers (the American cousin of our digestive biscuits), wrapped in foil and cooked in the heat of the fire. Obviously you could try this on a barbecue, but I have tinkered with the concept and come up with this.

For a 28 x 18cm baking tray you need:
★ 75g butter
★ 200g digestives or Graham crackers
★ 150g dark chocolate
★ 4 tablespoons milk
★ 200g marshmallows (mini ones, if possible)

Melt the butter and smash up the biscuits by breaking them between your hands (you could use a food processor, but be careful not to grind them up too finely). Mix the butter and biscuits together in a large mixing bowl and set aside.

Melt the chocolate with the milk in a bowl set over a pan of simmering water or in a microwave. Be careful not to stir it too much, as overworked chocolate will curdle (if it does, add a couple of tablespoons of hot water from a just-boiled kettle). Once the chocolate has melted, fold in the marshmallows. As soon as they begin to give a little, rather than actually melt completely, remove the pan from the heat. Now fold the biscuits, chocolate and marshmallows together and press the mixture into a 28 x 18cm baking tray lined with baking parchment. Leave in the fridge until the chocolate has set; this takes less than an hour, which makes this a good spur-of-the-moment concoction. Enjoy, and give my regards to your dentist.

MACAROONS.

I love ice cream with macaroons. A warning: these are nothing like shop-bought macaroons. I only say that because sometimes, despite the unquestionable virtue of 'home made', it can be disappointing. All of us have a fondness (sometimes secretly) for one industrial taste or another – I mean things like synthetic pink ice cream or 'banana' milkshakes. Mine might just be almond essence. I like its marker-pen headiness. I love those awful Bakewell tarts you get in boxes. You have to eat them with builder-strength tea and the icing peels off the cake and sticks to your teeth. It's heaven. I digress. These macaroons don't taste of almond essence and they are great. If you want it, you'll have to add it yourself.

For 16–18 macaroons you need:
★ 100g ground almonds
★ 150g golden caster sugar
★ 1 level tablespoon cornflour or arrowroot
★ 1 egg white

Preheat the oven to 150°C/Gas Mark 2. Mix the almonds, sugar and cornflour or arrowroot together in a bowl. In a separate bowl, whisk the egg white until it has formed soft peaks, then fold it into the almond mixture as carefully as you can, so as not to lose the airiness. Blob teaspoon-sized portions on to a baking tray lined with baking parchment. Place in the oven and bake for 20–25 minutes, until the macaroons are golden brown on top. Transfer to a wire rack and leave to cool.

ICE CREAM 'SHAKES'.

I can't contemplate anything else with a burger night (see page 202). The thick American-style shake has, thankfully, now usurped our own old-fashioned milk shakes. These were dubious concoctions of lurid powders whisked into milk (with varying degrees of success). The great thing about doing your own versions of a thick shake is, of course, that you can get quite inventive.

The ice cubes may seem like an odd addition to ice cream, but they give a little texture to the finished drink. The quantities that follow will make two shakes. If there are more than a couple of you, make the shakes in these batches of two. It is surprisingly easy to overfill a blender and you'll know if you have because that initial 'rev' of the blades will decorate your T-shirt. Or ceiling. Or both. The following 'recipes' are really just lists of what goes into my favourite concoctions. You could make each one more 'adult' by adding a shot of booze. Kahlua goes with anything chocolatey, and rum will turn the tropical shake into something very like a Piña Colada. Crikey. Did I just say that?

For a basic shake for 2 you need:
★ 2 generous scoops of ice cream (of your choice)
★ 3 ice cubes
★ 250ml milk

Whiz the ice cream and ice cubes in a blender. Once you have a rough purée, you can slowly add the milk.

CHOCOLATE AND BANANA SHAKE.

Use a really dark, chocolatey ice cream for the best results.

You need:
★ 1 ripe banana
★ 2 generous scoops of chocolate ice cream
★ 3 ice cubes
★ 2 tablespoons plain yoghurt (optional,
   but it intensifies the banana taste)
★ 250ml milk

Mix as for the basic shake, adding the banana and yoghurt with the ice cream and ice.

TROPICAL SHAKE.

You could use any fruit juice for this, but pineapple is my favourite.

You need:
★ 1 ripe banana
★ 2 generous scoops of vanilla ice cream
★ 3 ice cubes
★ 250ml pineapple juice

Mix as for the basic shake, adding the banana with the ice cream and ice cubes.

MARATHON SHAKE.

Those of us over a certain age will remember when Snickers was called Marathon. I can live with the bar changing its name, but I can't bring myself to call this a Snickers shake. Don't be put off by the peanut butter. The end result is not at all claggy.

You need:

- ★ 1 ripe banana
- ★ 2 generous scoops of chocolate ice cream
- ★ 1 tablespoon peanut butter
- ★ 1 tablespoon golden syrup
- ★ 3 ice cubes
- ★ 300ml milk

This shake is best if you blitz the banana, ice cream, peanut butter and syrup before adding the ice cubes. Then proceed as for the basic shake.

PLAYING WITH FROZEN BERRIES.

Here is a handful of puds that are one up on 'zshushing' up ice cream. They all rely on frozen berries. If you are lucky enough to grow your own soft fruit, or at least to pick your own, you will know that freezing is a good way of dealing with the glut you sometimes get at the end of summer. Soft fruit is one of the easiest things to freeze, requiring no blanching. If, like the rest of us, you have to buy berries in, you will know how expensive the fresh ones can be. And how hit-and-miss in terms of quality. But frozen berries are great, especially if you have a mini repertoire of what to do with them. They provide a good stash of fruit for last-minute puds, and a taste of summer throughout the darker months.

You could use fresh berries for these recipes, obviously. If you do, cook them very lightly first (for no more than 5 minutes) with a scant amount of sugar and a squeeze of lemon juice. They won't disintegrate, but it will get their juices flowing.

CARLA TOMASI'S ITALIANATE SUMMER PUDDING.

Carla Tomasi was the first chef I worked for. She is from Italy, where they are world champions at throwing sweet courses together. Just think of the popularity of tiramisu. Less well known, but just as good, is the Italian take on a Brit classic, trifle, which they call *zuppa inglese* (literally, 'English soup'). And even less well known is this – Carla's own take on another British favourite, summer pudding.

You can buy Madeira cake just about anywhere, but you could improvise as well. You need a fairly plain, loaf-shaped sponge. I have used those marbled chocolate sponges before, which looked a bit lurid (like a mad carpet bag) but tasted great.

For 4–6 people you need:
★ 500g bag of frozen summer fruit
   (or a similar weight of fresh fruit)
★ 100g golden caster sugar
★ 50ml water
★ 125ml marsala or Madeira wine
★ juice of ½ lemon
★ 250ml double cream (or half cream
   and half mascarpone cheese)
★ 1–2 Madeira cakes (depending on size),
   cut into slices about 5mm thick

Put the fruit into a colander with a bowl beneath it to catch the juice as it thaws. Gently heat the sugar and water in a pan, stirring occasionally, until the sugar dissolves and you have a very light, clear syrup. Allow this to cool. Add the marsala, lemon juice and the juice from the berries and set aside.

Beat the cream until it leaves a trail behind the whisk, but don't fully whip it. Line a 750–900ml pudding basin with cling film, allowing enough surplus overhang to bring it back over the top of the bowl later.

Dunk each slice of Madeira cake in the boozy, syrupy mix (just briefly, so it doesn't become too soft to work with), then press it on to the sides and base of the lined bowl.

Fold the fruit and cream (and mascarpone, if using) together and fill the inside of the bowl. Now dunk more slices of cake and use them to cover the top. Bring the cling film over the top of the pudding and place in the fridge to set. Overnight is ideal, but a couple of hours will do it. Reserve any excess syrup mix.

When you want to serve up, remove the cling film from the top of the pudding and invert the bowl over a plate. Tap it a few times with your knuckles but don't try to prise it from the bowl. It will come away eventually. Paint any dry-looking patches of cake with the remaining syrup. In fact, you can douse the whole thing with whatever is left!

RASPBERRY TRIFLE.

An ersatz version of *zuppa inglese*. I like to use Madeira cake for the base, but you could just as easily go for sponge fingers.

You need to make a custard for this, unless you are happy to buy it in. If you do buy one, make sure it is a thick, fresh type. The recipe below is for confectioner's custard (*crème pâtissière*).

How you serve this is up to you. Occasionally I like to put trifle in wine glasses and serve it as individual portions – a bit kitsch, perhaps, but sometimes that is what you want from this type of pud.

For 6–8 people you need:

★ 2 tablespoons golden caster sugar
★ 250ml marsala or Madeira wine
★ 100ml water
★ a sliver of orange zest (optional)
★ 1 Madeira cake, broken into smallish pieces
★ 500g raspberries, thawed if frozen
★ 300ml double cream
★ a small bar of very bitter chocolate (optional)

For the custard:

★ 6 egg yolks
★ 100g golden caster sugar
★ 50g plain flour
★ ½ vanilla pod
★ 300ml whole milk
★ 200ml double cream

First make the custard. Beat the egg yolks, sugar and flour
together until pale and creamy. Slit the vanilla pod open
lengthways with a sharp knife and scrape the seeds into the
mixture. Heat the milk and cream in a saucepan until they reach
scalding point (the mixture will fizz against the side of the pan).
Remove from the heat and pour very slowly on to the egg
mixture, stirring it thoroughly as you go. Return the whole thing
to a gentle heat and cook, stirring constantly, until the custard
has thickened considerably. This doesn't take long. Making
crème pâtissière is easier than egg-only custards because the
flour stabilises the mixture, but be careful not to let it catch on
the bottom of the pan. The custard is ready as soon as the
spoon starts to leave a trail in its wake as you stir. Allow it to

cool completely before you use it, stirring occasionally to prevent a skin forming.

Heat the sugar, marsala and water with the orange zest, if using, until the sugar has completely dissolved and you have a clear syrup. Leave to cool.

Arrange the broken pieces of cake in the bottom of a suitable bowl and pour over enough of the syrup to soak them completely. Scatter the raspberries over the cake and cover them with the custard. A word of advice: if you are preparing the trifle more than an hour or so in advance of serving it, stop with the custard. Add the cream only when you are about to serve up. Whipped cream can overstiffen and crack if left in the fridge (it can also taste 'fridgey').

Shortly before serving, whip the cream until it is just beginning to set and top the trifle with that. I like to decorate the cream with some shavings from a bar of very bitter chocolate.

FROZEN SUMMER BERRIES AND WHITE CHOCOLATE SAUCE.

Based on a famous dish from the Caprice and the Ivy restaurants in London, this is one for people who really don't like making pudding. It is fast becoming a classic, and quite right too. It is a near-perfect combination of sweet and sour, hot and cold, and it's a cinch to make. One caveat: get grown-up white chocolate for this, rather than Milky Bar, which behaves quite differently when it melts.

The fruit should still be frozen when you put the pudding together, so if you use fresh berries instead, arrange them in a single layer on a large tray so they don't clump together and put them in the freezer until hard. Avoid outsize specimens, or cut them in half so that they thaw at the same rate as the other berries.

For 4 people you need:
- ★ 500g bag of frozen summer fruit
- ★ 300ml double cream
- ★ 200g white chocolate, broken up

If the berries are clumped together in the bag, just thump it gently with a rolling pin to separate them. Keep it in the freezer until you serve up. Heat the cream until it is just bubbling slightly against the side of the pan, then remove it from the heat and stir in the chocolate immediately. Arrange the berries on individual plates and drizzle the white chocolate sauce over them. The chocolate starts to melt the berries and they in turn start to thicken the sauce. By the time you have guzzled the lot, it looks like carnage on a plate. Heavenly.

TWO SIMPLE (BUT RATHER POSH) CHOCOLATE PUDS.

This is chocolate at its most intense. The chocolate in these puds should be fairly fearsome and sophisticated. You must use a serious brand.

These recipes are easily made on a whim, if you have eggs, butter and sugar in the house.

CHOCOLATE SOUFFLÉ CAKE.

This is really a baked chocolate mousse. What is wonderful about it is the total lack of flour, which gives it an intensely chocolate taste. The darker and moodier this cake the better, so for the coffee I make a strong espresso.

For 8–10 people you need:

★ 6 eggs, separated
★ 125g icing sugar (set aside 1 heaped tablespoon)
★ 200g bitter chocolate
★ 125g unsalted butter
★ 2 tablespoons strong black coffee

Grease a deep 20cm springform cake tin and line the base with baking parchment. Preheat the oven to 180°C/Gas Mark 4.

Beat the egg yolks and icing sugar in a large bowl until pale and fluffy. Melt the chocolate and butter in a bowl set over a pan of simmering water or in a microwave, then stir in the coffee. Now, while the chocolate mix is still warm, beat it into the egg yolk mixture.

Whisk the egg whites with the reserved tablespoon of icing sugar until you have a meringue with very soft peaks. Fold this meringue into the chocolate and egg yolk mix as gently as you can, to keep it airy. The easiest way to do this is to take 1 or 2 heaped tablespoons of the meringue and whisk them in fairly briskly to loosen the chocolate mix, then after that go as gently as you can, using a spatula or a large metal spoon.

Transfer the mixture to the cake tin and bake for 30 minutes. No peeking, by the way, as this cake really needs constant heat. Even if it seems very wobbly after half an hour, take it out of the oven. Leave it to cool completely before removing it from the tin. As the cake cools, the centre collapses and becomes dense. Once cold, it is ready to eat but, if you leave it until the next day, the flavour becomes somehow more intense.

CHOCOLATE AND HAZELNUT TORTE.

Here is another intensely flavoured chocolate cake, also made
without flour. You could substitute almonds for the hazelnuts.
Be sure to use whole nuts, as ready-ground ones will not give
the same texture.

For 8–10 people you need:
- ★ 200g whole hazelnuts
- ★ 200g bitter chocolate
- ★ 200g unsalted butter, softened
- ★ 200g golden caster sugar
- ★ 5 eggs, separated

Grease a deep 20cm springform cake tin and line the base with
baking parchment. Preheat the oven to 150°C/Gas Mark 2.

Roast the hazelnuts in a roomy baking tray for 10 minutes.
Transfer them to a colander whilst still warm and shake the skins
off. This is easy. Put the colander in an empty sink and either
shake it gently or hold it with one hand, tapping it with a wooden
spoon with the other. The skins will fall through the holes in
the colander. You needn't lose every last shred of skin. (Some
people say that the skin on nuts is bitter when they have
been cooked.)

Blitz the hazelnuts in a food processor until roughly ground.
Do the same with the chocolate. Use the 'pulse' function so
that you don't over-process them and end up with Nutella.

Beat the butter and sugar together until pale and fluffy. Beat
in the egg yolks one by one, then fold in the nuts and chocolate.
In a separate bowl, whisk the egg whites until they form soft
peaks. Add a heaped tablespoon to the chocolate and nut mix
and whisk it in fairly briskly to loosen the mixture. After that, use

a spatula or a large metal spoon to fold in the rest of the egg whites as carefully as possible, so you don't knock out any air.

Put the mixture into the cake tin and bake for 45 minutes, until the cake is set and slightly crisp on top. To check it is ready, insert a skewer into the centre; it should come out clean. Allow the cake to cool completely before removing it from the tin.

As if you needed telling, this cake is delicious with a good scoop of ice cream. A coffee-flavoured one will add to its general air of sophistication.

MORE NUTS.

Here, to round off with, are two very easy puddings that rely on nuts. Once again, if you have a good stock of these in your kitchen, you are minutes away from simple but impressive cooking.

APRICOT AND ALMOND PUDDING.

This is based on a delightful recipe from Claudia Roden. Besides being very user-friendly (especially if you use dried or tinned apricots), it has a slightly split personality. In summer you could serve it cold with cream and perhaps some fresh raspberries. In winter, make the hot sauce and serve the whole thing straight from the oven.

For 4–6 people you need:
- ★ 100g unsalted butter, softened
- ★ 150g golden caster sugar
- ★ 3 eggs
- ★ 150g ground almonds
- ★ 2 or 3 drops of almond essence

★ 1kg apricots, halved and stoned (if using dried Hunza apricots, soak them in warm water for 30 minutes first)
★ 2 tablespoons icing sugar

For the sauce:
★ 200g apricot jam
★ 3 tablespoons water
★ 1–2 tablespoons kirsch or apricot schnapps

Preheat the oven to 180°C/Gas Mark 4. Beat the butter and sugar together until pale and fluffy, then beat in the eggs one by one. Mix in the ground almonds and almond essence, then transfer the mixture to a greased 20cm baking dish or an oval gratin dish. Arrange the apricot halves on top, cut-side up, and press them down slightly. Bake for 45 minutes, until golden brown, then remove from the oven.

Meanwhile, to make the sauce, gently heat the jam, water and kirsch or schnapps together until the jam has dissolved. Serve the pud dusted with the icing sugar and pour the sauce around each portion. If custard is more your thing, you could use that instead – it's very 'nursery food'.

A PERSIAN BAKLAVA.

Because you can buy such good ready-made filo pastry just about everywhere, I thought I should include a recipe for baklava, which is more of a sweetmeat than a real dessert. I like to make this kind of thing if I am feeding a large group of people and, besides, I can't think of a more fitting way to round off a feast such as the kebab night on page 213. You could pair the baklava with a tub of plain yoghurt and some grapes or slices of watermelon to provide a sort of sweet buffet.

It is possible to have everything you need 'in' for this dish, especially if you have a store of nuts and keep the pastry in the freezer. You will need to defrost it before use, and annoyingly there always seems to be too much. One way round this is to cut the frozen wrap of pastry 'sheets' in half, right through the centre, which will give you smaller sheets.

You can buy baklava quite easily these days if you live near a Turkish or Greek delicatessen, but this home-made version is less dense and buttery and (as a result) less sickly. Fans of Middle Eastern cookery might like to know that it is based on a recipe from Margaret Shaida's book, *The Legendary Cuisine of Persia* (Penguin Books, 1994).

To fill a 28 x 18cm baking tray you need:
★ 150g almonds, roughly ground
★ 150g walnuts, pistachio nuts or hazelnuts, roughly ground
★ seeds from 6 cardamom pods, crushed
★ 150g granulated or caster sugar
★ 75g unsalted butter, melted
★ 6 sheets of filo pastry (cut to fit your baking tray;
   only don't be too exact about it)

For the syrup:
★ 150g granulated or caster sugar
★ 1 tablespoon runny honey
★ 6 tablespoons water
★ 2 tablespoons rose water or 2 tablespoons fruit juice
★ 2 tablespoons pistachio nuts, roughly crushed
   (you can buy these ready in Middle Eastern stores)

Preheat the oven to 190°C/Gas Mark 5. Have everything ready before you deal with the filo pastry, which can dry out and go brittle very quickly.

Combine the nuts, cardamom and sugar and set aside. Line the base of a 28 x 18cm baking tray with baking parchment. Brush the parchment with some of the melted butter and lay a sheet of filo pastry over it. Brush that with butter, then lay another sheet of filo on top and brush that with butter, too. Top with half the sugar and nut mixture, pressing it down as firmly as you can. Lay another sheet of pastry over that, brush it with butter and top it with another sheet. Brush that with butter and add the remaining nut and sugar mixture. Press it down again and top with another sheet of pastry. Brush that with butter and add your final sheet of pastry. Brush it with butter and prick it all over with a fork. With a sharp knife, cut the baklava into diamond shapes or squares, making sure you cut through all the pastry layers. Bake for 20 minutes or until golden brown on top.

Meanwhile, make the syrup. Put the sugar, honey, water and rose water or fruit juice in a pan and heat gently until the sugar has dissolved. Simmer very gently for about 10 minutes to thicken the syrup. When the baklava comes out of the oven, pour the syrup over it, then sprinkle the chopped pistachio nuts over the top. Leave to cool before serving.

ACKNOWLEDGEMENTS

Producing *Cupboard Love* was an absolute pleasure thanks to the following people: Richard Atkinson is a wonderful editor with unquestionable judgement when it comes to the essential things in life (i.e. food and pop music). I couldn't have written this book without him. Jane Middleton prevented me from rambling over a literary precipice. And made me lunch. Jason Lowe and Georgia Vaux added their magic ingredients, with glamorous assistant Natasha Plowright. Some time ago I built a small shrine to my agent Lizzy Kremer. I worship at it daily. I definitely owe Camilla Stoddart several glasses of something really expensive (this is an understatement). David Eyre, Trish Hilferty and Carla Tomasi continue to inspire me every time I walk into the kitchen. Thank you for reminding me why I love Peckham: Sally at Persepolis; Tony at East Dulwich Deli; everyone at Wing Tai; all the stallholders at the Farmers' Market. Thank you for having me: Auriol Bishop, Nicola Doherty, Kerry Hood, Henry Jeffreys, Briar Silich and the rest of the brilliant team at Hodder; Mickey B. whenever and wherever; Digby Trout and Martin Fletcher at Higher Combe; Matthew Drennan, Mitzie Wilson and Seamus Geoghegan at *Delicious*; Sarah Smith at *Style*; Leslie Plommer and Merope Mills at the *Guardian*; Rachel Simhon and Casilda Grigg at the *Telegraph*; Carolyn Cavele and the team at Food Matters; Simon Casson and Amy Lamé at Duckie; Kit and the

Widow; Hilary and Roy King at the Red Pear. Thank you for your help and advice: Ben's Fish; John Cunningham; Lottie Davies; Will Eaves; Richard Evans; Mary Fitzpatrick and Bill Morton; Kathryn Flett; Lulu Grimes; Charlie Hicks; Doug Kean; Pat Llewellyn and Ben Adler; George Manners; Angela Martin; Barry Moore; Neal's Yard Dairy; Polly Powell; Nick Ragget; Danny Riordan; Wendy Sayell; Hitesh Shah. I hope my parents are as proud of this book as the last one. Their support and encourage-ment has been invaluable. Spades of gratitude and lots of love (not of the cupboard variety) to all my other friends and family. Forgive me for not listing everybody by name.

INDEX